Migration and Remittances

Migration and Remittances

Inter-Urban and Rural-Urban Linkages

Jayasri Ray Chaudhuri

Sage Publications
New Delhi ▪ Newbury Park ▪ London

Dedicated to the process of development

First published in 1993 by

Sage Publications India Pvt Ltd
32 M-Block Market, Greater Kailash I
New Delhi 110 048

Sage Publications Inc
2455 Teller Road
Newbury Park, California 91320

Sage Publications Ltd
6 Bonhill Street
London EC2A 4PU

Published by Tejeshwar Singh for Sage Publications India Pvt. Ltd., phototypeset by Pagewell Photosetters, Pondicherry and printed at Chaman Enterprises, New Delhi.

Library of Congress Cataloging-in-Publication Data

Ray Chaudhuri, Jayasri, 1959-
Migration and remittances: inter-urban and rural-urban linkages / Jayasri Ray Chaudhuri.
p. cm.
Includes bibliographical references.
1. Rural-urban migration—India—Durgapur. 2. Migrant remittances—India—Durgapur. 3. Durgapur (India)—Economic conditions. I. Title.
HB2100.D87R39 1993 307.2′4′095414—dc20 92–34738

ISBN: 81–7036–316–0 (India)
0–8039–9458–3 (U.S.)

Contents

List of Tables

Note: Tables which do not have their source specified refer to the sample survey data.

List of Figures

Note: (1) All time series figures refer to the period 1930–1990.
(2) Figures which do not have the source of data specified are based on the sample survey data.

Acknowledgements

This book owes its existence to the sincere, patient, hospitable and intelligent cooperation of the 7000 residents in Durgapur who answered my questionnaires on migration and remittances. They are the ones who have been subject to probing questions about their private lives without any promise of return or gain of any kind. There lies my first and foremost obligation and gratitude.

I also wish to thank all the organisations and institutes, listed below (located in Delhi, Calcutta and Durgapur) for extending kind assistance in procurement of information, both published and unpublished. Special thanks to some of the officials, referred to below alongside the institutes, who were directly involved with this work.

1. Census organisation of India: special thanks to Mr. V.S. Verma (Registrar General, Delhi), Mr. B.K. Roy (Dy. Registrar General—Map, Delhi), Mr. Rama Rao (Assistant Registrar General, Delhi), Mr. Tomar (Dy. Director, Delhi), and Mr. A.K. Dutta (Dy. Director, Calcutta).
2. Postal Department of India: special thanks to Mr. Ojha (Additional Post Master General, Calcutta), Mrs. M. Dutta (Director of Accounts, Calcutta), Mr. A.K. Moitro (Accounts Officer, Calcutta), Mr. Bireswar Ganguly (M.O. section, Calcutta), Mr. S.K. Brahmo (Calcutta), Mr. Subodh Mukherjee (Calcutta), Post Master (Durgapur) and all the employees of the 28 post offices of Durgapur, especially those of the Main Post Office in Durgapur 1.
3. Durgapur Notified Area Authority: special thanks to Mr. Debabrato Banerjee (Vice Chairman), Mr. Tapan Adhikary (Executive Officer), Mr. B.K. Chaudhuri (Secretary). Thanks to Kamal Mukherjee (for printing of questionnaires), Pratap Singh Lama, Mr. Sukhen Bhowmick and Mohummad Samser Khan (for providing security during the surveys). I am very grateful to this organisation for providing accommodation in their guest house during the second phase survey, for arranging local guides in all the areas outside industrial townships during both the surveys and for allowing me to use their

printing facilities free of cost for printing the questionnaires in both the phases.

4. Asansol Durgapur Development Authority (Durgapur): special thanks to the Chief Executive Officer and Mr. S. Kar (Planner-in-charge), especially for providing blue prints of maps of local areas free of cost.
5. Housing Directorate of West Bengal (Durgapur): special thanks to the Executive Officer and draftsman Mr. Dilip Chakraborty (for duplicating the maps of some of the areas for my survey).
6. Durgapur Steel Plant: special thanks to Mr. B.N. Raha (Town Administrator), Mr. S.K. Ghosh (Estate Manager, Town Administration), Mr. P. Chowdhury (Manager, Personnel), Mr. A.M. Dey (Manager, Finance) and P.K Banerjee (Assistant Manager, Finance).
7. Durgapur Projects Limited: special thanks to Dr. A.N. Sanyal (Public Relations Officer), A.K. Mitra (Controller of Finance), Debasis Sinha (Deputy Controller of Finance and Accounts) and Mr. P.K. Ghosh (Town Administrator).
8. Alloy Steels Plant (Durgapur): special thanks to Mr. M. Ganguli (Executive Director) and Mr. S.S. Panja (Chief Personnel Manager).
9. Steel Authority of India Limited (Durgapur): special thanks to Mr. S.N. Choudhury (S.R.M) and Mr. G.S. Dhir (Marketing Executive) for permitting me to get computer printouts from their printer free of cost.
10. Mining and Allied Machinery (Durgapur): special thanks to Mr. N.C. Bhattacharjee (Chief Town Administrator) and Mr. A.K. Chakraborty (Public Relations Officer).
11. Planning Commission of India (Delhi): special thanks to Mr. S.R. Hashim and Dr. B. Ray Chaudhuri.
12. Institute of Public Finance and Policy (Delhi): special thanks to Mr. Hiranya Mukhopadhyay.

I am very grateful to Mr. Sujit Ukil and Mrs. Rubi Ukil for their enormous help during both the phases of fieldwork in Durgapur. Moreover they provided accommodation and food to my research team during the first phase survey in 1987. I am also very grateful to Mr. Tapash Dutta and his wife Mrs. Sanchita Dutta for their help during my visit to Delhi. I thank my parents and uncles for assisting me in organising the fieldwork and Shyamsundar Panda for special assistance in the field.

I owe special thanks to my field assistants Miss Ilina Nag, Miss Mahuya Palit, Miss Nandini Goswami and Miss Debjani Guha for sincere and expert assistance given in running the survey and tabulation of data. Thanks to all the local assistants, especially, Mr. Swapan Pal, Mr. Nayan Rakshit, Miss Sumita Saha, Miss Chhanda, Mr. Biswajit Dutta, Mr. Jyotish

Das, Mr. S.R. Das, Mrs. Tulsi Das, Mr. Ratan Dasgupta, Mr. Nirmal Kar, Mr. Satya Bose, Mr. Chitta Das, Mr. Pannalal Balmiki, Mr. Shanti Pan, Mr. Damodar Kesh, Mr. Jagdish Saraiya, Mr. Sambhu, Mr. Das and Bamapada Ruidas and Mr. Sunil Dutta. Their sincere help and effort made it possible for me to conduct the fieldwork.

In the current world no work is possible without finance. I am grateful to the Government of West Bengal (India) for funding my research in Cambridge. I thank Smuts Memorial Fund, Philip Lake Fund (Department of Geography) and Newnham College in the University of Cambridge (UK) for financing all expenses in India during fieldwork. Finally my thanks to Charles Wallace Trust and Leche Trust for financial help during the last few months before completion of this book. I thank Mr. S. Mukherjee of the High Commission of India, London for his assistance.

For academic guidance, I sincerely acknowledge the effort of my supervisor Professor Graham Peter Chapman. I owe my knowledge of computing and statistics to his patient and excellent teaching abilities. Moreover, I thank him for permitting and helping me to use some of his Fortran programs I am also grateful to him for his constant encouragement and for the interest that he has shown in this research project. Since I permitted him to use the census data collected by me in Delhi, he arranged it to be typed into the computer by Dr. H.N. Misra. I acknowledge the time saved as a consequence.

I will always remember with respect and gratitude Professor R.J. Chorley for support and help, whenever needed, for academic or any other purposes. In addition I thank my graduate tutors of Newnham College, Dr. I.B. Henderson and Dr. Judith Ennew for their help and support on all occasions. My thanks to Mr. Ian Agnew for drawing most of my maps and diagrams which did require a lot of patience! My special thanks to Mr. Arthur Lucas, Mrs. Veronica Kemp, Maria Constantinou and Jane Robinson for being kind and helpful friends throughout my stay in Cambridge. In addition I would like to thank Dr. Alan Baker and all the other academic and non-academic staff of the Department of Geography who have helped me in Cambridge.

I would like to thank Professor Sudipto Mundle (Institute of Public Finance and Policy, India and a visiting Fellow in Department of Economics, Cambridge) and Dr. Nigel Crook (Department of Economics, School of Oriental and African Studies) for giving me very valuable guidance in economics, as my topic of research required substantial knowledge of economics.

I have not forgotten the contributions of my friends Sheila and Leigh in helping me with computation! Neither have I forgotten Sue and Debashish for their help with typing of the final draft. My thanks to Dr. Deepa Nag for encouragement and support during the last few months of research. I am very grateful to Dr. V.K. Kumra for helping me to edit the final draft of this book and thanks to Dr. Sukumar Sen for his help in organising the fieldwork. My thanks to the University of Cambridge and Newnham College for all the research facilities provided.

Finally I acknowledge the contribution of the ferocious dog (which chased me out of a respondent's house at 9 pm.) in warning me 'not to trespass'—an advice to be given consideration while wondering about the 'ethics of survey'!!!

Preface

The population of India for 1989 has been 835 million, only 26 per cent of which is urban. While the urban proportion of the population has undergone very little change in the last three census decades, the growth of cities of enormous population size in absolute terms has raised questions regarding the dispersal of urban growth to smaller centres and the impact of in-migration to cities.

On the hypothesis that remittances (or the income transferred by the migrants to areas outside the town) play an important role in regional development, this study focuses on the development of the gross remittance linkage from an urban centre through its working migrants, employed within its municipal or corporation boundaries. The case study selected is Durgapur, a public sector steel town developed during the Second Plan period of post-Independence India. The town is located in the state of West Bengal in eastern India. The study aims at understanding the extent of redistribution of personal income of the migrant labour force from a new town which was initiated by government investment and the associated growth of employment.

With the above mentioned objectives this book focuses on three aspects of town growth and its impact:

1. A macro level grouping of Class 1 towns (population more than 100,000 according to the Census of India) on the basis of selected socio-economic and migration characteristics. The purpose is to determine the place of Durgapur and the role it plays in absorbing migrants in relation to other Class 1 towns of India.
2. A micro-level study of the trend of migration to Durgapur since its inception, the characteristics of the migrants and an examination of Durgapur's role in the rural-urban labour transfer mechanism.
3. A micro-level study of the strength and character of remittance linkage of the town with other rural and urban areas outside its municipal boundaries; addressing the following issues: (*a*) the strength of the remittance linkage, (*b*) the types of remittance linkage—rural or urban, (*c*) the spatial distribution of the remittances and their significance in generating a multiplier effect on income in different areas within India.

1

Introduction: Models of Migration and Regional Growth

Introduction

Rural-urban migration takes place within specific scenarios of regional economic development. A three-component model can be envisaged consisting of an Urban Centre (UC) defined by its municipal or corporation boundary and a Rural Hinterland (RH), the first two components which together constitute a region, and the third component, the external context, represented by the Rest of the World (RoW). Any of these three components may be growing healthily or declining, and the links between any two of these three may be weak or strong.

Suppose RoW has strong demand linkages with the UC, but RH has weak economic relationships with UC and is stagnating. It is not difficult to imagine that migration from RH to UC will be strong, but investment in UC can remain high because of its trading links with RoW. Some of the migrants may remit income to RH, but the effective reduction in demand at UC is not significant compared with external RoW demand. Such a model possibly represents pre-Independence India with its colonial trading and administrative centres like Calcutta, Bombay, Delhi and Madras.

In an alternative scenario links between RH and UC on the one hand and RoW on the other may be weak, so that the regional economy is more closed. Suppose investment in UC is relatively high and investment in RH is weak, perhaps because of a shift in industrial policies. The demand from RH for UC's goods and services will be weak: and the more so, if the urban-rural terms of trade has shifted in favour of high priced urban commodities. UC's demand may grow if the local income-multiplier effect of its investments is high, but there may be a countervailing process: migration from RH to UC results in large-scale remittances from UC to RH for rural consumption purposes. Thus the local multiplier is severely reduced, but to the extent that remittances are not invested in RH, RH does not generate growth and an increased demand for UC's goods and services in the long run. Apparent urban growth (in numbers) seems matched by regional stagnation in different parts of the country. Such a model would perhaps roughly fit the economic situation which has evolved in India after Independence.

Hence transfer of labour force in a developing economy can be expected to result in redistribution of finance which may affect the effective demand for commodities and services both in the short and long run. The extent to which finance is rechannelled through personal income transfer by migrants and the impact of this rechannelled finance in the short and long run can partly determine the contribution of migration to regional growth (the region being already defined as UC and its RH). However this aspect of migration has not been incorporated into formal models of economic growth and migration as will be seen in the following sections.

Theoretical Background

Types of Linkages and Economic Theories of Regional Growth

The rural hinterland of an urban centre may be defined by the spatial extent of different types of linkages from the urban centre. Such linkages may be of the following types:

1. Physical linkage in terms of connecting roads, railways, telephone lines etc.
2. Commodity linkage which include flow of commodities to and from the spatial unit under consideration.
3. Service linkage.
4. Human linkage which consists of: (*a*) commuters and (*b*) migrants; linkage development via commuters and migrants may result from the motivations of purchasing and/or selling commodities and/or services or from other types of occupational motivations.
5. Monetary linkage or the flow of capital in exchange of commodities, services or labour: flow of capital in exchange of labour can take the form of remittances which can be defined as personal income transferred to areas outside the spatial unit.

Development of any of these linkages between two spatial units can be expected to have an impact on both ends in socio-economic and physical terms. Thus planners and economists have tried to modify or induce linkage development with the expectations of improving the living conditions of the people within the spatial units at both the ends. The primary concern especially in the developing countries has been to provide an impetus to economic growth mainly in terms of income and purchasing power amongst the inhabitants within the spatial units. Divergent trends of economic growth between regions or similar types of spatial units (identified on the basis of various criteria) have resulted in the formulation of various types of models in economics and econometrics, the purpose being to identify the key determinant variables responsible for stagnation or growth so that the determining variable or variables can be controlled to give the optimum growth rate in the selected region.

It is interesting to note that almost all the major economic theories like Economic Base theory, Export Base Model, Sector and Stage theories (Chand and Puri 1983; Glasson 1978) highlight the development of trade and physical linkages as determinants for the promotion of economic growth. The Economic Base theory assumes an increase in basic activities to start with, while the regional trade multiplier assumes an increase in investment and export. Both of them, however, do not investigate the causes which trigger off increased demand bringing about an increase in basic activity and export. The Export Base model on the other hand attributes the increase of demand for exports to: (*a*) increase in per capita income in the exogenous sector when the income elasticity of demand for exports is high; (*b*) the growth of population in the case of low income elasticity of demand; (*c*) depletion or exhaustion in other areas producing the same item; (*d*) improved transfer facilities and lowered delivery costs which may make marginal producers unable to compete; (*e*) technology which has found new uses of the exported commodity. The Sector theory emphasises development of transport, increased specialisation, growth of trade and tries to explain changes in demand in different sectors in terms of income elasticity of demand.

Flow of capital and labour have been incorporated in the Neo-classical model which was first developed by R.W. Solow and T.W. Swan and later modified by Borts and Stein (Chand and Puri 1983). According to this Neo-classical model labour will flow from low to high wage regions and capital will flow from high to low wage regions. However this theory does not elaborate on the mechanisms of capital transfer.

Leontief has analysed diffusion of growth in terms of demand for input from other regions by an industry, thus including linkage development via trade and perhaps migration of labour as input in the production process. Myrdal in his theory of Cumulative Causation (Myrdal 1957), put forward the concept that spread effects of growth from progressive regions operate through: (*a*) increased demand for agricultural products and raw materials, (*b*) advanced technology made available to lagging regions. Hirschman (1958) has used the term 'trickling down' to suggest forces which mainly operate through: (*a*) inter-regional trade, (*b*) transfer of capital to backward regions and (*c*) absorption of disguised unemployment and increase of marginal productivity of labour and per capita income due to migration from the hinterland to the growth centre. The effect of the first two mechanisms given by Hirschman depends largely on the existence of complimentaries between the industries in the growth centre and the hinterland.

Growth Poles and Spread Effects

The Growth Pole theory originally developed by Perroux in 1955 claims that development is unbalanced. It takes place first at key nodes from which developmental impulses spread to other objects but which being themselves best placed for further development are likely to become cumulatively more developed. He writes: 'growth does not appear everywhere all at once: it appears in points or growth poles with varying intensity: it spreads via various channels and with varying effects . . .' (Perroux 1964, cited in Moseley 1974: 4).

Perroux has been concerned with development, not just growth in quantitative terms. In his concept, development includes the process of structural change as well. He stresses that the propensity of the key nodes to adopt innovations assures their development. According to him innovations, new ideas, new processes are the driving force of development. Though Perroux did acknowledge that growth poles would also exist in geographical space, Boudeville (Glasson 1978) explicitly extended the original theory to include more comprehensively the geographical dimension. Following Darwent (1969, cited in Glasson 1978), Moseley (1974) and Glasson (1978) have used the term 'growth centre' for the geographical entity. According to Hermansen (1972) a nodal region qualifies to be called a development pole only when it contains propulsive firms within leading industries.

The growth of such poles can have two discernible impacts:

1. 'Polarisation' of other economic units into the pole of growth results due to various agglomeration economies. This will lead to geographical polarisation with the flow of resources to and concentration of economic activity at a limited number of centres within a region.
2. 'Spread effects' cause the dynamic propulsive qualities of the growth pole to radiate outward into the surrounding space.

As pointed out earlier Myrdal has used the term 'spread effects' and Hirschman has used the term 'trickle down forces'. Myrdal writes:

> the whole region around a nodal centre of expansion should gain from the increasing outlets of agricultural products and be stimulated to technical advance along the line . . .
>
> The spread effects of momentum from a centre of industrial expansion to other localities and regions, operating through increased demands for

their products and in many other ways, weave themselves into the cumulative social process by circular causation . . . . (Myrdal 1957: 31)

However Myrdal believed that such spread effects will be offset by the backwash effects leading to divergence rather than convergence. If the peripheral goods are primarily agricultural goods with low income elasticity of demand, the increased demand for such goods resulting from an increase in the prosperity of the centre may not materialise. In addition, the selective out-migration of capital and skilled labour from the poor region may reduce the ability of the poor region to compete. Hence, according to him there is a net movement of population, capital and goods in favour of the progressive region.

An increase in income (which may bring about an increase in demand for commodities) amongst the people in the hinterland can be induced through inter-regional trade and transfer of capital by the following mechanisms:

1. Increase in demand for agricultural goods from the growth centre under study which results from population growth in the growth centre and higher purchasing power of the labour force engaged in the industrial sector. However, the fact that agricultural commodities have low income elasticity of demand may deflate the amount of increase. Increase in the number of people in the urban centre can stimulate such demand and migration implies reallocation of agricultural commodities for consumption rather than absolute increase. However if a large proportion of migrants are from other urban units, which may be the case for workers in highly technical and innovative firms and industries, there will be no substantial increase in the demand for food from the urban sector.
2. Increase in income may be induced in rural areas by government manipulation of commodity terms of trade through differential pricing policy for agricultural and non-agricultural commodities so as to ensure higher returns for agricultural commodities and/or making urban commodities and services available at cheaper prices.
3. Propensity of growth centre firms to buy materials or services from outside an urban unit. Moseley has pointed out:

> It is indeed backward linkage which is most important in this context: the amount of 'leakage' of such purchases being a crucial factor in the stimulation of regional growth . . . . Forward linkage may be an important stimulus, if the provision by growth centre firms of cheaper and more accessible inputs stimulates peripherally located firms to greater levels of production . . . but the stimulus is likely to be small. (Moseley 1974: 132)

Empirical studies in Britain suggest that local purchasing tends to constitute only a small percentage of the total. Similarly in Durgapur (in India) it has been pointed out that large-scale industries tend to procure their spare parts from Calcutta rather than the neighbouring areas. Such links are likely to develop with other urban units.

4. The consumption expenditure saved due to out-migration can increase the disposable income. Though this does not increase the total income of the area, it may result in reallocation of finance for alternative uses which may increase output and per capita income. This is an indirect effect of the growth of an urban unit and increased migration.
5. Finally in developing countries like Nigeria, Kenya, Botswana, Ghana and India income may be increased by remittances flowing from the migrants to their relatives living outside the urban centre. Though studies have been made on spread effect via personal expenditure of the workers in the commuter zone, nowhere in the literature of growth pole and growth centre policy has remittance been considered as a mechanism for bringing about spread effect from a growth centre. This lapse may be attributed to the fact that the theory has emerged and has been empirically tested in developed countries in areas where the social customs and family structure do not require personal income transfer to family members on a regular basis. Though the importance of impact via labour market has been accepted, the lack of conception of the possibility of development of remittance linkages led to the conclusion that 'the commuting hinterland is the most important single index of the extent of the centre's impact' (Moseley 1974: 144).

In the studies made in developed economies the only processes by which impact may spread via labour markets are:

1. Reduction of underemployment so that per capita incomes would rise.
2. Expenditures by commuters in their areas of residence.
3. Spread of innovations and adoption of new techniques have been emphasised in the context of increased output both in the hinterland and growth centres.

However even in developing countries the commuting zone is likely to benefit the most as a major part of the income earned by the commuting recruits is likely to be taken back to the place of residence without placing a strain on the civic amenities required to be provided by the authorities of the newly-built towns. On the other hand in the case of migrants, personal income transfers representing only a proportion of the migrant's income may reduce the local multiplier effect in the urban area while the remittances may not be invested in increasing the output in the rural hinterland so that its impact is only confined to a temporary increase of consumer goods in the short run.

Therefore a hypothetical scheme of a five tier hierarchy of growth centres in India as advocated by Misra (1972), will hardly be viable if the mechanism of spread of growth is not understood. Misra emphasises centrality rather than growth, does not define terms like 'growth', 'centre' and 'poles' and fails to specify the criterion for the identification of growth foci (Wanmali 1983). He advocates provision of various services at different hierarchical levels with different population thresholds but does not question the economic viability of such provisions in terms of demand for them and purchasing power of the consumer. Harriss, while discussing the concept of growth centres in India, has pointed out that if growth centres are to be markets for the wholesaling of agricultural produce, they should be located in relation to the centre of gravity of projected marketed surpluses and not in relation to spatial gaps in the settlement systems (Harriss 1976), thus emphasising the supply side rather than demand. However she has also pointed out that towns to a small extent serve and are served by those in the rural hinterlands which can afford to avail themselves of urban facilities. The type and price of the demanded commodity or service have to be taken into account (which may be affected by the development of migration and remittance linkages) as well as other factors like local preferences for particular markets by particular groups of people.

Rothermund (1980), in his study of rural stagnation in the Dhanbad district of Bihar in eastern India has highlighted how the bottlenecks in the existing physical and commodity linkages result in variations in prices and insufficient access to markets by the farmers. The farmers start operating in a non-integrated market and are often isolated resulting in economic stagnation in the rural areas. The entrepreneurs have mostly migrated from outside the district, while the industrial wage employees seldom invest in agriculture in the surrounding areas. His study has however, not dealt with the development of remittance linkages from the mining and industrial centres under study. Though this study emphasises the lack of spread effect from the mining and industrial centres in the district, these centres were not strictly speaking planned growth centres.

On the other hand Dienemann (1980) has shown that even after import of commodities, Rs. 37 million remained in Dhanbad district and so he concludes that: 'a multiplier effect in the positive direction (due to the parts of income remaining in the region) can still be discerned in the commercial sector' (Dienmann 1980: 295–96). Dienemann has highlighted the development of remittance linkage of the mining and industrial centres in Dhanbad district and has shown that the linkage is weak with rural areas within the district as most of the remittances flow to areas outside the district. Harriss (1984) in her study of commodity linkage of a small town

Arni in south India, has concluded that though the town does have a generative function on its hinterland through transfer of wages, its parasitic role in terms of commodity linkage is greater. However she has not made a detailed study of remittances and the small town might not have been suitable for the study of migration and remittance linkages.

The above section highlights the fact that remittance linkage has not been given attention in the major theories of regional economic growth and therefore it is necessary to investigate the importance of remittance linkage from empirical studies in order to ascertain the necessity for its incorporation in a formal theory of regional economic growth. Hence this research aims to focus specifically on the development of remittance linkage via the migrant labour force of an urban centre as such a linkage can be expected to initiate an increased demand for commodities. Since the potential of a town to develop remittance linkage depends upon its labour absorption capacity, it is necessary to investigate the strength of the migration linkage before estimating the strength of the remittance linkage.

Models of Migration

Theoretical explanations of rural-urban migration dates back to the late 1880s when Ravenstein first proposed his 'laws of migration' according to which migrants move from areas of low opportunity to areas of high opportunity and the choice of destination is regulated by distance. Lee in 1966 put forward his ideas of 'push' and 'pull' factors.

The first well-known economic model of migration has dealt with the concept of the shift of labour force from a rural labour-surplus agrarian sector to the urban industrial sector. The Lewis–Fei–Ranis (cited in Todaro 1980) model developed in the late 1950s and 1960s saw positive effect from such a transfer as surplus labour is expected to be absorbed in the rapidly growing, more productive, urban industrial sector in which marginal product was positive and rapidly growing as a result of capital accumulation and technological progress.

Lewis assumed that urban wages would have to be at least '30 per cent' (cited in Todaro 1980: 21) higher than average rural incomes to induce workers to migrate from their home areas. At the assumed constant urban wage, the supply of rural labour was considered to be perfectly elastic, indicating that the supply of labour was not constrained and as much labour was available as required, so that the supply curve plotted against wage on the y axis is horizontal. It was further assumed that the capitalist would reinvest all the profits in the modern sector. This process of modern sector growth and employment expansion was assumed to continue until all 'surplus' rural labour has been absorbed in the urban industrial sector. This model considered migration as an equilibrating mechanism which through transfer of labour from the labour-surplus to the labour-deficit sector eventually brings about wage equality in the two sectors. The model is based on the concept of a dual economy, comprising a subsistence, agricultural sector characterised by underemployment and a modern industrial sector characterised by full employment.

However the rate of growth of employment in the modern industrial sector has generally not been sufficient in developing countries to absorb the increasing labour supply resulting from both natural population increase in the urban sector and net rural-urban migration. Moreover there has been the labour saving bias of most modern technological change. The result has been: (*a*) the growing prevalence of 'urban surplus' labour; (*b*) the institutionally determined urban wages tend to rise even where substantial urban open unemployment exists.

In the face of substantial rural-urban migration, which occurs despite rising levels of urban unemployment and underemployment, experienced by the developing nations in the 1960s, Todaro (1980) developed a model to explain this paradoxical relationship. Todaro's model postulates that migration proceeds in response to urban-rural differences in expected rather than actual earnings. Expected gains are measured by: (*a*) the difference in real incomes between rural and urban job opportunities; and, (*b*) the probability of a new migrant obtaining an urban job, which is assumed to be related to the urban unemployment rate.

Migration rates in excess of the growth of urban job opportunities are rational and probable in the face of expected large positive rural-urban income differentials. High rural-urban migration can continue even when high urban unemployment rates exist and are known to the potential migrants. If the migrant anticipates a relatively low probability of finding regular wage employment in the initial period, but expects this probability to increase over time as he broadens his urban contacts, it would be rational for him to migrate.

Todaro's basic model and its extensions consider the urban labour force as distributed between the relatively small modern sector and a large traditional sector (Harris and Todaro 1970). While wage rates in the modern sector are affected by both market and non-market forces, wage rates in the traditional sector are determined solely by competition. As a result the latter are substantially lower than those in the modern sector. Most urban in-migrants are assumed to be absorbed by the traditional sector while they seek employment opportunities in the modern urban sector (Oberai and Bilsborrow 1984). Falling job probabilities resulting from rising urban unemployment will be a factor in discouraging migration.

This model, therefore, emphasises the negative impact of migration in terms of increasing unemployment, underemployment and urban poverty in the destination. Apart from implying increased demand for employment, migration also results in increasing demands for civic amenities in the centres of in-migration, not only to cater to the desires of the migrants but also to maintain proper sanitation and health condition in the urban centre. This in turn involves increasing public expenditure in absolute terms. The unemployed and underemployed tend to settle in illegal squatter colonies, thereby avoiding tax payment, but increasing the pressure on the existing system of civic amenities accompanied by deterioration of sanitation and health. Moreover in-migration, by creating a glut in the labour market, tends to increase inequality in income between the two urban sectors mentioned above which have two wage rates. The wage rate in the modern sector rises under the influence of non-market forces whereas it remains stagnant or falls in the traditional sector.

A major weakness of the Harris–Todaro model is its assumption that potential migrants are homogeneous in respect of skills and attitudes and have complete information for working out the probability of finding out a job in the urban formal sector. Moreover it does not consider non-economic factors such as pressure of population, resulting in high man-land ratios, fragmentation of landownership, inequalities in distribution of land-ownership, institutional mechanisms which discriminate in favour of the owners of wealth, technological change biased against labour etc. (Oberai and Bilsborrow 1984). They write:

> A better understanding of the causes of migration requires an analysis of macro-economic and institutional factors that generate rural-urban differentials. A distinction is needed to be drawn between socio-economic structural factors and the specific mechanisms (unemployment, wage differentials, etc.) through which the structural factors operate (Oberai and Bilsborrow 1984: 17).

The Harris–Todaro model (with its permanent rural traditional and urban modern sectors) has been extended and modified by a number of economists. Steel and Takagi (1976, also cited in Todaro 1980) examine some of the properties of the Harris–Todaro model when first an 'urban intermediate sector', (productive small-scale enterprises using 'non-modern' technology) is explicitly incorporated into the framework to give it three sectors; and then a rural non-agricultural sector and an urban 'non-productive', 'informal sector' are included to yield a five sector model. Their conclusion is that

> the presence of an intermediate sector, which produces manufactured goods in small scale establishments combining moderate amounts of capital with labour, substantially alters the two sector analysis of the urban unemployment problem of Harris–Todaro. When labour can choose only between agriculture, manufacturing and unemployment, any attempt to reduce urban unemployment by expanding job opportunities is likely to aggravate it through increased rural-urban migration

> . . . . This paper demonstrates that unemployment can nevertheless be reduced without sacrificing output growth (or at worst with very little cost), through expansion of the intermediate sector (Steel and Takagi 1976, cited in Todaro 1980: 43).

Despite many modifications of the basic Todaro/Harris–Todaro model, the fact remains that

> its fundamental contribution—i.e., the idea that migration proceeds primarily in response to differences in 'expected' urban and rural real incomes and that as a result of this the observed accelerated rates of internal migration in developing countries in the context of rising urban unemployment are not only a plausible phenomenon but are in fact entirely rational from the private 'expected' income maximisation viewpoint of individual migrants—remains widely accepted to this day (Todaro 1980: 45).

Lipton (1977) emphasised the negative impact of rural-urban migration in the source or origin area of the migrants. According to him rural-urban migration occurs in response to rural-urban inequality derived from 'urban bias', which manifests itself in disproportionately low investment in the rural and especially the agricultural sector, in 'price twists', especially low farm output prices which discourage farmers, in over-taxation and under-provision of public benefits from that taxation, over-valuation of local currencies and higher investment in urban areas. Such a process results in sucking away the brighter and more skilled villagers, including potential rural leaders to the 'urban bias'. Since more education means increasing rural-urban migration, the better off gain most. Only after considerable sacrifice, in the form of costs incurred to secure education, are the private returns (in terms of remittances or higher income earned by an educated migrant) likely to justify the whole exercise of emigration for education.

Educated migrants transfer their demand for service labour townwards and their remittances to better off families can sometimes buy capital to replace labourers. The external costs of rural skill drain must fall on the countryside (and the external benefits on the initially richer, more unequal towns). If the majority of skilled persons leave villages, their replacement may be a major problem; their rewards will rise, quality deteriorate and intra-village inequality between skilled and unskilled will grow. As for unskilled workers, their substantial random rural emigration might perhaps help those who stay to raise wages. According to Lipton the promising, self-advancing forms of migration takes place amongst better off villagers (though often from villages of low average income per person).

Lipton has put forward two objections to relying on remittances as a cause of intra-rural or rural-urban equalisation: (*a*) total net remittances are very small compared with rural income and often negative; (*b*) positive remittances go disproportionately to the better off. To support his first point he has cited the proportions from (*a*) a survey in Ranchi in 1961 which stated that only '3 per cent' of the migrants sent 'Rs. 16 a month' while '86.1 per cent' did not remit at all (Lipton 1977: 326) and (*b*) the survey in Gujarat and Rajasthan in north-west India where the average share of inremittances in the village income was '6.5 per cent' (Lipton 1980: 11) and (*c*) Tamil Nadu in southern India where the average contribution of remittances was only '1.3 per cent' (Lipton 1977, 1980: 11). First, all the cited data were collected in the 1950s and early 1960s when high migration towns characterised by high level of migrants and migrant labour force have probably not developed in those parts of India. As stated earlier the remittance potential of the towns can be expected to be a function of its potential to absorb migrating labour force. If migration is a function of distance as postulated in Ravenstein's gravity model, the absence of nearby towns (capable of absorbing migrant labour force), in a certain region, is likely to deter migration from villages and thereby keep the remittance receipt low. Inequality or even marriage migration can encourage migration to low migration towns which may cause outflow of remittances from the villages. Regional concentration of high and low migration towns in India in 1971 is investigated in Chapter 3. Later surveys in Punjab (Oberai and Singh 1983) contradict both the points of Lipton.

Byres has further pointed out that the same study of the Institute of Development Studies also refers to a village in Maharashtra, where 44 out of 65 households received regular remittances, 16 villages in Delhi to which migrants remitted between 26 per cent and 69 per cent of their income and in four of them migrants remitted 50 per cent or more. Apart from India, the study also refers to examples from Nepal, Kenya, Uganda, Ghana and Pakistan which have not been taken into account by Lipton.

Lipton's theory seems to depend primarily on one set of Indian data collected in the 1950s and 1960s whereas other empirical studies are required in other parts of the country, especially in the vicinity of high migration towns to put forward a generalisation about the impact of remittances. He has also highlighted the low, often negative value of the net remittances, the empirical evidence coming from the same datasets collected in the northwestern and southeastern Indian villages. The authors who conducted the study in Gujarat, Rajasthan and Tamil Nadu write:

> Data on outremittances are available only for the villages covered by Sardar Patel University of AERC (covering Gujarat and Rajasthan) and Madras AERC. In the case of Sardar Patel AERC, out of 8 reporting villages, in one outremittances exceeded inremittances; in another these two were almost evenly balanced; and in two others the

> former constituted one-third or more of the latter. In the case of Madras AERC the nine reporting villages were equally divided into those where outremittances exceeded inremittances and those where the former were less than the latter (Connell, Dasgupta, Laishley and Lipton 1976: 105).

Lipton in his book in 1977 referred only to the data from Tamil Nadu to make the point that the net remittances into the village was negative and did not refer to the other dataset from northwestern India. In 1980 he writes: 'Of nine villages in Tamil Nadu, with available data, four are net outremitters' (Lipton 1980: 13).

Since it is not possible to divide nine villages into two equal parts as suggested by Connell *et al.* (as quoted above), there seems to be a lot of confusion in simple data statements given by Connell *et al.* and Lipton. If we assume that Lipton's statement about four villages being net outremitters in the Tamil Nadu dataset to be correct and combine it with the figures given for Gujarat and Rajasthan (quoted above), then it seems that out of 17 villages studied, inremittances to villages exceeded outremittances in 11 villages, they were equal in one village and in only five villages outremittances exceeded inremittances.

Byres in his criticisms on Lipton's hypothesis of 'urban bias' writes: 'The evidence in question is fragmentary and localised . . . and not, perhaps susceptible to universal generalisations of the kind made by Lipton' (Byres 1979: 231). According to him Lipton's examples have been chosen because they happen to illustrate the point at hand (or seem to) and Lipton happens to have become familiar with the limited piece of evidence in question. Baker and Harriss (1980) have criticised Lipton's urban bias for using material from India only when it suited his purpose and they have given empirical evidence against the concept of 'price twists' in the Indian context.

Lipton has also pointed out that if migrants send in substantial net remittances, the remaining villagers can achieve a given level of living with less income and effort and are thus encouraged to substitute leisure for effort. However such remittances might be needed if villagers are to pay for physical capital, thereby bringing technical progress to the rural area. If remittance income goes to better off villagers, that is bad for intra-rural equality, but could be good for production. It is the investment plan of the village poor that is financially constrained. Moreover remittances are used first to pay off debts, followed by consumption which 'often absorb 90 per cent or more of the village's remittances' (Lipton 1980: 12), conspicuous consumption to maintain status, for example, high payments of bride price and luxurious housebuilding. Finally, chain migration rests on education financed by remittances. Sometimes such use of funds comprises genuine investment in socially productive human capital, but it also represents acquisition of paper qualifications which increase the qualifiers prospects of income only by reducing non-qualifier's prospects resulting in an increase of educated jobless.

> Investment is only the fourth priority for remittances, and it is often used outside the village; or in mere capital transfer rather than capital creation (notably purchase of land); or to hire workers . . . . where once family labour was used; or for labour replacing mechanisation rather than the generation of extra output or the better use of scarce land inputs (Lipton 1980: 12).

The rural-urban or foreign origin of the consumer or investment goods obtained by remittances is relevant to the welfare of the rural economy. It may reduce demand for rural commodities and raise the cost of living. On the other hand if the village offered high-yielding outlets for investment of surpluses, they would have been invested there and not financed out-migration. Bigger and better-off farm families with monopsony power in local factor markets and with rising supervision cost, will tend to select productive investments which reduce labour/land and labour/capital ratios.

Remittances, then, according to Lipton, are unlikely to do much to reduce rural poverty, either by financing productive and labour intensive investment or by being sent directly to the rural poor. Poor rural migrants have lower propensities to remit. He, however, acknowledges that poorer villages and poorer people can sometime gain from the remittances since remittances per migrant seem to increase with the size of the nuclear family. In the Indian sample remittances per villager were significantly higher in villages with high landlessness and high female and child labour rates. Finally, remittances per head are higher for poorer villages in the Indian sample so that circulation of cash remittances within the village may in part trickle down to some of its working poor.

In spite of these criticisms the fact remains that remittances can be expected to initiate demand for commodities, though how this demand is met will depend upon other types of linkages like physical linkage, commodity linkage and service linkage of the receiving area. The type of commodity demanded will be constrained by income and initial consumption, environmental and local factors, social obligations, value system and obligations of the people in the particular area as will be discussed in the next chapter. Per recipient, remittance may not be large enough to make huge investment privately to increase production of the commodity and hence an increase in demand can lead to local inflation unless the government creates facilities for their provision or production in the region. Thus it must be remembered that remittance linkage works alongside other types of linkages, though in areas where there is no remittance linkage to trigger off demand at the local level, alternative means of increasing demand have to be devised on a priority basis.

The rural landscape may be differentiated by environmental and socio-economic factors which may dictate particular types of farming requiring different types of input in terms of labour and technology. This in turn may affect the amount of investment that can go into agriculture in a particular region, the incidence of surplus labour and the necessity and benefits that can accrue from migration. However his emphasis on restructuring of the Indian education system to eliminate the urban bias by including agriculture based studies at the primary level requires more attention (Lipton 1968). It is no doubt necessary to invest in rural areas, but it must be remembered that investment cannot be spread equally throughout all areas.

The initial economic inequalities which have been precipitated over space through historical, environmental and social factors have to be accepted and plans formulated on their basis. Such inequalities include development of linkages (including remittance linkages) of unequal strength in different parts of the country which have to be given due consideration at the time of allocation of funds to different rural areas. Within the given constraints of particular regions, agricultural production can be increased up to a certain amount and industrial commodities have to be produced simultaneously to meet the various types of demand of the people as acknowledged by Lipton (1977).

If we take the 'urban' to mean a spatial unit where the majority of the people are engaged in non-primary occupations, investment in processing of commodities in a rural area may gradually turn it to an urban unit after a certain length of time (as associated activities of marketing and transport grows) which will then attract migrants if economic inequalities still persist, unless the migration linkage is traced to its source and investment diverted to that spatial unit. Baker and Harriss (1980) have criticised Lipton's definitions of 'urban' and 'rural' as they emphasise the existence of an undifferentiated rural sector consisting of landless agricultural labourers and an urban sector consisting of monopoly industries, politicians, business-men and organised labour. Rural landlords are thought to be bought off by urban interests and have been called 'crypto-urbanites'.

Sufficient amount of empirical information exists to illustrate that the strength of the remittance linkage in terms of proportion of village income, the value of net remittance (outflow from town to village minus inflow from village to town), proportion of urban migrants receiving and sending remittances vary from village to village and town to town. It is not possible to arrive at a general conclusion for the whole of india or the developing countries or the world from such 'scanty' and piecemeal information. Moreover in order to generalise and theorise from empirical information it is essential to question the definition of the term remittances used by different studies while designing the questionnaire. The questionnaire design may not take into account all the channels through which remittances can flow and consequently there may be underestimation of the strength of the linkage (as shown in Chapter 5). Therefore, while the empiricist who collects the empirical information must have a deep understanding of the society, the theoretician must also have a depth of knowledge about the country and society from which the empirical information have been collected in order to assess and evaluate the comparability and relative importance of the collected data. Byres while criticising Lipton's 'urban bias' writes: 'There is no sense of a detailed knowledge of the countries—their history, social structure, contemporary evolution' (Byres 1979: 217).

Lipton evidently ignored the possibility that regional variations might exist in the strength of the migration and remittance linkages within a country, especially a large country like India. Such variations in the strength of remittance linkages are highlighted in the next section as well as the next chapter. Therefore planning has to take into account the existing migration and remittance linkages in different parts of India as well as understand what types of urban units are likely to give rise to what type of migration and remittance linkages so that decisions can be made regarding the allocation of funds to different spatial units within the country for different purposes.

Migration and Remittances

In the late 1970s the International Labour Organisation turned its attention to the importance of migrant's remittances both at the national and international levels, for example, the detailed study in Punjab in India (Oberai and Singh 1981) and the remittances sent from Gulf countries to countries of South Asia (Amjad 1989). Studies have been undertaken from both rural and urban points of view in different developing countries. The significance of remittance in local rural economies has been illustrated by studies in different parts of India. Estimates from six villages in Garhwal district in northern India reveal that domestic income derived from migrants' remittances is higher than that obtained locally (Whittaker 1984: 129). In village level studies in Gujarat and Rajasthan, remittances as percentage of village income seem to vary between zero and 39 per cent, while around Madras, Orissa and West Bengal the figures vary between zero and 7 per cent (Connell, Dasgupta, Laishley, Lipton 1976: 107-9). In the context of Punjab in north-western India the author writes: 'data on remittances indicate a large transfer of resources to the rural areas of Ludhiana district from outmigration' (Oberai and Singh 1983: 104).

On the assumptions that some of the basic postulates of the migration theories discussed above, hold good in the real world and remittance linkage of varying strengths are likely to develop from different types of towns, this book aims to measure some of the characteristics of migration and remittances in a post-Independence industrial new town in India. The case study selected is Durgapur, a public sector steel town developed during the Second Plan period of post-Independence India. The town is located in the state of West Bengal in eastern India. The objective is to throw light on the possibility of using some of the theoretical concepts in urban planning. The important concepts that the subsequent chapters are expected to highlight are:

1. Potential of Class 1 towns to activate the labour transfer mechanism in different parts of India with special reference to a micro-level analysis of the potential of a post-Independence, industrial new town selected for the case study. The case study is expected to highlight the length of time over which the labour absorption capacity of such a town is likely to operate, given a certain trend of investment in industries within the geographical boundary of the urban unit. This draws upon the concept of transfer of labour from the rural to the urban sector elaborated in the Lewis-Fei-Ranis model discussed above.
2. On the assumption that labour migrates with the expectation of finding a job in the destination urban unit (i.e., with the probability of finding a job being less than 1), the case study is expected to measure the proportion of job-sought migrants compared to definite-job migrants (i.e., whose probability of finding a job is 1 as explained in Chapter 4) in different phases of town growth. The objective is to examine how the basic concept of Harris–Todaro model operates over time within a defined geographical space and how such proportions can help in planning of intra-town allocation of space for people who otherwise tend to squat.
3. On the assumption that migration is likely to result in the flow of remittances in both directions, this book is expected to examine the strength of the remittance linkage which has developed from the industrial new town selected for case study. As pointed out earlier, though such a study might throw some supporting or contradictory light on the theory of urban bias by Lipton, an isolated empirical study cannot support or disprove the theory at an aggregate level. Any attempt to draw an overall conclusion by comparing with the other existing empirical studies is likely to be erroneous because of the different definitions of remittances used by the different researchers at the time of formulating the questionnaires as discussed in Chapter 5. In order to theorise from empirical information it is essential that the same questionnaire is run in different places.

2

Remittances

Introduction

The analytical interest in remittances stems from the concern with their potential impact on various behavioural and structural phenomena. This chapter deals with the definition of the term 'remittance', empirical information collected and analysed by various researchers, the problems associated with research in this area and the objectives and methodology of research in this book.

Remittances associated with migration have been cited as a key benefit for areas of out-migration, not only by replacing foregone income, but augmenting savings, investment and technological innovation. An Egyptian study by Abou-Zaid in 1963 has claimed that rural-urban remittances have encouraged risk-taking and supplied credit for equipment hire or purchase. Simmon in his study in the Indian context in 1966 has pointed out that remittances led to a shift in the cropping pattern to higher risk cash crop while according to Srivastava (1968) remittances have enabled farmers to purchase labour saving machinery. The above-mentioned examples have been cited from Standing (1984).

Several studies have reported an impact on income distribution. In rural Punjab in India the data suggested that remittance income represented a larger proportion of household income among the poorest groups. The same was concluded in a survey of out-migration in Java (Hugo 1978). It might be the case that the impact of remittances may seem to be reducing income inequality because some poorer groups receive proportionately more than richer groups. However the larger absolute amounts received by the more affluent enable them to strengthen their control of the local economy through investment, while the poor may need the income to reduce debts or to purchase food. Thus remittances may reduce inequality in consumption, but increase structural inequality in the rural economy. It is also the case that the loss of income by the remitting migrant contributes to a worsening of income distribution in their destination. Data from the ILO study in Ludhiana, Punjab, demonstrates this well.

Definition and Impact of Remittance

The dictionary meaning of the term 'remittance' is 'a sum of money sent from one place or person to another; a quantity of some article sent in this way', (Shorter Oxford English Dictionary, 1964). In most empirical and analytical studies remittances are defined as personal income transfers directly associated with migration. Standing (1984) has pointed out that by no means are all remittances to areas of out-migration or in-migration personal, private transfers. Migrant associations have collected money and goods to send back for social projects in a home village or to particular groups or households in need (for example, Hart 1971; Mangin 1970; Skeldon 1980 cited in Standing 1984). In some cases as in large parts of Africa, membership of ethnically based home place associations in cities and towns is specially compulsory for migrants (for example, Little 1965; Gugler 1971 cited in Standing 1984). However it is possible that collective transfers are made mainly in times of rural stress and do not represent continuous redistribution of income earned from employment within the urban centre under study. Moreover in-migration surveys have varied from including only monetary transfers to also including goods of whatever value and purpose (gifts, loans or any other). The problem of including goods is the subsequent difficulties in valuation as the value may be fixed at the prices prevailing in the source or destination area. Moreover the prices of different commodities change over time at different rates in different parts of the country. This may raise problems in the valuation of the commodities.

Remittance Categories by Migration Category

When a migrant leaves a village, initially outflows will exceed inflows to the rural area, in that the migrant will normally take savings or have the journey financed by donations from relatives or by means of a loan. Subsequently after reaching the urban area, the migrant may continue to receive support from the rural area, either while searching for a source of income or while receiving schooling or training. But gradually the rural outflow will be expected to decline and in most cases will be reversed as remittances to the rural area begins. The way in which this will happen and its impact on the rural area will depend on the type of migration involved. Standing (1984) distinguished five categories of migrants, each of which will be discussed in turn to examine its relationship to remittances.

1. If the migrant is a seasonal or successful 'target-income' migrant worker a reverse flow to the rural area could be expected fairly quickly, the migrant's propensity to save could be expected to be high and the subsequent return to the rural area would be associated with a flow to the village of accumulated savings and acquired assets. So in the case of 'target' circular migrants, assuming their earning expectations were realised, the net flow of remittances would be positive for the rural area.
2. In the case of longer-term migrants, after an initial period the migrant may cease to send remittances. This type of behaviour was suggested in the International Labour Organisation's Kenya migration survey. Another plausible pattern is for the flows to decline gradually.

   On the other hand in the migration survey in Punjab in western India, the data suggest that after about three years of absence migrants started sending remittances and that thereafter the proportion remitting did not decline with time (Oberai and Singh 1980). An earlier study of Bombay suggested that those absent for more than 20 years continued to send remittances regularly (Prabhu 1956). A more recent survey in Delhi revealed no evidence of a decline in remittances over time in the city (Banerjee 1981).
3. Family members follow after an interval taking family savings and assets, once the migrant is established in the urban area. Definitionally, in that case there is a net loss of income for the rural area, if it is assumed that the remittances are sent mainly to immediate family members (which is not always the case). However some rural-urban remittance from the migrant to the family member precedes the migration of the family members.
4. In this case the entire family migrates together and there are no remittances.
5. Unsuccessful migrants induce rural outflow but do not produce a subsequent income transfer to that area because their migration yields little or no income or because they lose contact or interest in their areas of origin.

Gross versus Net Remittances

The above-mentioned categorisation evidently emphasises the importance of the outflow of remittances from the urban centre and most of the studies have been made in terms of flows in that direction only. The gross out-remittance[1] as distinct from net out-remittance from the town is expected

[1] Gross remittances or gross out-remittances from a town refer to the total remittances sent from the town under study to areas outside the town. Net remittances or net out-remittances refer to the total remittances sent from the town under study minus the total remittances sent to the town.

to be a significant measure of remittance linkage because of the following reasons:

1. If a migrant receives financial support from the source area, he is unlikely to send back remittances. So the net remittance will be negative and gross remittance zero.
2. If the migrant receives commodities and does not remit back, net remittance will be negative and gross remittance zero.
3. If the migrant receives commodities for selling in the town he is likely to send back a part of the earnings from the operation. It is assumed that unprofitable sales would not be sustained long. If the commodity sold has been produced with factors of production obtained in the rural areas, any gross remittance sent back will be equal to the net remittance as there is no monetary outflow from the rural area for purchase of commodities. On the other hand if some of the factors of production are obtained from urban areas the net remittance will be less than the gross. However in both the cases the net remittance is likely to be positive.
4. If the migrant receives goods for private consumption while remitting income, the net remittance will be less than the gross. However if the inflow is to support the person in the urban centre his out-remittance from the urban centre is likely to cease so that his gross remittance becomes zero and his net out-remittance is likely to become negative.

The above-mentioned gross and net remittances refer to values at the level of an individual migrant. An aggregation of the gross and net remittances of all migrants in a spatially defined areal unit will give the amount of gross and net remittances from that unit as a whole. A measure of gross out-remittance from a spatial unit is likely to group together the source areas which receive zero or negative net remittance on the one hand and areas which receive positive net remittance on the other hand to give fairly reliable, (but not an accurate understanding) of the extent of receipts of particular areas from an urban centre.

Gross Remittances

Size of Gross Remittances

As described in the former section the gross remittance is the first important component and it can be expected to vary according to variations in the propensity to remit on the part of urban migrants in different towns in different regions and the number of migrants. Different indices of propensity to remit can be constructed such as:

1. Proportion of migrants or earning migrants or earning male migrants who remit (n/m where n is the total number of remitters and m is either total number of migrants, earning migrants or earning male migrants);
2. average amount of remittance per migrant or earning migrant or male earning migrant (x/m where x is amount remitted).

These three variables may be combined as given below to give the towns gross remittance:

$$\sum_{j=1}^{n-1} R_{nj} = (n_n/m_n)*(x_n/m_n)*m_n = n_n\,x_n/m_n$$

where R_{nj} is the value of remittances from town n to all other places (rural and urban, j = 1 .... n–1).

Five major empirical studies[2] have tried to identify the determinants of a migrant's propensity to remit in terms of both number and/or amount. These studies consider several variables in relation to remittances, which will be reviewed here.

1. The size of income of the migrant at the destination has been considered in all the four studies. In Rempel and Lobdell study in Kenya (1978 based on survey in 1968 in eight largest urban centres) the correlation coefficient between amount of income earned and proportion of income remitted is positive. In Johnson and Whitelaw's study (1974, based on survey in Nairobi in 1971) and Oberai and Singh's study (1983, based on survey in Ludhiana in Punjab in India in 1976–77) these two variables have a negative correlation. On the other hand the total amount remitted per month gave positive correlation with the income of the migrant in all the five studies.

   Oberai and Singh have analysed the propensity to remit in terms of

[2] The five empirical studies on remittances are:

1. The Kenyan survey carried out by H. Rempel, J.R. Harris and M.P. Todaro in eight largest urban centres in December 1968 which provided the data for analysis by H. Rempel and R. Lobdell (Rempel and Lobdell 1978);
2. The Kenyan survey in Nairobi during Spring 1971 by the Institute of Development Studies (University of Nairobi) provided data for analysis by G.E. Johnson and W.E. Whitelaw (Johnson and Whitelaw 1974).
3. The survey in Pakistan by Mohammad, Butcher and Gotsch conducted in 1973 and analysed by them (Rempel and Lobdell 1978);
4. The survey conducted in Delhi from October 1975 to April 1976 by B. Banerjee provided data for analysis by B. Banerjee (Banerjee 1981); and,
5. The survey conducted in Ludhiana city in Punjab in India by the International Labour Organisation in collaboration with the Department of Economics of Punjab University (India) in 1976–77 which has been analysed by A.S. Oberai and H.K.M. Singh (Oberai and Singh 1983).

'likelihood to remit' separately to show that it has a positive correlation with the income received at the place of residence. It increases at a diminishing rate with increase in income up to a certain level.

2. The length of time the migrant has been a resident in the town has been considered by (*a*) Rempel and Lobdell (Kenyan study); (*b*) Johnson and Whitelaw (study in Nairobi); (*c*) Banerjee (1981, based on survey in Delhi in 1975–76); (*d*) Oberai and Singh (Ludhiana). In Rempel and Lobdell's study both the proportion of income remitted and the total remittance have negative, but insignificant correlation with the migrant's length of residence in the town, possibly because the survey included migrants who have been residents in the urban centres only for five years. However in the other Kenyan study, Johnson and Whitelaw have shown that the proportion of income remitted decreases with increasing length of urban residence.

   Banerjee's study in Delhi indicates that remittances increase at an increasing rate with the length of urban residence. Oberai and Singh conclude: 'The data on years since inmigration indicate that recent inmigrants send as much as longstanding inmigrants although the proportion of income remitted declines with the length of stay in the city' (Oberai and Singh 1981: 311). In terms of likelihood of sending remittances the length of stay in the urban area is negatively correlated (Oberai and Singh 1981).

3. Landownership has been considered as an important variable though differences exist in the exact definition of the variable. Rempel and Lobdell define it as 'land possessed by the migrant that produces cash crops or food for family members'; Johnson and Whitelaw have defined it as 'one if any member of the individual's family is cultivating land outside of Nairobi, zero if otherwise'; Banerjee defines it as 'amount of land owned by the migrant's family at the time of migration, in acres'; Oberai and Singh record it as '1 if owned land in previous place, 0 otherwise'.

   In Rempel and Lobdell's study both amount remitted and proportion of income remitted have no significant relationship with landownership whereas in Johnson and Whitelaw's study the relation between the proportion of income remitted and landownership is significant and positive.

   In Banerjee's study the relationship between the amount remitted and landownership is insignificant. In Oberai and Singh's study amount of remittance, proportion of income remitted and likelihood to remit, all have positive, but insignificant correlation.

4. Family structure both in the urban destination area and rural area have been analysed by all the studies. Rempel and Lobdell have analysed it in terms of: (*a*) marital status, (*b*) whether wife is a resident in a rural area. Johnson and Whitelaw have split it up into

four variables: (*a*) number of wives in Nairobi, (*b*) number of wives outside Nairobi, (*c*) number of children living in Nairobi, (*d*) number of children living outside Nairobi. Mohammad, Butcher and Gotsch (based on a survey in Pakistan in 1973 and cited in Rempel and Lobdell 1978) have considered two variables: (*a*) wife and children present with the migrant, (*b*) the size of the migrant's extended family in the home area. Banerjee's study includes four variables: (*a*) if the migrant is married and living with his wife in the city, (*b*) if the migrant is married and has left his wife in the rural area, (*c*) a measure of dependency burden in the urban household given by (number of nonworkers/(number of workers + 1)), (*d*) a measure of dependency burden in the rural household given by (number of nonworkers/(number of workers + 1)). Oberai and Singh have considered six variables: (*a*) household size, (*b*) if married head living with wife and children, (*c*) if married head living alone here, (*d*) if unmarried head, (*e*) if wife, child or parent of the head, (*f*) if brother, sister or relation of the head.

In Rempel and Lobdell's study the remitting propensities of married men were not significantly different from that of single men. Sixty per cent of the married men had a wife resident outside Nairobi. These men remitted significantly more than either other married men or single men. In Johnson and Whitelaw's study there is no significant difference in the proportion of income remitted by men with wives resident in Nairobi and men with wives resident outside Nairobi. Significant differences appear for the men who have to pay child care costs for children resident outside Nairobi. The latter hold in the study made by Mohammad, Butcher and Gotsch though they do not differentiate between wife's and children's residence possibly because separation of the mother from the child is inconceivable in Pakistan.

Banerjee's study shows that *ceteris paribus* migrants who have their wives living with them in the city remit less than migrants living as non-familial units. The latter group of migrants, who have left their wives in the rural area, will have a greater commitment to remit than unmarried migrants. The remittances are significantly positively correlated with dependency burden in the rural household and significantly negatively correlated with the dependency burden in the urban household. Oberai and Singh's study in Ludhiana shows that: (*a*) married heads living with own family remit a significantly smaller percentage of their income, (*b*) unmarried in-migrants send on an average a larger amount and higher proportion of their income than married migrants.

In terms of likelihood to remit: (*a*) household size has a significant negative effect, (*b*) married heads living alone are more likely to send remittance than married heads living with wife and children, (*c*) the coefficients of unmarried heads and non-nuclear members are also positive and significant.

Only this study in Punjab seems to indicate the importance of remittances by brothers, sisters and other relatives or non-nuclear members and measures the importance of remittance sent by wife, parent or son.

5. Level of education has been considered by Rempel and Lobdell, Johnson and Whitelaw and Banerjee in terms of 'years of formal education completed by the migrant'. Oberai and Singh correlate the decision to remit with four education levels viz. (*a*) no formal education, (*b*) has less than high school education, (*c*) has high school education, (*d*) graduate and above.

In the studies by Rempel and Lobdell and Johnson and Whitelaw the coefficients for education have a positive sign and are significant. Rempel and Lobdell have pointed out that:

> contrary to expectation, the education of the migrant and the urban income earned are not highly correlated in our sample (0.04). It would appear that the better educated choose to remit a larger proportion of their urban income even though their superior educational qualifications do not serve to provide them with above average urban income opportunities at this early stage of urban residence. This implies remittances represent a repayment of a social debt incurred in obtaining education. This is the interpretation Johnson and Whitelaw [1974: 476] attach to the positive sign for the coefficient for their educational variable (Rempel and Lobdell 1978: 332).

Banerjee's study in Delhi confirms this significant and positive relation of level of education with the propensity to remit. However in their study in Punjab Oberai and Singh note a contrary finding:

> The average remittance varies significantly with the level of education, but since the average income also rises with education, the proportion of income remitted remains more or less the same for all educational levels. In other words the propensity to remit does not depend on the level of education, although the absolute amount remitted varies because education affects the level of income (Oberai and Singh 1983: 316).

In terms of likelihood to remit on the part of a migrant 'education of inmigrants appears to be negatively associated . . . . This may signify a smaller degree of attachment to the home area' (Oberai and Singh 1983: 310).

6. Permanent or temporary nature of migration has been taken into account by Rempel and Lobdell and Banerjee in terms of the migrant's intention of living permanently in the urban centre. In Rempel and Lobdell's study this variable does not have a significant relation with the amount remitted or proportion of income remitted. On the contrary in Banerjee's study this variable has a negative and significant correlation, 'indicating that *ceteris paribus*, migrants who plan to settle in the city remit Rs. 19/month less than those who intend to return to the rural area' (Banerjee 1981: 348).
7. Whether the migrant has moved to obtain cash for a specific purpose has been used as an additional variable by Banerjee and it shows a significant positive correlation with the amount remitted.
8. The income of the home family has given a negative correlation with the total amount remitted in Mohammad, Butcher and Gotsch's study.

Oberai and Singh have taken into consideration some additional variables for explaining propensity to remit from Ludhiana city in Punjab. These are as follows:

9. Distance of migration has been analysed in terms of whether the migrant has in-migrated from outside Punjab. In terms of proportion of income remitted those who have migrated from within the state have the same propensity to remit as those who have migrated from outside the state, although the absolute amount remitted by the former is slightly higher because of their higher average incomes.

   In terms of likelihood to remit the distance variable has a significant positive correlation indicating that the long distance migrants from outside the state are more likely to send remittances.
10. Rural or urban character of the place of last residence has been incorporated in terms of whether the migrant has in-migrated from rural area. The results show that those from urban areas send larger amounts than those from rural areas, but since they also have higher average incomes, the proportion of income remitted is not significantly different between the two groups.

    In terms of likelihood to remit those from rural areas are more likely to remit than those who have migrated from urban areas.
11. Nature of employment has been analysed in terms of whether the migrant has a permanent/regular job/work and the relationship is insignificant in terms of proportion of income remitted. However in terms of likelihood to remit there seems to be a weak relationship with permanent nature of work as it is significant in two equations and insignificant in the third.

Apart from regression results the tabulated data indicate the following points: (*a*) permanent employees remit larger amounts than temporary and seasonal employees, but their propensity to remit in terms of number of remitters is about the same; (*b*) self-employed migrants are less likely to remit and remit significantly smaller proportions of their income than the wage earning in-migrants; (*c*) sector-wise, in-migrants employed in the formal sector remit larger absolute amounts, but there is no significant difference in the percentage of income remitted compared to the informal sector; (*d*) professional and administrative workers remit larger absolute amounts than other occupational categories, but the proportion of income remitted is not significantly different among different occupational groups.[3]

On the basis of these observations Oberai and Singh conclude: 'the proportion of income remitted does not depend on the nature and type of employment and that observed differences in absolute amounts remitted are largely due to differences in the levels of income' (Oberai and Singh 1983: 316-17).

12. The influence of caste has been analysed in terms of four caste groups viz: (*a*) belongs to high caste, (*b*)belongs to cultivating caste, (*c*) belongs to artisan caste, (*d*) belongs to low caste. Caste does not appear to have a significant influence on the amount or percentage of income remitted. However in terms of likelihood to remit it has been shown that: '*ceteris paribus* high cultivating and artisan castes are 4 to 8 per cent less likely to send remittances than the low caste' (Oberai and Singh 1983: 310).
13. Age of the migrant has given insignificant coefficients for amount and proportion of income remitted. However, in terms of likelihood to remit, age has a significant and negative correlation indicating that increasing age is likely to reduce the likelihood to send remittances perhaps because beyond a certain age, the in-migrants may no longer need to support aged parents back home since they may not be alive.

Another element which determines the gross remittance is the total number of migrants which will depend upon the propensity of a town to absorb migrants especially working migrants. Some of the determinants of the propensity to absorb migrants may be as follows:

1. Employment opportunities available in the town in terms of type and number;
2. poverty in the hinterland specially rural hinterland;
3. education level in the hinterland;
4. diffusion of information in the hinterland;
5. number of contacts in the town; and,
6. distance from the rural areas.

[3] The other occupational categories are tabulated in Oberai and Singh (1983: 301).

The results of the various surveys discussed above highlight numerous similar and dissimilar trends among the determinants of remittances in different spatial contexts. The conflicting conclusions might be explained only by putting the individual town analysis in a regional context at a chosen level.

Use of Gross Remittances

The use to which the monetary remittance is put by the recipients is likely to depend upon the following factors:

Initial consumption pattern of the recipient: Where the recipients are below the poverty line the income elasticity of demand for agricultural commodity mainly food will be high. This will increase the local consumption expenditure on food.

On the other hand with an increase in income status of the recipients, the expenditure of remittances will gradually shift to the purchase of clothes, medicine, durable household goods, house improvements and construction and luxury consumption. In the case of landowning classes mainly above the poverty line a proportion can be expected to be spent on seeds, fertiliser, pesticides, water procurement and hiring of labour. The priority given on expenditures on any of these agricultural inputs will depend partly on: (*a*) available disposable income including the remittance; (*b*) specific requirements of particular crops; (*c*) out-migration of family labour and/or innovations in agriculture and/or purchase of land by the large landholders from the small landholders which may lead to increased demand for hired agricultural labour and sharecropping. If this increase in wage labour is induced by reduction of family labour and innovations then it will act as an employment multiplier; (*d*) size and fragmentation of farms will affect the propensity to adopt mechanisation even when substantial amount of capital is available through remittance. Where farm conditions are suitable mechanisation can be implemented only by rich farmers as it involves release of large amount of capital to finance it.

Availability of the desired commodity or service: The above-mentioned expenditures will materialise only if they are available in the area. Hence the initial consumption pattern may trigger off demands which can lead to establishment of wholesale and retail units as well as service centres. It must be pointed out that demand for education is likely to lead to out-migration rather than increase of the facility at higher levels. At lower levels it may result in an increase in the demand for stationery goods, books and light either with kerosene or electricity. Hence an employment multiplier comes into operation which may not increase the total output in the area, but increases the per capita employment and income potential.

Propensity to save and compulsory ceremonial duties: Apart from current consumption expenditure, another element which will compete with the propensity to invest will be the propensity to save. The propensity to save is likely to be influenced by two factors: (*a*) income level and current consumption (savings may be defined as: S = Y − C where S is savings, Y is income and C is consumption expenditure); (*b*) compulsory ceremonial duties especially payment of dowry for the daughters' marriage. However the rigidity of such obligatory social duties may vary from region to region and caste to caste. The ratio of number of daughters and sons a person has is likely to be directly proportional to the propensity to save in the Indian context. A daughter usually represents outflow of money from the household while a son represents inflow. Hence the sex distribution of the next generation in an Indian household is likely to influence the net outflow from a household. Hence remittances may help to augment the savings rather than investment or current consumption expenditure, thus resulting in no immediate multiplier effect. However such savings herald an increase in short run consumption expenditure in future though its effect on the demand for urban or rural commodity is difficult to generalise. Regional variations in social norms may result in different propensity to invest the remittance money. Though within an area the propensity to save for dowry is likely to extend over all income groups, the absolute value will vary with income. As one moves down the income levels the propensity to invest may completely disappear under the social pressure explained above.

Value system and attitude towards different types of occupation: The propensity to invest will also depend upon the attitudes of the people towards different types of work and the general value system. Emphasis on intellectualism in certain regions may make white collar jobs and professional work like doctor, lawyer, professor, teacher more respectable than having a local 'business'.[4] Moreover this may partly be an outcome of colonial rule as the term 'business' degenerated to trading activities rather than augmenting the production of processed commodities. Since such activities generally require no particular educational level and technical skill the labour supply for them is always high. Though the context has changed the perceptions tend to linger resulting in an aversion for specific occupations in different regions, thereby affecting the propensity to invest. In addition the risk and labour involved may be more strenuous than protected wage earning employment. Moreover perceptions of sin and corruption may vary from region to region and under the government system of taxation self-employed people may be tempted to various illegal practices. This can affect the local perception of the occupation. Illegal

[4] The term 'business' is a local usage in India for any self-employed person other than professionals requiring technical skills.

activities in different forms may exist in other occupations as well, but accountability may make it less widespread and obvious. This affects the respectability of an occupation in the perception of the people.

Finally the inherent nature of a person may tend to shirk risks. If at the initial stage people of a certain region are subjected to more accountability in wage-earning occupations, the general fear of risk may be transmitted from one generation to another with a psychological multiplier effect.

The evolution of a psychological aversion for production and trading is exemplified by West Bengal in India. Prior to the advent of the British rule the area specialised in cotton cultivation, spinning and trading of cotton yarn. With the advent of the British rule, the purposeful disruption of the local trade by the foreign power and the inherent desire of the people to be closer to power in terms of person and space resulted in a transfer of occupational preference from self employment to white collar jobs, the impact of which still tends to linger in the value system of the area.

Hence propensity to save becomes a function of income, consumption, intensity of social obligations, perceptions of people about the different occupations.

On the assumption that under similar combination of events the rate of return on the investment use k is constant across regions, the variations in the exact use conditioned by the regional variations in the combination of events become important in the understanding of transmission of spread effect through remittance linkage. Empirical surveys of remittance usage in different regions of India can help in the understanding of usage functions highlighting the regional similarities and dissimilarities. An attempt will be made in Chapters 5 and 6 to compare the findings of the present survey in Durgapur in West Bengal with that of Ludhiana in Punjab made by International Labour Organisation in 1976–77.

Net Remittances

Finally the net remittance from a town will depend on the propensity of the migrants to receive money. Several authors have considered flows in both directions and have concluded that some rural areas are net losers in the process. One example is a study from six villages in western Nigeria by Essang and Mabawonku. Similarly a study of a village in Taiwan by Chen in 1971 and a survey of 300 households in Jeonlabag-do Province (Korea) support net outflow from rural to urban areas. The role of financing the education of out-migrants also play a prominent role in rural to urban flows as evident in India. After assessing the data from Indian village studies Connell *et al.* conclude that if the majority of the more expensively educated children do not return then the village can be a net loser, even when the migrants send back substantial remittances (1975, cited in Rempel and Lobdell 1978).

However on the basis of the survey of Ludhiana district taking the rural aspects into consideration, Oberai and Singh conclude that the outflow to out-migrants from rural areas is insignificant. Only 8 per cent of the out-migrants received such payments and the amounts remitted were also small (Oberai and Singh 1983). Banerjee's study in Delhi revealed that only 1.6 per cent of the sample were receiving remittances from the rural area.

Stark has argued that the rural to urban financial flow is for a limited time period while the return flow continues for a number of years (Rempel and Lobdell 1978). Therefore over a longer period the rural area is unlikely to be the loser. However the determinants of flow from a rural to an urban centre has not been analysed in detail.

Research Objectives, Collection of Empirical Information and Associated Problems

With the objective of ascertaining the potential of a town to absorb migrant labour force and the consequent development of a remittance linkage with other spatial units, this book focuses on three aspects of town growth and its impact:

1. A macro level grouping of Class 1 towns (population more than 100,000 according to the Census of India) on the basis of selected population and migration characteristics. The purpose is to determine the place of Durgapur and the role it plays in absorbing migrants in relation to other Class 1 towns of India.
2. A micro-level study of the trend of migration to Durgapur since its inception, the characteristics of the migrants and an examination of Durgapur's role in the rural-urban labour transfer mechanism.
3. A micro-level study of the strength and character of remittance linkage of the town with other rural and urban areas outside its municipal boundaries; the aim being to answer the following questions: (*a*) Does a town specialised in heavy industries develop a strong remittance linkage? (*b*) If it develops remittance linkage, what type is it—rural or urban? (*c*) How are the remittances spatially distributed and what is their significance in generating a multiplier effect on income in different areas within India?

In order to fulfil the above-mentioned objectives it was necessary to collect empirical information of two types. Consequently this book depends heavily on two major sources of data.

Secondary Data from Official Sources

The macro-level analysis of towns mentioned above required town-level data on migration and socio-economic variables. This dataset was obtained from the Census of India. Since all the 1981 census volumes were not available in published form until 1989, the first fieldwork included a trip to Delhi to collect the data from the unpublished volumes. It must be noted that the migration variables at the town-level was not available for 1981 as the census authorities have opted to omit that level of information from the 1981 schedule. For 1981, migration data is now available at the district level. However, since this study focuses on measuring the potential of individual towns to absorb migrants, the district level data is not relevant. Further details of this dataset will be discussed in Chapter 3.

Though doubts are always expressed about the authenticity of published data, the census data includes 100 per cent enumeration of the population in terms of the selected variables. The town is usually divided into blocks and local officials are paid to do door to door counting. Since most of the variables are non-monetary and the survey is being done by the government there is likely to be no 'no responses'. The enumerator can hand in wrong figures without counting, but the likelihood of such a possibility is low. I have seen the raw data sheets of the enumeration done in Durgapur for 1981 census and it gives detailed information of each house along the roads including the squatter settlements in different localities. Though some of the floating population might not have been recorded, the total figure is so large for Class 1 towns with more than 100,000 people, that the error expressed as percentage of the total population is likely to be very small. Hence inter-town comparisons of migration and socio-economic characteristics given by the census are likely to highlight the general trend.

The state level estimates of rural poverty have been used for forming an idea about the backdrop against which the different types of towns have developed. Poverty has been measured in terms of percentage of rural or total population of each state below the poverty line as given by the Planning Commission of India on the basis of the National Sample Survey data for 1972–73, 1977–78 and 1983–84. The absence of more detailed district level data makes the analysis problematical.

The poverty line has been defined by the Planning Commission of India as the amount of money required to provide a monthly calorie intake of 2400 per person in rural areas and 2100 per person in urban areas. This Planning Commission data on the number of people below the poverty line is based on the National Sample Survey data on household consumer expenditure and for updating the poverty line over the different years for which the estimates are made, the Central Statistical Organisation's Private Consumption deflator is used. Thus this measure implies an average level of absolute poverty which is determined on the basis of food intake, a basic necessity for the physical existence of all human beings.

Poverty can be defined in various ways in both relative and absolute terms. Attempts have been made by individual researchers to use different definitions for poverty to suit their own research objectives at the particular level chosen for their study. Such isolated micro-level definitions, however fail to give an overall picture of the levels of poverty in different parts of India. To have an idea about the relative levels of poverty in different parts of a large country, it is necessary to make sample surveys in different parts of the country with a consistent definition of poverty. Such an objective can be realised only by official data collection agencies having the required expertise, manpower and money for the purpose. The statistical methods used for data collection by the National Sample Survey Organisation in India are very sophisticated and reliable. It is the only available data on poverty suitable for inter-state comparison in India and deals with absolute poverty in terms of nutrition requirement for survival. Hence this data have been used in my study of large towns located in different states of India.

Moreover for practical purposes, (unless the aim of the study is to highlight the inability of a definition to fulfil the objectives of a particular research at a particular level), it is more useful to accept the basic definitions used by the major planning authorities in the country, so that the result of the research can be used for comparison with other studies or official reports necessary for planning. It is necessary to create new definitions only when a particular definition is not fulfilling the research objectives of a particular analysis. Otherwise unnecessary duplication of definitions may create more confusion.

Apart from the above-mentioned data, this study has also used state-level data on per capita state domestic product, per capita consumption expenditure and consumer price index numbers (for West Bengal and Bihar) which will be discussed in the relevant sections in Chapter 5. Unpublished aggregate yearly figures of money transfer via money orders to and from Durgapur were obtained from the Main Post Office in Durgapur. This unpublished data is an accurate record of all transfers via money orders, required by the postal department for their own calculations of receipts of revenue accruing from it. Hence there is no question of errors.

Primary Data

The micro-level analysis of migration and remittance characteristics of Durgapur required the running of a two-phased questionnaire survey in Durgapur, as detailed data on these variables are not available from any official source. The designing and running of a household survey have to follow the following steps:

1. Formulation of research objectives and central questions which the research based on the survey is expected to answer;
2. developing an appropriate questionnaire design;
3. determining a sample size which would be representative as well as cost effective;

4. determining a sample design to distribute the sample throughout the town;
5. creation of a survey infrastructure;
6. selection and training of research assistants;
7. running the questionnaire which is bound to be fraught with problems.

The step 1 mentioned above has been discussed in the previous section. Steps 2 to 4 involved technical and statistical expertise and their details will be discussed in the relevant sections on data analysis in Chapters 4 and 5. Steps 5 to 7 required organisational aptitude. The following discussion gives a general description of the last three steps for the two-phased survey conducted in Durgapur in 1987 and 1989.

Creation of survey infrastructure: As the representativeness of a survey requires a large sample size, it is essential to plan carefully the details of the infrastructure prior to launching of the survey; the purpose being to minimise time and cost. The distribution of the sample in different parts of the town depends upon at what level the study aims to estimate the required variables. Since my objective was to estimate the variables for the town as a whole, the sample had to be distributed in different parts of the town amidst different income and occupational groups. This required an enormous amount of intra-town movement which was expected to and did make the survey expensive and time-consuming, especially because Durgapur covers a large area with scattered residential areas and the topography is undulating. The infrastructure included the following components:

1. Fixing the exact areas within the town which were to be surveyed and determining the exact proportion and number of households to be surveyed in each area.
2. Procurement of area maps with the required details, the requirement in this case being roads within the selected areas and/or types of quarters in different townships reflecting the economic status of the occupants or landuse maps with plots indicating residences and fields. Some of the maps were available from local planning authorities like Asansol–Durgapur Development Authority, Housing Directorate and the industries. Where the maps were not available rough sketches showing the roads were drawn by hand.
3. In order to ensure the response and understanding of all categories of people, some form of authorisation by the acknowledged local institution or government is required. Apart from the authorisation letter from the department of Geography at Cambridge, the Chief Town Administrators of DSP, DPL, ASP and MAMC (abbreviations given in Appendix 5) issued letters requesting the residents of the respective townships to cooperate in the survey. Since ABL has been closed

during the one year period preceding the first survey, the authorities could not be approached. These letters proved to be very useful because the official stamp made people more respectful even when they could not read the language.

Outside these industrial residential areas the Vice-Chairman of Durgapur Notified Area Authority kindly consented to arrange local help provided prior information was given about the date and area of survey. Local guides were essential for being introduced in the locality, as well as for security, since some of the areas were locally notorious for illegal activities and were not safe, especially for a woman interviewer. Security was of utmost importance during the second phase as it was essential to interview the earning migrant and majority of them were available in their residences only after office hours in the evenings. The problem was however to synchronise the time of the survey with the convenience of the guide (as he/she was often employed) and with the person to be interviewed.

4. Printing of questionnaires in bulk had to be organised, but it was thought to be prudent to print a few at the first instance as there is always the possibility of mistakes or changes in the questionnaire depending on the responses in the first few days.
5. Arrangement of intra-city conveyance by car was necessary as the sample design was to cover different areas of the town, some of them being quite far flung. As mentioned earlier the topography of Durgapur is very undulating and the residential areas have developed disparately with very long distances between the industrial townships, (which is itself an oft-quoted criticism of the town planners) Moreover during the second phase survey the migrants identified in the first phase had to be contacted and in most cases it was necessary to return at an appointed time to interview the working migrant. Industrial labour tend to work in different shifts and hence there was no guarantee as to the number of times the same house had to be revisited. The person to be interviewed often forgot about the appointment and fresh appointments had to be made. Some people were reluctant to give information during the second phase and had to be given time to decide, thereby necessitating returning to the same house several times. In the cases where discrepancies were noted in the questionnaires another interview had to be arranged. All this necessitated hiring a car. The presence of a driver was necessary for security as well in unknown areas.

   However hiring a car with a driver was very expensive and a detailed organisation of all the links in the infrastructure was essential for a smooth and quick functioning of the entire system.

Selection and training of research assistants: Since the sample size was expected to be 1500–2000 households in the first phase, it was necessary to appoint research assistants, not only for interviewing, but also for other paperwork like stapling of questionnaires, tabulation of data etc. Local assistants, even if less qualified, had to be appointed as they were expected to have local knowledge about the different areas. Moreover in some areas an educated woman interviewer was too conspicuous to allow relaxed conversation with the respondent. This was true in some of the squatter settlements of milkmen located in the steel town and along Grand Trunk Road. In such areas a local male interviewer was accepted more easily.

Training of the research assistants involved the following points.

1. Acquainting them with the topic, objectives and methodology of research was essential in order to convince people of the relevance and authenticity of the project and to deal with counter questions from the respondent. It proved to be a difficult task as the male local assistants who could be recruited at the given wage had not studied geography, economics or statistics. This was due to the fact that geography is heavily biased towards female students; whereas students in economics are usually high in demand or are students with no spare time.
2. Explaining the questions, the range of probable responses, the possibility of unexpected responses, the justification, logic and purpose of each question and the method of quick cross-checking of the questions in order to test the authenticity of replies in the field was a part of the training. Emphasis had to be laid on the necessity to be honest. A few questionnaire forms had to be filled in for practice by each assistant.
3. They had to be rehearsed in conversation, the method of coaxing out replies by indirect questions and to pinpoint relevant answers from long, rambling and indecisive replies. The opening conversation had to be polite and persuasive to surmount initial suspicions and reluctance to give information to strangers.

The selection of research assistants depended on the type of work and the qualities it required. Two types of work were required: (*a*) interviewing, (*b*) tabulation of the filled in questionnaires. Two of the research assistants were to tabulate the questionnaires in the evenings and were asked to take rest after their shift of interview in the mornings. Tabulation in the field was considered to be necessary because of the following reasons:

1. It would help to find out and correct the mistakes immediately;
2. it helped in understanding the different handwritings;
3. it kept the full team alert, sincere and honest;
4. it helped in getting a daily, overall view of the variety of responses; and,

5. it enabled easy movement of data back to England as it would have been expensive and difficult to carry back 7000 sheets of paper in each phase. During the first phase the variables were handwritten on paper, while in the second phase the data (consisting of 550 cases with 109 variables) were directly fed into a portable computer. Thus in the second phase the entire inputting of data was done by me, while an assistant dictated from the questionnaires. To my horror, on return to Cambridge, I discovered that there were difficulties in transferring the data to the mainframe and it took me three months to get the data ready for analysis (on the mainframe).

Graduation was the minimum qualification required, though preference was given to students of geography, economics and statistics. Two female candidates were recruited from Calcutta in the first phase as people tend to be less suspicious of young female students. Second phase survey was mainly done by me, though in some areas I had to depend on a local male research assistant because of his possibility of getting a better response as explained earlier. It was deemed inadvisable to recruit female interviewers in the second phase as the survey had to be conducted at different times of the day, mostly after dark and guardians would not allow them to participate in such work. It was also too much of a responsibility for me to guarantee security. The interviewer was expected to have an intelligent, quick-witted, smiling, pleasing and persuasive personality to invoke confidence in the respondent. Patience and commonsense were essential attributes, especially to deal with unpleasant respondents, some of whom could become insulting. Tabulation in the first phase demanded an understanding of the research topic and an ability to cross-check answers to locate discrepancies. Hence the tabulators had to be better qualified and trained in geography or economics. It was preferred that the interviewer could speak fluently in English and Bengali, together with some grasp over Hindi.

In the first phase two first class female graduates in geography were taken from Calcutta and had to be provided with food and accommodation. Hiring female candidates proved to be difficult because of Indian conservatism. Two other male local candidates were hired easily. They were less qualified. In the second phase one male candidate from the first phase was re-employed and two female candidates were employed in shifts to help in computerisation of data, questionnaire stapling etc.

Running the questionnaire: The initial plan was to do the survey in two shifts i.e., from 8 am to 1 pm and from 4 pm to 6 pm as the intervening period is usually allocated for short naps. Each interviewer was expected to fill up 10 questionnaires per day. However towards the end of the survey the time had to be reduced to one shift as the interviewers were becoming extremely exhausted.

Embarrassingly, questionnaire survey involves manipulation of the psychology of the respondents which invariably raises doubts regarding the ethics of survey. Since the entire research project depended upon the responsiveness of the inhabitants in Durgapur, the quality of response and sources of error will be discussed in the next two subsections.

Responses: To the surprise of all interviewers the residents of Durgapur seemed to be very responsive and helpful to both the phases of questionnaire survey. It was encouraging to find an active interest in the topic, though it required elaborate explanations regarding the practical implications of the study. Noting a certain amount of scepticism regarding 'planners, researchers and their abstract theories', all interviewers were directed to emphasise the implications of the study in real life.

Interesting questions were asked by both literate and illiterate respondents regarding the procedure of generalisation from the interview of a small proportion of the total population. My theoretical knowledge of probability sampling was forced to descend to the wordly realities as it had to be explained in simple terms to be understood by the people, some of whom have not been tormented by the hieroglyphics of script! To my immense satisfaction they understood and responded! The fact that an Indian, especially a Bengali woman had the 'courage' to move alone in unknown areas, sometimes in squatter settlements, often after dark, brought forth surprised and admiring remarks as well as eager responses to the research questions.

However life was not all rosy! Though the fact that I was working in a foreign university evoked respect, especially amongst the educated upper class, it also gave rise to suspicions regarding my true identity. In some areas, especially amongst the lower middle income group of industrial workers I was accused of being a 'CIA' agent. On grounds of such a suspicion one of the respondents in the Coke Oven Colony refused to answer. This problem was partly overcome by informing them that I was a government scholar and had been lecturing in one of the well-known colleges of Calcutta. Since the Vice-Chairman of Durgapur Notified Area Authority who organised local guides was a Marxist Party leader, in some areas I had to convince the people that I had no political affiliations whatsoever.

The non-Bengali women mostly refused to answer and in such cases effort was made to meet the male members even during the first phase survey. My general impression was that the non-Bengali population was more conservative than the Bengali population and since their value system did not understand the necessity of a young woman to move unreservedly from door to door for the purpose of a study, they were very reserved and required an enormous amount of coaxing. In some cases the male research assistants were more effective, especially during the first phase. As majority of the non-Bengalis were self-employed, they were afraid of income tax enquiries. In such cases attempt was made to avoid revealing my link with the government. The most difficult area was Karangapara, a densely populated bazaar, with non-Bengali businessmen. Both the phases of survey, especially the second one was frustrating as well as frightening and at one point of time I was advised by the local guide to leave the area from the survey. To the astonishment of the local people I persevered!

During the first phase there was an initial hesitation to give their names and addresses and they had to be persuaded that this was an initial survey and names were required for returning for the second interview, to take place after one year. During the second phase the identity was not recorded on the questionnaire. The average time taken for each questionnaire during the first phase was 10–30 minutes, depending upon how hospitable the person was. On several occasions I had to drink 10 cups of tea, in spite of feeling sick as I did not want to hurt the respondent and thereby spoil the survey. The second phase questionnaire took 45 minutes approximately.

The responses varied from person to person, question to question and community to community. The questionnaire should be so designed as to deal with a wide range of answers, neither losing any information nor deviating from the point. Open questions tend to record a wide range of answers without biasing the respondent, though at times gentle prompts and suggestions are required. In order to prompt the interviewer should be conversant with the variable and must be well-informed about local conditions in order to judge the authenticity of the replies, for example, due to lack of prior knowledge the answers to the query about office designation were vague on the first day.

In many houses the interviewed person failed to recall the year of arrival. Subsequently approximations were insisted upon or the age at arrival was recorded so that the year could be calculated from the person's present age. For females from rural areas they had to recall how many years they have been married and after how many years of marriage they arrived in Durgapur. They often did not know their present age. So the age had to be calculated from their age at marriage, the age of their children and general appearance. Surprisingly they seemed to know their age at marriage as that was a major landmark in their lives.

Women were often afraid to reveal or were ignorant about their husbands' past and present occupations. I was chased away with abuses in one house by the housewife because she felt insulted that I had wanted to interview her husband while the door was slammed on my face by another housewife because she was afraid that I would enquire about her husband's side business which is illegal for a government worker. I discovered this from the local people.

The names of the villages from which they migrated were sometimes incomprehensible because of difficulties of understanding various accents or due to the lack of knowledge about each and every small village in India.

Some did not know the name of the district from which they have migrated. The agricultural landholders in the fringes were afraid that land ceilings were being checked, while the question on number of children (as an answer sheet had to be filled for each member in the first phase) and the age at marriage made them alert on account of legislation of adult marriage and propaganda of family planning.

Due to increasing regional disturbances the Sikhs were afraid to answer while the former refugees from Bangladesh and East Pakistan enquired whether they would be evicted. In general, the upper income and the lower income groups were very cooperative, while the middle and especially the lower middle income group was very suspicious. Allotting proper research assistants to the suitable groups, without letting the assistants understand, required subtle diplomatic instructions, for example, the qualified women assistants from Calcutta brought enthusiastic response from the educated managerial and administrative employees, while the local assistants got better response amongst the squatters.

Contrary to the initial plan, a pilot survey of the second phase was not conducted as it did not seem prudent to disturb and irritate people many times. During the second visit most of the respondents remembered the first phase survey.

Sources of Error: Since the first phase survey was concerned with qualitative variables the chances of obtaining erroneous responses were negligible. As discussed in the earlier section the age and husband's designation given by the respondents might not have been accurate and the year of migration might have deviated by one or two years. The sensitivity of the respondents to different questions has been quantified and will be discussed in Chapter 4. However a study based on a large sample size is likely to highlight an authentic general trend in spite of minor errors.

The second phase survey results were expected to have more important sources of error as this questionnaire concentrated on extracting monetary information about remittances and income. Hence in this phase the structure of the questionnaire was of great importance as discussed in Chapter 5. There was however no way of verifying the value of remittances recorded in the survey. The questionnaire could only make sure that the possible links have been recorded and personal knowledge of the prices of commodities, cost of living etc., had to be used for cross-checking. The first page asked questions about family members residing outside Durgapur and their source of earning. Then if the respondent refused to reveal the monetary link with family members living outside the town, he/she was cross-questioned about the source of income of the member living outside. On the basis of local knowledge about the structure of family dependence it was assumed that parents, brothers/sisters, sons/daughters, in-laws were likely to receive remittances and the respondent was questioned and coaxed to give a fairly truthful answer. As to the value of the remittance, three examples are given below to illustrate the procedure of cross-checking.

1. Suppose a respondent in Durgapur had a daughter studying in a private school in Calcutta who lived in a hostel. The migrant gives a very low value. He is then asked to give breakdowns of tuition fee, hostel charge, book purchase, clothes purchase per month or year. The total then demonstrates the real value and then the migrant is asked to explain the deviation.
2. Suppose a respondent sends money to a village for the maintenance of his/her mother and the cultivation of five acres of land and there are doubts about the value given. He is asked what crops are cultivated during the year and how many times per year. Then he is asked to give the breakdown of the cost of cultivation per acre on heads like seed, fertiliser, pesticide, water and labour. It was easy to calculate the expected amounts after the questionnaire has been run for the first few days because similar results tend to emerge as more and more people are asked the same questions. In fact towards the end of the survey I was able to calculate accurately the likely production of paddy given the location of the land and the inputs. Non-respondents who own land or are in similar professions were asked to give their opinion about the values given by the respondents.

   It was important that I did not bias the respondent with my estimate and so the strategy was to coax him to give more breakdowns of the total expenses and the expenses made from the remitted money without revealing my estimate. The method used for cross-checking the income variables will be discussed in Chapter 5.
3. Sometimes a local, experienced person who knew the respondent, was asked about the authenticity of the data and if the figure given by the respondent was found to be incorrect further investigations were made. One example was an industrial worker who gave a very small amount of transfer to the rural area and did not want to disclose his side business as an agent arranging sale of residential land. From his friends I came to know that he was building a house in his village. So I visited his family and had a casual conversation (not as an interviewer) with his daughter and wife. The exact amount of money transferred to the rural area and his income were thus ascertained.

Finally, the respondents were also hesitant to reveal the size of landholdings of the recipients of the remittances because of the land ceiling legislations in India. In those cases they had to be convinced that they had the option of not revealing the names and addresses of the recipients. Therefore, though the questionnaire had intended to record the addresses of the recipients with the objective of tracing them for interview, that question had to be omitted for many respondents. Direct questions regarding the temporal variation in the proportion of income remitted was not asked because it was expected that the answers would have been vague and unreliable as the respondent would not have been able to calculate or remember past figures. Instead, current values of remittances sent by migrants who have migrated at different points of time (those who have migrated in the last few years, 10–20 years ago, 20–30 years ago etc.) were expected to reveal a temporal trend in the propensity to remit as the migrant's length of residence in the town increased.

Though the results derived from a survey dataset of this type invariably lacks accuracy, they can still be expected to reveal fairly reliable patterns, especially when the sample size is very large. While presenting and analysing such a dataset doubts can arise regarding the validity of using decimal places, since such fractions may imply pseudo-precision. The decision to include decimal places depends upon two other factors:

1. The purpose of using the value, for example, the fact that only 26 per cent of the population of India is urban can be used to highlight the smallness of the proportion and for this purpose the decimal place may not be important; on the other hand if a proportion value is used for the purpose of estimation of an absolute value, the decimal place may be important.
2. The size of the absolute value from which a proportional estimate is to be derived is an important consideration, for example, 13.41 per cent of the total income generated by the town (amounting to more than 1000 million of rupees in the case of the sample survey in Durgapur) is bound to be a very large number; removal of 0.41 per cent (in order to have a rounded figure of 13 per cent) may result in an underestimation of over Rs. 8 million. If the data is being tabulated for the first time it is essential that the loss of information is minimum so that the subsequent studies which use the data for comparison have the option of rounding off the fraction themselves. Use of the fraction leaves the reader the option to include or exclude the marginal Rs. 8 million. On the other hand if the absolute value is small, for example, 13.41 per cent of Rs. 10 is likely to differ very little from 13 per cent of Rs. 10 so that the decimal places can be omitted.

On the basis of the above-mentioned points it was decided to use one or two decimal places while tabulating the values of the variables pertaining to migration and remittances in Chapters 4 and 5. Though this is a standard convention followed in statistical presentation of data by researchers and official sources, it must be remembered that the decimal places should not be taken to imply accuracy at that level.

Concluding Remarks

Remittances will depend upon the economic and family background of the migrants to a particular destination area. The type of the urban destination areas in terms of employment opportunities and accommodation available may affect the attributes of the migrants. Therefore different towns may develop remittance linkage of varying strength and characteristics. Some towns may absorb more migrants from other urban areas and thus may tend to develop stronger remittance linkage with urban rather than rural areas. Some regions may become strongly linked with the urban centres through remittances while other areas may fail to do so. Thus variations in remittance linkage may become a factor behind regional disparity.

Surveys have shown that the strength of the rural-urban remittances vary from country to country. In Ghana a survey of urban households with in-migrants suggested that nearly two-thirds sent or took money home and over half claimed to do so every month. In a large survey in Tanzania a majority of the migrants in urban areas reportedly sent or took money home, but less than 40 per cent did so regularly, once a year or more. In Kenya gross rural-urban remittances were found to be substantial. All the above mentioned examples have been cited from Standing (1984).

The study in Ludhiana reveals that 16 per cent of the migrants sent back remittances and 18 per cent of the migrant workers did so (Oberai and Singh 1981). In Delhi about 66 per cent of the earning male migrants interviewed seem to remit to origin areas (Banerjee 1981). This book provides empirical evidence of the development of remittance linkage from a planned, post-Independence, industrial new town in India. Bearing in mind all the methodological and data problems involved in this study, it is possible, however, to give only an approximate idea of the strength and characteristics of the remittance linkage. The comparability of the aggregate data with studies made in other areas depends upon the definition of remittances and questionnaire design which will be discussed later.

3

Regional Differences in Migration Characteristics of Large Indian Towns

Process of Urbanisation in India

India has a population of 835 million (estimate for 1989 in *Asia 1990 Yearbook*) and the process of urbanisation in India has not been rapid. Table 3.1 shows the gradual increase in the proportion of urban population to the total from 18 per cent in 1961 to 19.8 per cent in 1971 to 23.3 per cent in 1981 (the estimate for 1989 being 26 per cent). This increase in the urban proportion could be accounted for, in theory, by natural increase only if there is a sufficient disparity in natural rates of increase of urban and rural population. If we assume the converse, that the natural rates of increase in the two sectors are exactly the same, all of the change in the urban proportion would be accounted for only by migration. Using this latter hypothesis we can calculate the Crude Numbers of Estimated Migrants from urban to rural areas in each of the last three census decades (Table 3.1). This shows that as many as 10 million people might have migrated in the period 1961–1971, although this very large absolute number resulted in an increase of only 3.2 per cent in the percentage urban. Using 1981 as an illustrative base for a hypothetical calculation, to bring the proportion of urban population to 50 per cent would require a shift of 150 million people from the rural to the urban sector. This indicates the enormity of the problem of increasing urban employment opportunity adequately if, as many predict, the rate of urbanisation increases.

Theoretically the migrant attracting capacity of towns may result from one or more of the following factors:

1. Expansion of employment opportunities which would be remunerative enough to attract migrants.
2. The size and character of the unemployed indigenous labour force available in the towns.

Table 3.1

Trend of Urbanisation in India

Year	*Urban percentage in total population*	*Percentage increase of total population in the decade*	*Urban population in millions*	*Predicted urban population*	*Crude est. of urban migration in the decade*	*Change in urban percentage*
1881	9.2	–	–	–	–	–
1921	11.4	–	–	–	–	–
1931	12.1	–	–	–	–	–
1941	14.0	–	–	–	–	–
1951	17.3	–	–	–	–	–
1961	18.0	21.6	78.93	75.95	2.98	0.8
1971	19.8	24.8	109.09	98.50	10.00	1.7
1981	23.3	25.1	156.40	135.68	20.72	3.2

Note: Est. stands for estimate.
Source: Census of India 1971 and 1981; General Population Tables; Series I, Part II-A(i).

3. The size of surplus labour pool and poverty level of the rural hinterland.

This chapter examines the regional variations in the pattern of absorption of migrants by 'Class 1 towns' of India and the associated occupation characteristics of the towns. The increasing importance of these large towns is demonstrated by the fact that they accounted for 48.9 per cent of the total urban population of India in 1971, and by 1981 the proportion has increased to 59.8 per cent. Table 3.2 shows the change in the average size of Class 1 towns in the last three decades. Durgapur, the case study selected for this book became a Class 1 town in 1971. Hence this chapter also identifies the role of Durgapur in the urban system of Class 1 towns. However, since the data for migration was available at the town level for 1971 only, a more current picture of the urban system is not available.

Methodology of Analysis

The secondary data for the migration variables at town level were available for 1971 only, whereas the data for socio-economic variables at town level were available for both 1971 and 1981. Hence it was not possible to measure the change of migration variables of Class 1 cities between 1971 and 1981. The selected migration variables for 1971 are:

1. Percentage of migrants to total population.

Table 3.2

Decadal Increases in Population per Town in Class 1 Towns of India

Year	*Urban Population/Class 1*	*Difference*
1951	312,200	
		16,060
1961	328,260	
		25,000
1971	353,495	
		82,213
1981	435,708	

Class 1 Town: Town having more than 100,000 people (census definition).
Source: Based on Chand and Puri (1983), Table 2 and Table 3 and Census of India 1981, *General Population Tables*.

2. Percentage of migrant workers to total workers.
3. Percentage of urban migrants to total migrants.
4. Percentage of male migrants to total migrants.

The selected socio-economic variables for 1971 and 1981 are:

1. Percentage of population engaged in primary activities; the term 'primary' includes the census figures of those engaged in agriculture, livestock rearing and orchards.
2. Percentage of working population engaged in mining activities.
3. Percentage of working population engaged in domestic industries.
4. Percentage of working population engaged in organised industries.
5. Percentage of working population engaged in construction work.
6. Percentage of working population engaged in trade.
7. Percentage of working population engaged in transport.
8. Percentage of working population engaged in other services.
9. Total population.
10. Percentage growth rate in 1961–71 and 1971–81.

The variables of migration and socio-economic characteristics, as listed above, were inspected for skew and transformed as shown in Tables 3.3a, 3.3b and 3.3c. The β_1[1] index of the migration variables indicate a fairly normal distribution for the 1971 data of 146 Class 1 towns. In contrast to the

[1] β_1 index $= \frac{\pi_3^2}{\pi_2^3}$ where $\pi_2 = \frac{\Sigma (X_i - \bar{X})^2}{N}$ and $\pi_3 = \frac{\Sigma (X_i - \bar{X})^3}{N}$

i.e., the second and the third moments about the mean ($\bar{X}$); X_i is the value of the ith observation. Egon Pearson tabulated the confidence limits for this measure and the modified version given in table G. Norcliffe 1982: 249 has been used in this analysis.

Table 3.3a

The Skewness of the Selected Migration Variables—1971

Migration variables	*β_1 Index*
Percentage of migrants	0.12
Percentage of migrant workers	0.09
Percentage of urban migrants	0.08
Percentage of male migrants	0.00

The β_1 value 0.22 is taken as the critical value at 1% level for 150 observations according to Table. G*. Norcliffe, 1982, p. 249.
Source: Based on data from Census of India, 1971, *Migration Tables*.
* This table is used for all subsequent statistical significance tests for β_1.

Table 3.3b

Skewness and Transformations of the Socio-Economic Variables—1971

Untransformed socio-economic variables (1971)	*β_1 Index*	*Transformations*	*β_1 Index*
Per cent in primary	0.90	Logarithms	−0.06
Per cent in mining	69.18	Logarithms	−0.12
Per cent in domestic industry	5.97	Logarithms	0.04
Per cent in organised industry	1.44	Logarithms	0.00
Per cent in construction	65.24	Logarithms	0.14
Per cent in trade	0.01	*	*
Per cent in transport	6.88	Logarithms	0.07
Per cent in services	0.41	Square roots	0.00
Per cent growth rate (1961–1971)	26.73	Logarithms	0.19
Total population	35.38	Logarithms	2.89

* No normalisation required.
Source: Based on Census of India, 1971, *General Economic Tables*.

migration variables the socio-economic variables of 146 Class 1 towns for the year 1971 proved to be highly skewed. This necessitated normalisation through transformation as indicated, to meet the assumption of normality for using the Pearson Product Moment Correlation Coefficient. However the relationships have also been tested with the Spearman's Rank Correlation with untransformed data. The untransformed data have also been used for mapping the combinatorial groups of towns which forms the focus of the present analysis (see next section). Comparability of census definitions of occupation categories has been discussed in Appendix 1.

Finally state level estimates of rural and total poverty have been used for forming an idea about the backdrop against which the different types of

Table 3.3c

Skewness and Transformations of the Socio-Economic Variables—1981

Untransformed socio-economic variables (1981)	*β_1 Index*	*Transformations*	*β_1 Index*
Per cent in primary	21.39	Logarithms	−0.03
Per cent in mining	32.25	Logarithms	0.94
Per cent in domestic industry	6.04	Logarithms	0.00
Per cent in organised industry	1.10	Square roots	0.00
Per cent in construction	6.24	Logarithms	−0.39
Per cent in trade	−0.10	*	*
Per cent in transport,	2.88	Square roots	0.26
Per cent in services	0.23	Square roots	−0.02
Per cent growth rate (1971–1981)	7.56	Logarithms	0.15
Total population	34.84	Logarithms	1.59

* No normalisation required.
The β_1 value 0.16 is taken as the critical value at 1 per cent level for 200 observations.
Source: Based on Census of India, 1981, *General Economic Tables*.

towns have developed.[2] Poverty has been measured in terms of percentage of rural or total population of each state below the poverty line as given by the Planning Commission of India on the basis of the National Sample Survey data for 1972–73. The absence of more detailed district level data makes the analysis problematical. The occupation variables of the towns

[2] As shown in Figure No. 3.1 each town has been described in terms of the selected variables, for example, Durgapur is above average in percentage of migrant, percentage of migrant worker, percentage of urban migrant and percentage of male migrant and thus it is a High Migration Town (Type A) and it is within the subtype designated as CC15. The rural poverty figures of the state in which the town is located has been recorded against each classified town. Then an average value of the poverty data, tabulated for a particular group of towns (for example, Type A towns) was obtained for that group or class of towns by taking N as the total number of towns in that class or group of towns, for example, High Migration Towns or Type A. Similar average poverty values were obtained for the other types of towns, for example, Low Migration Towns (Type B), Older Migrant Centres (Type C) etc. These average poverty figures were compared to give some understanding of a likely association between poverty levels and types of towns.

Similarly average poverty values for all towns having above average male migrants within the Type A towns were compared with the average poverty values for all towns having above average female migrants within Type A towns as shown in Table No. 3.9b. Such average poverty values were obtained for different groups of towns identified by a single or combination of attributes or variables at different levels (Tables 3.7, 3.8a, 3.8b, 3,9a etc.).

Similar combinatorial grouping was done with occupation characteristics of the towns and average poverty values were obtained for town types identified on the basis of the occupation variables, for example, average poverty values of towns having above average primary activity (in terms of percentage of workers employed in primary occupation) or above average construction work (in terms of percentage of workers employed in construction work) etc. as shown in Table 3.10.

have been analysed as a mathematical mapping of 'traffic' variables on the 'backcloth' of rural and total poverty of particular states in which the towns are located. Such a procedure has highlighted (below) some interesting and plausible divergences, for example, towns having above average rural migrants exhibited a higher rural poverty value compared to those having above average urban migrants. However it is not possible to test the strength of that relationship by any standard statistical method.

Classification of Town by Migration Type

The untransformed migration variables shown in Table 3.3a have been 'sliced' so that for each town the variables are recorded as having a positive or negative standardised score (z-score) i.e., above or below average. These binary variables then give rise to sixteen possible combined categories (CC), which have been labelled in the range CC 0 to 15, in Figure 3.1a. The sixteen possible CCs are reduced to give four town migration types, by using only two of the binary variables, the percentage of migrants in a town, and the percentage of employed migrants. These two give an indication of the level of migration and the 'success' of the migrants in the urban economy. The four types are:

High Migration Towns: With above Average Percentage Migrant, above Average Percentage Migrant Employment (Type A)

This identifies towns which draw significantly upon the rest of the country to satisfy labour force requirements. All of them have percentage migrant and percentage migrant worker above average. This implies migrants have a greater share of urban income compared to other towns. Such towns provide a strong earning capacity for the migrant population and may function as newly growing remitting towns; surplus labour absorption being their primary function. The map shows that the regions of higher in-migration are Delhi and Punjab, Gujarat, Central Madhya Pradesh, most of Maharashtra, Bangalore and environs, the general Damodar region, and coastal Andhra, plus a few smaller areas like western Tamil Nadu and coastal Orissa. 36 per cent of the total Class 1 towns fall in this category.

Within this town type the towns with CC 13 are likely to have the greater impact on rural areas as they are above average in percentage rural migrant compared to the towns in CC 15 which can be expected to be more imbedded into the urban system and are likely to develop stronger links with other urban centres in that system as they are above average in percentage urban migrants. In contrast those categorised as CC 12 and CC 14 (accounting for 33 per cent of the number of towns in this town type) have a higher proportion of female migrants and on the assumption that female migrants have a lower propensity to remit they can be expected to develop weaker remittance linkage compared to CC 13 and CC 15.

Low Migration Towns: With below Average Migration and Migration Employment (Type B)

They can be expected to play a far less significant and more passive role in the surplus labour transfer mechanism as the functioning of the urban employment centres in these towns have either ceased to depend on or have never depended upon migrating labour force. They constitute 43 per cent of the Class 1 towns. Compared to the previous group of high migration towns, these towns are associated with higher levels of rural and average poverty (see below). The distinct groups which show up on the map are in:

1. The Ganges Valley in Uttar Pradesh and Bihar
2. Rajasthan
3. North Karnataka and west Andhra Pradesh, which constitute the dry Deccan interior.

The first regional group coincides with areas of low urban/rural population potential identified by Chapman and Wanmali (1981) shown in Figure 3.2. It seems that these areas are under-urbanised (this is not necessarily a tautology), there is in particular a lack of small towns, and there is no regional urban system exerting pull. The other regional groups are in areas of high urban/rural population potential as identified by Chapman and Wanmali, and the explanation is more problematical. In these areas however the potential to small urban places is higher, and it is conceivable that the smaller rather than the larger urban centres have been growing here most.

Older Migrant Centres: With below Average Migration but above Average Migrant Employment (Type C)

Most of the Class 1 towns of West Bengal including Calcutta fall in this category, thus presenting a contrast to Delhi and Bombay (both high migration type). They account for only 9 per cent of the Class 1 towns of India. The implications of this combination may be: high in-migration levels in the past account for the persistence of the high level of migrant workers, resulting in strong but possibly declining remittance linkage; the high level of non-migrant population forecasts a decreasing participation of migrants in the total labour force in the future. This in turn implies a declining role of these towns in labour absorption mechanism and further weakening of remittance linkage in the near future.

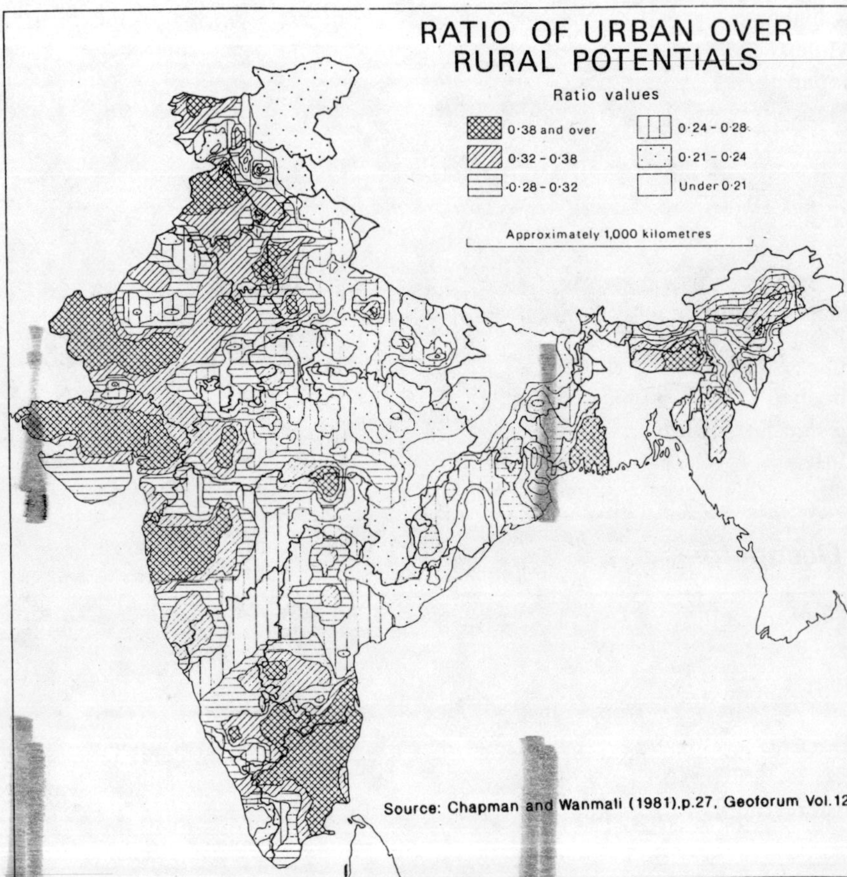
RATIO OF URBAN OVER RURAL POTENTIALS
Ratio values
0·38 and over
0·32 – 0·38
0·28 – 0·32
0·24 – 0·28
0·21 – 0·24
Under 0·21
Approximately 1,000 kilometres
Source: Chapman and Wanmali (1981).p.27, Geoforum Vol.12

Fig. No. 3.02

Stagnating Recipients of Migration: With above Average Migration but below Average Migrant Employment (Type D)

A higher proportion of the earning is retained by the indigenous population, while there is a need for the absorption of migrants in the labour force by expansion of employment. Towns of this type constitute 12 per cent of the Class 1 towns of India. Like the towns classed as CC 1 in the low migration category, those categorised as CC 5 have above average nonworker migrants, male migrants and rural migrants implying the possibility of a negative impact on both the urban destination area and rural source area. However 63 per cent of the towns in this group are classed as CC 4 with above average female migrant and rural migrant, followed by CC 6 with above average female migrant and urban migrant which constitute 25 per cent of these towns while only 12 per cent of them are above average in male migrants. Hence these towns have very little role in the labour transfer mechanism. An obvious small regional group is around Madras, and suggests that to some extent this is tied up with the well known north-south differences in India with respect to sex-ratios.

Occupation Characteristics of Different Types of Towns

The remaining variables are concerned with employment characteristics. These show distinctive patterns for the four types of towns noted above, as summarised in Table 3.4.

Occupation Characteristics of High Migration or Type A Towns

Interesting features of type A towns in this table are:

1. 67 per cent of these Type A towns are below average in primary activity compared to 60 per cent of all towns.
2. 89 per cent of the Type A towns are below average in domestic industries compared to 65 per cent of all towns.
3. 62 per cent of the Type A towns are below average in transport compared to 60 per cent of all towns.
4. 91 per cent of the Type A are below average in mining possibly because mining is concentrated in a few urban centres resulting in a highly skewed distribution. However 45 per cent of the mining towns with above average mining activity fall within this group of high migration towns.
5. 53 per cent of the Type A towns are above average in organised industry compared to 42 per cent of all towns.
6. 51 per cent of the Type A towns are above average in construction compared to 39 per cent of all towns.

Table 3.4

Town Migration Types and Occupation Characteristics

Socio-economic variables	*Z-score*	*% Of all towns*	*% Type A towns*	*% Type B towns*	*% Type C towns*	*% Type D towns*
Primary activity	+	39.73	32.73	42.86	7.69	75.00
	–	60.27	67.27	57.14	92.31	25.00
Mining activity	+	7.53	9.09	4.76	15.38	6.25
	–	92.47	90.91	95.24	84.62	93.75
Domestic industry	+	34.93	10.91	52.38	23.08	56.25
	–	65.07	89.09	47.62	76.92	43.75
Organised industry	+	47.47	52.73	31.75	69.23	31.25
	–	57.53	47.27	68.25	30.77	68.75
Construction work	+	39.04	50.91	30.16	7.69	56.25
	–	60.96	49.09	69.84	92.31	43.75
Trade	+	50.00	50.91	44.44	76.92	50.00
	–	50.00	49.09	55.56	23.08	50.00
Transport	+	39.73	38.18	41.27	53.85	31.25
	–	60.28	61.82	58.73	46.15	68.75
Services	+	45.89	50.91	50.79	23.08	25.00
	–	54.11	49.09	49.21	76.92	75.00

Source: Based on data from Census of India.

7. 51 per cent of the Type A towns are above average in other services, compared with 46 per cent of all towns.
8. 51 per cent of the Type A are above average in trade compared with 50 per cent of all towns, indicating a more balanced situation unlike the other occupational characteristics cited above.

82 per cent of these Type A high migration towns are above average in either or both organised industry and construction. Changes noted between 1971 and 1981 are as follows:

1. Domestic industry has increased in 59 per cent, decreased in 33 per cent and remained the same in 8 per cent of the towns.
2. Organised industry has increased in 61 per cent, decreased in 37 per cent and remained the same in 2 per cent of the towns.
3. Construction has increased in 59 per cent, decreased in 35 per cent and remained the same in 6 per cent of the towns.
4. In contrast trade has decreased in 56 per cent and increased in 44 per cent of the towns.
5. Similarly transport has declined in 69 per cent of the towns.
6. Service has also decreased in 59 per cent of the towns.

Transport, services and trade still seem to be lagging behind. The trend is further illustrated by the variations in mean values of different occupation categories between 1971 and 1981. Organised industry, domestic industry and construction have registered an increase in average proportions while primary activity, mining, services, transport and trade have declined in proportion.

Occupation Characteristics of Low Migration or Type B Towns

These Low Migration Towns are occupationally distinct from the former group and the significant features are:

1. 68 per cent of these Type B towns are below average in organised industry compared to 58 per cent of all towns.
2. 70 per cent of these Type B towns are below average in construction compared to 61 per cent of all towns.
3. 51 per cent of the Type B towns are below average in services compared to 54 per cent of all towns.
4. 59 per cent of the Type B towns are below average in transport compared to 60 per cent of all towns.
5. 56 per cent of the Type B towns are below average in trade compared to 50 per cent of all towns.
6. 52 per cent of the Type B towns are above average in domestic industries compared to 35 per cent of all towns; it must be noted that above average domestic industry seems to be associated with a slightly higher rural and total poverty values than the average values of towns with below average domestic industry.

The High and Low Migration Towns are distinctly different in terms of domestic industry and to some extent in organised industry and construction. Table 3.5a shows that the mean for domestic industries in the Low Migration Towns for 1971 is 6.97 per cent while it is as low as 2.81 per cent in the High Migration Towns. Moreover both percentage migrants and percentage migrant workers correlate negatively with employment in domestic industries.[3] On the other hand the correlation coefficients of construction employment and percentage migrants and migrant workers are positive and significant at 1 per cent level (Table 3.12b).

The significance of domestic industry, construction and organised industry employment for distinguishing intergroup differences in 1971 is further

[3] The relationships being significant at 1 per cent level by both Spearman's Rank Correlation and Pearson Product Moment Correlation Coefficient methods.

Table 3.5a

Intra-group Occupation Means by Town Types—1971

Occupation	*Type A town*	*Type B town*	*Type C town*	*Type D town*
Primary activity	6.83	7.75	3.40	10.24
Mining activity	1.21	0.94	0.36	0.13
Domestic industry	2.81	6.79	2.85	7.00
Organised industry	25.73	21.55	26.34	20.74
Construction work	4.73	3.10	2.77	3.74
Trade	19.63	20.32	23.31	21.34
Transport	11.42	11.30	17.29	11.44
Services	27.67	28.23	23.71	25.42

Source: Based on data from Census of India.

revealed by the one-way analysis[4] of variance performed for all the occupation categories (shown in Table 3.6a). The F-ratio for domestic industry

[4] In one-way analysis of variance the means of several samples from different population are compared. In it the total sum of squares is broken into two sources—the variation due to the factor (i.e. the differences among the samples) and the variation due to random error (i.e. variation within a particular sample). Each sum of squares has a certain number of degrees of freedom associated with it as shown in the table below.

Source	Degrees of Freedom (DF)	Sum of Squares (SS)
Factor	a–1	$\Sigma_i n_i(\bar{x}_i-\bar{x})^2$
Error	n–a	$\Sigma_i \Sigma_j (x_{ij}-\bar{x}_i)^2$
Total	n–1	$\Sigma_i \Sigma_j (x_{ij}-\bar{x})^2$

In the above table x_{ij} is the jth observation in the sample i, $\bar{x}_i$ and n_i are the sample mean and sample size for sample i, a is the number of samples, n is the total number of observations and $\bar{x}$ is the mean of all n observations. Each sum of squares is divided by its corresponding degrees of freedom to obtain mean square (MS).

$$\text{F-Ratio} = \text{MS Factor/MS Error}$$

It is very large when MS Factor is much larger than MS Error i.e. the variations amongst the samples is larger than the variation due to random error. In such cases the null hypothesis that all the samples have the same avarage will be rejected. How large the F-Ratio must be in order to reject the null hypothesis is determined by the F-table.

Figures 3.3a and 3.3b summarises the results separately for each occupation category by year and town types. The sample size, the sample mean, the sample standard deviation and a 95 per cent confidence interval are given for each occupation category. Each confidence interval is calculated by the formula:

$$\bar{x}_i - ts_P/\sqrt{n_i} \text{ to } \bar{x}_i + ts_P/\sqrt{n_i}$$

Here $\bar{x}_i$ and n_i are the sample mean and sample size for level i, s_P = Pooled STDEV = $\sqrt{\text{MS Error}}$ is the pooled estimate of the common standard deviation, σ and t is the value from a t-table corresponding to 95 per cent confidence and the degree of freedom associated with MS Error. These intervals give some idea of how the population means differ (Ryan, Joiner and Ryan 1976).

Table 3.5b

Intra-group Occupation Means by Town Types—1981

Occupation	*Type A town*	*Type B town*	*Type C town*	*Type D town*
Primary activity	6.72	7.53	6.07	10.39
Mining activity	1.13	0.91	1.19	0.09
Domestic industry	3.90	6.21	3.48	6.99
Organised industry	27.20	24.19	31.12	22.04
Construction work	4.75	4.17	4.01	4.20
Trade	19.40	20.14	20.88	21.74
Transport	10.98	10.24	12.33	11.11
Services	26.70	26.20	20.95	23.42

Source: Based on data from Census of India.

Table 3.6a

One-way Analysis of Variance Showing the Variation between High and Low Migration Towns with Respect to Proportion of Working Population in Different Occupations

Occupation	*Values of F-ratio for Type A and Type B town migration types*	
	1971	*1981*
Primary activity	1.09	1.02
Mining activity	0.05	0.04
Domestic industry	24.02**	21.00**
Organised industry	3.85*	2.07
Construction work	7.64**	2.64
Trade	0.74	0.80
Transport	0.01	0.70
Services	0.10	0.10

** Significant at 1 per cent level.
* Significant at 10 per cent level.
Type A towns: High Migration Towns.
Type B towns: Low Migration Towns.
Refer to Figure 3.3a.
Source: Based on data from Census of India.

employment between the two groups of towns is highly significant at 1 per cent level and the accompanying diagram (Figure 3.3a) shows the distinctively higher position of this variable in the low migration towns. The F-ratio for construction is also significant at 1 per cent level and the diagram shows the lower position of the low migration towns, though the divergence between the two groups is not so wide as domestic industry. On the other hand the F-ratio for organised industry is significant only at 10 per cent

The Variation Between High and Low Migration Towns in 1971 and 1981
(As shown by one-way analysis of variance)

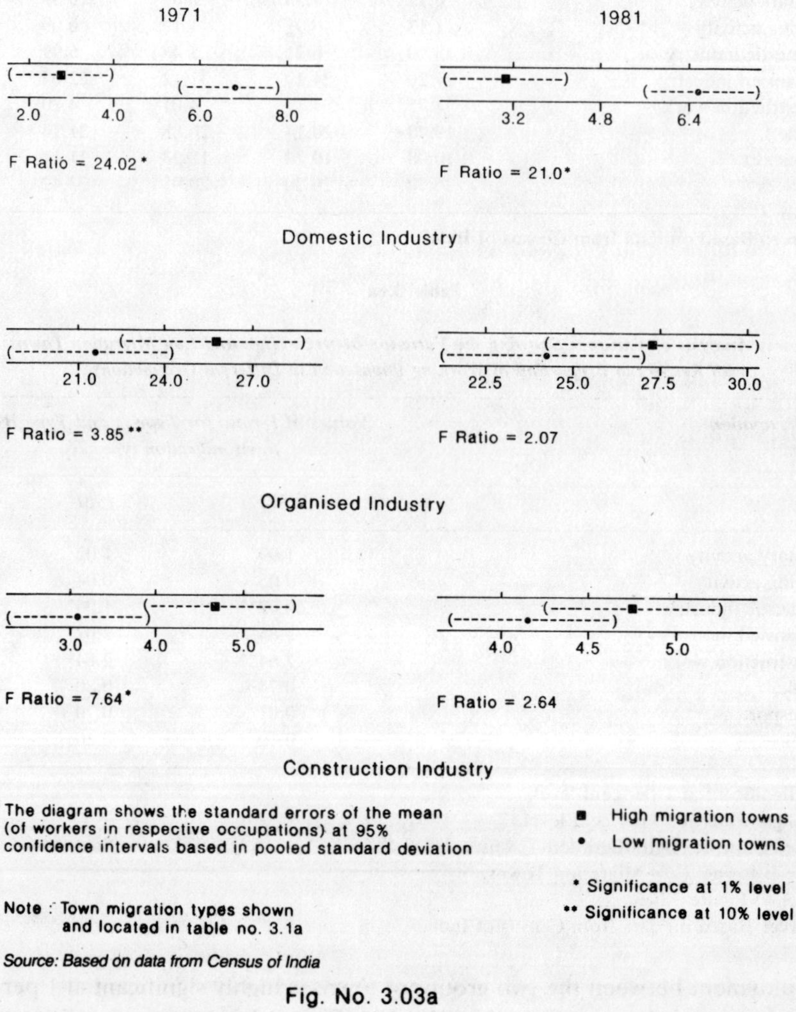

The diagram shows the standard errors of the mean (of workers in respective occupations) at 95% confidence intervals based in pooled standard deviation

■ High migration towns
• Low migration towns

* Significance at 1% level
** Significance at 10% level

Note : Town migration types shown and located in table no. 3.1a

Source: Based on data from Census of India

Fig. No. 3.03a

level and the zone of overlap in the diagram signifies the existence of a group of towns in both the low and high migration categories which have similar proportions in organised industry. The differences in the migration parameters in this group have possibly resulted from the effect of other variables.

In the low migration group of towns the employment proportions have shown the following trends between 1971 and 1981:

1. Construction has increased in 79 per cent of the towns.
2. Organised industry has increased in 77 per cent of the towns.
3. Services has increased in only 26 per cent of the towns while in 73 per cent it has decreased.
4. Trade has increased in 47 per cent and decreased in 48 per cent of the towns.
5. Transport has increased in only 34 per cent and decreased in 63 per cent of the towns.
6. In both the groups of towns primary activity has declined.

A one-way analysis of variance with 1981 occupation data (Table 3.6a and Figure 3.3a) for high and low migration towns reveals that after a decade domestic industry continues to be distinctly higher in the low migration towns, the F-ratio being highly significant at 1 per cent level. However the F-ratio for construction and organised industry are no longer significant at even 10 per cent level indicating considerable amount of temporal variation in these two occupation proportions in the two groups of towns. Such variations are bound to result in as well as reflect changes in the migration characteristics.

A similar one-way analysis of variance between the two decadal years in each group for all the occupation categories (Table 3.6b) seems to indicate that more significant changes have been taking place in the low migration categories of towns. The highly significant F-ratio (at 1 per cent level of significance) for construction indicates a significant difference in this occupation proportion between 1971 and 1981, the diagram indicating a higher proportion in construction in 1981 (Figure 3.3b). For this variable the F-ratio for the High Migration Towns is 0 indicating little or no significant changes in construction activity. Similarly the F-ratio for low migration towns is 1.97 in organised industry compared to 0.39 for high migration towns. There seems to be an increase in the proportion of this variable in Low Migration Towns between 1971 and 1981.

In contrast transport and services have declined in proportion by 1981 in the low migration towns. Though the F-ratios are not yet significant at 10 per cent level, they are much higher than the high migration towns. For transport the F-ratio in low migration towns is 1.56 compared to 0.19 for high migration towns. Similarly for services the figure in low migration

Decadal Variations in Occupation in Three Town Migration Types
(As shown by one-way analysis of variance)

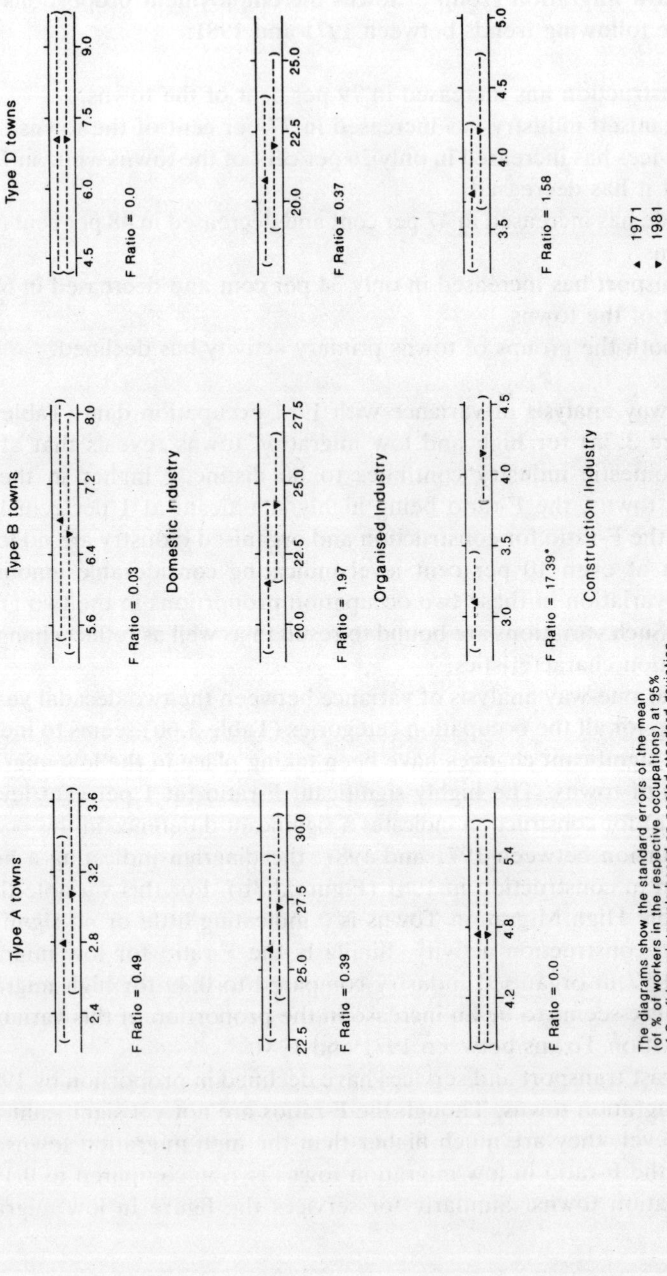

The diagrams show the standard errors of the mean
(of % of workers in the respective occupations) at 95%
of Confidence intervals based on pooled standard deviation

Note : Refer to table No 3.06b

Source: Based on data from Census of India

Fig. No. 3.03b

Table 3.6b

One-way Analysis of Variance Showing the Decadal Variation in the Proportion of Working Population in Different Occupations in Three Town Migration Types

Occupation	*Values of F-ratio for 1971 and 1981 occupation proportions*		
	Type A towns	*Type B towns*	*Type D towns*
Primary activity	0.02	0.08	0.01
Mining activity	0.00	0.00	0.24
Domestic industry	0.49	0.03	0.00
Organised industry	0.39	1.97	0.37
Construction work	0.00	17.39**	1.58
Trade	0.06	0.07	0.13
Transport	0.19	1.56	0.06
Services	0.23	2.01	2.02

** Significant at 1 per cent level.
Type A towns: High Migration Towns.
Type B towns: Low Migration Towns.
Type D towns: Stagnant Recipients of Migration.
Note: Type C towns or Old Migrant Centres were excluded as the number of observations were too small (12) to be representative in this statistical test.
Source: Based on data from Census of India.
Refer to Figure 3.3b.

towns is as high as 2.01 compared to 0.23 in the high migration towns (Table 3.6b).

Occupation Characteristics of Older Migrant Centres or Type C Towns

Their interesting occupational characteristics are:

1. Construction has ceased to be an important function and 92 per cent of them are below average with respect to this variable compared to 61 per cent of all towns.
2. Trade appears to be significantly high; 77 per cent of the towns being above average in trade compared to 50 per cent of all towns.
3. 69 per cent of them are above average in organised industry compared to 42 per cent of all towns.

The occupation means for 1971 show that this group of towns are significantly low in primary activity compared to the two other groups. Domestic and organised industry seem to be at similar levels with the high migration category, but construction and services seem to be lower than both the high and low migration categories discussed earlier. On the other hand transport and trade appear to be higher compared to both the earlier categories (Table 3.5a). However change between 1971 and 1981 (Table 3.5b) reveals the conspicuously increasing trend of primary activity in 80 per cent of the towns in this group. The mean has also registered an increase from 3.40 per cent to 6.07 per cent. This has been accompanied by an increase in domestic industry in 70 per cent of the towns, though the variation in the mean values for 1971 and 1981 has been marginal. Primary activity and domestic industry in turn are normally associated with higher levels of poverty.

Occupation Characteristics of Stagnating Recipients of Migration or Type D towns

Occupationally this group has the following characteristics:

1. 75 per cent of them are above average in primary activity and the mean in this category for 1971 is 10.24 per cent, highest compared to the three other groups of towns.
2. 56 per cent of them are above average in domestic industries and like primary industries the mean is the highest compared to the three other groups of towns, amounting to 7 per cent.
3. 50 per cent are above average in trade, the mean being slightly higher than the three other groups.
4. 69 per cent of them are below average in organised industry and the mean for 1971 is only 20.74 per cent.
5. 69 per cent of them are below average in transport, but the mean is 11.44 per cent similar to the high and low migration groups.
6. 75 per cent are below average in services.

Town Migration Type, Poverty Levels, Urban-Urban and Rural-Urban Links

High Migration or Type A towns

Type A or high migration towns seem to be associated with lower levels of rural poverty compared to all the other town migration types as shown in Table 3.7. Within this town type it is quite clear (Tables 3.8a and 3.9a) that there is a higher level of rural in-migration where rural poverty is high (in towns of CC 13 and CC 12), but a higher level of migration from other urban centres where rural poverty is low (in towns of CC 15 and CC 14). The levels of rural poverty seem to be higher where towns have developed with higher male in-migrants compared to those with higher female in-migrants. It may be explained by the fact that female in-migration does not

Table 3.7

Relation Between Migration Type and Rural Poverty Level

Town migration type	*No. of towns in a given type*	*Average rural poverty of states of towns of given type*
Type A	55	51.5
Type B	63	54.2
Type C	12	57.3
Type D	16	57.7

Note: The values of average poverty are based on per cent of rural population below poverty line in the states.
The mean and standard deviation for all states are:
Mean = 44.23 per cent; Standard deviation = 16.77.
The Class 1 towns used in the analysis seem to be associated with higher levels of rural poverty, though the large standard deviation indicates that small inter-group deviation is likely to be insignificant. However it must be remembered that since the results are based on aggregate values at the state level in which the towns are located, they give only a rough idea about the situation. Under the current data constraints this is the best that could be done.
Source: Based on data from Census of India and Planning Commission.

Table 3.8a

Relation Between Categories of Migration Type A Towns and Rural Poverty Level

b2

Combined categories in town migration type A	*No. of towns of given type*	*Average rural poverty of states of towns of given type*
15	23	48.7
14	8	42.6
13	14	58.1
12	10	55.7

Note: Combined categories are defined and geographically located in Figure 3.1a.
Source: Based on data from Census of India and Planning Commission.

necessarily depend upon economic conditions as marriage can be expected to be the purpose of migration. On the other hand male in-migration for employment purposes may result from 'push factors' in the rural areas. Moreover towns with above average urban migrants outnumber those with above average rural migrants and this trend is very conspicuous amongst towns with higher proportion of male migrants. Therefore inter-urban link is likely to be stronger than rural-urban link, thus making the rural-urban labour transfer mechanism slower.

Within this town type the only area where towns with higher proportion of rural-urban link seem to outnumber those with higher proportion of urban-urban link is the enclave of industrial towns in the Damodar area covering parts of West Bengal, Bihar and Orrisa (Figure 3.1a). These towns seem to be dominated by male in-migration as well, thus indicating their active role in the labour-transfer mechanism. In contrast in Punjab and Maharashtra and in areas around Delhi and Bangalore, towns with higher proportion of inter-urban link seem to dominate, though they are all high in male in-migration as well.

Therefore in areas of higher level of rural-urban links, possibly associated with higher levels of rural poverty, it is necessary to concentrate on a rural-oriented strategy on a priority basis. On the other hand in areas with higher levels of urban-urban link, in order to reduce the pressure of in-migration to Class 1 towns perhaps more attention should be given to divert migration to smaller towns.

Low Migration or Type B Towns

The type B or Low Migration Towns characterised by rural and female in-migration seem to differ from the high migration towns in the following respects:

1. They are associated with higher poverty levels compared to the high migration towns (Table 3.7).
2. Unlike the high migration towns, it seems that there is no distinct relationship between town type and poverty levels probably because of the existence of uniformly higher levels of poverty in these areas so that the push factor operates everywhere, perhaps resulting in more step migration. Hence urban-urban migration has proceeded in areas of high level of rural poverty (Table 3.9a).
3. Towns with higher proportion of male migrants (CC 3 and CC 1) seem to be associated with lower levels of rural poverty compared to towns with higher levels of female migrants (as shown in Table 3.8b) which may reflect either (*a*) male migration for employment to these low migration towns takes place from higher economic class (the reason is highlighted later), while female migration for marriage means relief of burden to the migrant's parents and some amount of economic guarantee for the dependent migrant (*b*) male out-migration helps to lower the poverty levels. However in both the cases higher female migration from rural areas seem to be associated with similar rural poverty levels of approximately 57 per cent.

In contrast, male migration from rural areas in this group (CC 1) is associated with lower levels of rural poverty than high migration towns (CC 13) as shown in Tables 3.8a and 3.8b. This may be explained by the fact that the push factor is likely to operate strongly from poverty-stricken areas to towns where the expected probability of finding a job is higher as pointed out in the Todaro model (Chapter 1). This expected probability is

Table 3.8b

Relation between Categories of Migration Type B Towns and Rural Poverty Level

Combined categories in town migration type B	*No. of towns of given type*	*Average rural poverty of states of towns of given type*
3	13	51.5
2	18	55.0
1	9	50.0
0	23	56.7

Note: Combined categories are defined and geographically located in Figure 3.1a.
Source: Based on data from Census of India and Planning Commission.

Table 3.9a

Urban-Rural Migration Character of Four Town Migration Types and their Associated Level of Rural Poverty

Town migration type	*No. of towns of given type*	*Average rural poverty of states of towns of given type*
Type A towns with above average urban migrants	31	47.1
Type A towns with above average rural migrants	24	57.1
Type B towns with above average urban migrants	31	53.5
Type B towns with above average rural migrants	32	54.8
Type C towns with above average urban migrants	5	50.6
Type C towns with above average rural migrants	7	62.0
Type D towns with above average urban migrants	5	58.4
Type D towns with above average rural migrants	11	57.4

Source: Based on data from Census of India and Planning Commission.

likely to depend upon the indigenous labour supply in the town to which the migrant is supposed to migrate. Hence in older towns with a higher proportion of indigenous population (possibly providing the required supply of labour), migration in search of a job due to push from poverty-stricken areas is likely to be lower. Therefore migration will take place from better economic classes (perhaps from less poverty-stricken areas) whose certainty of finding a job will be higher perhaps due to higher education and skill level. Moreover in such cases only those who can economically afford to take the risk of migration will migrate.

In Bihar and Uttar Pradesh the number of towns with above average rural migrants outnumber those with above average urban migrants. These states are generally associated with higher levels of rural poverty. However rural in-migrants possibly consist of females because 8 out of 11 towns with

Table 3.9b

Sex of Migrants of Four Town Migration Types and their Associated Level of Rural Poverty

Town migration type	*No. of towns of given type*	*Average rural poverty of states of towns of given type*
Type A towns with above average male migrants	37	52.2
Type A towns with above average female migrants	18	49.9
Type B towns with above average male migrants	22	50.9
Type B towns with above average female migrants	41	55.9
Type C towns with above average male migrants	9	55.0
Type C towns with above average female migrants	3	63.0
Type D towns with above average male migrants	2	57.6
Type D towns with above average female migrants	14	57.7

Source: Based on data from Census of India and Planning Commission.

higher proportion of rural in-migrants have above average female migrants as well. On the other hand urban to urban migrants mainly consists of males. Amongst towns with higher proportion of male migrants the number of towns with both inter-urban links and rural-urban links seem to be equal.

On the other hand in the Rajasthan area female migration seem to dominate and inter-urban links are more conspicuous than rural-urban links. In south India the low migration towns are mainly characterised by female in-migrants from rural areas.

Hence in the Bihar-Uttar Pradesh region the planner's attention should be focused on increasing rural-urban migration to smaller sized towns. Since this region seems to lack smaller sized towns as pointed out earlier and the larger towns have low proportion of in-migrants it will be difficult to reduce rural poverty without initiating sectoral transfer of labour force. Increasing investment in the large towns may help to alleviate urban unemployment, but will have little impact in the rural areas.

Older Migrant Centres or Type C Towns

It is interesting to note that the older migrant centres or the C type of towns are associated with higher levels of rural poverty compared to the two former types already discussed. Within this town type those with higher proportion of rural migrants are associated with very high levels of rural poverty, the figure being 62 per cent compared to 57 per cent for high migration towns and 55 per cent for low migration towns. In contrast those with higher proportion of urban migrants are associated with a rural poverty level of only 50 per cent.

Table 3.10

Relation between Occupation Categories and Poverty Levels

Town type on the basis of occupation	*Z-score*	*No. of towns in given type*	*Average rural poverty of states of towns of given type*
Primary activity	+	58	54.7
	−	88	49.2
Mining activity	+	11	49.8
	−	135	51.5
Domestic industry	+	51	53.0
	−	95	50.5
Organised industry	+	62	51.2
	−	84	51.5
Construction work	+	57	49.9
	−	89	52.3
Trade	+	73	50.2
	−	73	52.6
Transport	+	58	52.7
	−	88	50.5
Services	+	67	50.0
	−	79	52.6

Source: Based on data from Census of India and Planning Commission.

Seventy-five per cent of these towns are above average in male migrants which are associated with lower levels of rural poverty (55 per cent) compared to those with above average female migrants (63 per cent), the trend being similar to the low migration towns. Though these towns are below average in migrant population rural migration seem to be continuing, possibly because the expectation of finding a job also depends upon the proportion of employed migrants who provide contact and job information. However with increasing participation of indigenous labour force in the employment opportunities the expectation of finding a job is likely to decline over time.

Stagnating Recipients of Migration or Type D Towns

This group of towns are dominated by female migrants from rural areas and are associated with high poverty levels. Urban and rural migration seem to take place against a backdrop of high poverty levels.

However propensity to migrate will vary according to the skill requirements of the particular occupation, availability of the required skills in the rural education system as well as the difference in the rate of diffusion of employment information to other urban centres compared to the other rural centres. It is however necessary to remind the reader that we do not have data for all urban places, only the largest ones. Hence it is possible that the smaller urban places in these regions have different characteristics from the ones we have ascribed to the towns in our dataset.

Durgapur in the National Urban System of Class 1 Towns

Durgapur in West Bengal is categorised as a high migration town with 1971 migration data having z-score values of above 0.68 (top 25 per cent of the towns) for percentage migrant and above 1.28 (top 10 per cent of the towns) for percentage migrant worker. It is characterised by the following occupational criteria according to 1971 data:

1. It is above average in organised industry, construction and primary activity.
2. It is below average in domestic industry, trade, transport, mining and other services.

Its position in relation to other towns with respect to organised industry and construction is understandable as it conforms with the industrial planning objectives associated with the inception of the town. Primary activity has a significant negative correlation with size of the town both in 1971 and 1981 (significant at 1 per cent level by both Spearman's Rank Correlation given in Table 3.11a and Pearson Product Moment Correlation Coefficient method given in Tables 3.11b and 3.11c). Hence in comparison to a larger and slower growing town like Ludhiana in Punjab and Jamshedpur in Bihar,it has higher proportion of labour force engaged in primary activity which is likely to decline in importance as the town grows in size.

Employment in trade is expected to increase as the demand for non-basic services increases with an increasing resident population. The negative correlation of trade with both growth and population (though only the first is significant at 1 per cent level in both the years) may indicate that trade is to a certain extent a function of time than size defined by total population as may be the case of transport as well. Hence larger and older towns like Calcutta and Ludhiana have higher proportions in trade.

Table 3.13 shows the decadal variation in the occupation structure of Durgapur. It establishes the trend of decline of primary activity. Though the proportions employed in domestic industry and trade have remained more or less the same (registering fractional increases only), the most conspicuous increase has been in service employment. After an initial spurt of growth, organised industry and construction employment seem to be registering a declining trend, which can be expected in the face of declining industrial investment as revealed by a survey by Webcon in 1977 (unpublished report in Asansol Durgapur Development Authority) and drive

Table 3.11a

Spearman's Rank Correlation of Selected Socio-Economic Variables

	1971		*1981*	
Socio-economic variables	*Growth*	*Population*	*Growth*	*Population*
Primary activity	−0.03	**−0.49**	−0.12	**−0.39**
Mining activity	**0.36**	**0.30**	**0.28**	0.17
Domestic industry	**−0.37**	−0.17	**−0.27**	0.06
Organised industry	0.17	**0.31**	0.16	**0.25**
Construction work	**0.39**	−0.11	**0.24**	0.00
Trade	**−0.25**	−0.18	**−0.26**	−0.15
Transport	−0.11	0.09	−0.09	0.17
Services	0.04	0.08	−0.07	0.15
Population	0.11	1.00	−0.11	1.00

Figures in bold indicate significant correlations at 1 per cent level (T-test) with Spearman's Rank Correlation.
Critical value for 1971: r = **0.21**; df = 150
(Note: df = N−2 = 144, but nearest value in the table has been taken)
Critical value for 1981: r = **0.18**; df = 200
(Note: df = N−2 = 204, but nearest value in the table has been taken)
Source: Based on data from Census of India.

towards modernisation in the industries in order to make the industries economically viable. It must be emphasised that transport which was already below average in 1971 declined further in 1981. It must be pointed out that the declining proportions of organised industry, construction and transport with simultaneous increase in domestic industry imply a declining role of the town in migrant absorption. While domestic industry has significantly negative relation with percentage migrants and migrant workers, services and transport have no significant relationships.

It is curious to note that the four other steel towns in eastern India and central India viz. Bokaro, Jamshedpur, Rourkela and Bhilai rank as 13 with above average rural migrants whereas Durgapur ranks 15 with above average urban migrants. In terms of occupation structure, Durgapur and Bokaro both are above average in primary occupation, organised industry and construction, but below average in mining, trade, transport and services. Jamshedpur being an older town, its inception dating back to 1910, is below average in primary activity, the other variables being the same. Rourkela has a slightly different structure as it has organised industry, transport and services above average. Percentage rural migrants is positively linked to primary occupation, domestic industry and trade (significant at 1 per cent level by both the methods) as shown in Tables 3.12a and 3.12b. On the other hand transport and services are significantly and positively related to percentage urban migrants. Organised industry and construction tend to have positive but weak relation with urban migrants. Thus the difference

Table 3.11b

Pearson Product-Moment Correlation Coefficients for Socio-Economic Variables—1971

*Transformed socio-economic variables**	*(1)*	*(2)*	*(3)*	*(4)*	*(5)*	*(6)*	*(7)*	*(8)*	*(9)*
(1) Primary	0.00								
(2) Mining	0.10								
(3) Domestic industry	**0.30**	0.13							
(4) Organised industry	−0.14	**−0.24**	−0.18						
(5) Construction	0.15	−0.09	−0.14	−0.02					
(6) Trade	−0.09	0.11	0.12	−0.14	0.01				
(7) Transport	−0.08	−0.05	−0.13	**−0.28**	−0.03	0.12			
(8) Services	−0.08	−0.13	−0.14	**−0.54**	−0.03	0.06	0.10		
(9) Growth	−0.04	−0.18	**−0.40**	0.13	**0.40**	**−0.34**	**−0.24**	0.01	
(10) Population	**−0.54**	**−0.25**	−0.18	**0.31**	−0.08	−0.08	0.05	0.05	0.05

Figures in bold indicate correlation coefficients significant at 1 per cent level.

Note: * Transformations for the selected socio-economic variables in this table have been given in Table 3.3b.

Source: Based on data from Census of India.

Table 3.11c

Pearson Product-Moment Correlation Coefficients for Socio-Economic Variables—1981

*Transformed socio-economic variables**	*(1)*	*(2)*	*(3)*	*(4)*	*(5)*	*(6)*	*(7)*	*(8)*	*(9)*
(1) Primary	0.00								
(2) Mining	−0.06								
(3) Domestic industry	0.12	−0.16							
(4) Organised industry	**−0.38**	−0.14	0.04						
(5) Construction	**0.21**	**−0.24**	−0.14	−0.20					
(6) Trade	0.04	**−0.20**	0.18	**−0.23**	0.08				
(7) Transport	−0.04	−0.16	−0.08	**−0.29**	0.11	**0.25**			
(8) Services	−0.15	**−0.20**	−0.08	**−0.43**	**0.31**	0.18	0.21		
(9) Growth	−0.15	**0.20**	−0.24	0.13	0.09	**−0.27**	−0.09	−0.09	
(10) Population	**−0.44**	**−0.29**	0.00	**0.27**	0.04	−0.05	0.11	0.15	−0.12

Figures in bold indicate correlation coefficients significant at 1 per cent level.

Note: * Transformations for the selected socio-economic variables in this table have been given in Table 3.3c.

Source: Based on data from Census of India.

Table 3.12a

Spearman's Rank Correlation of Migration and Occupation Variables—1971

	% Migrant	*% Migrant worker*	*% Urban migrant*	*% Male migrant*
Primary activity	−0.09	**−0.28**	**−0.37**	**−0.31**
Mining activity	0.20	**0.22**	0.10	**0.35**
Domestic industry	**−0.45**	**−0.52**	**−0.21**	**−0.39**
Organised industry	0.10	0.18	0.05	0.07
Construction work	**0.28**	0.20	0.12	0.16
Trade	−0.06	−0.05	**−0.22**	**−0.28**
Transport	−0.05	−0.04	**0.22**	0.07
Services	−0.05	−0.05	**0.24**	0.12

Figures in bold indicate significant correlations at 1 per cent level (T-test) with Spearman's Rank Correlation.
Critical value for 1971; r = **0.21**; df = 150
(Note: df = N−2 = 144, but nearest value in the table has been taken)
Source: Based on data from Census of India.

Table 3.12b

Pearson Product-Moment Correlation Coefficients between Migration and Occupation Variables—1971

Transformed occupation variables	*% Migrant*	*% Migrant worker*	*% Urban migrant*	*% Male migrant*
Primary activity	−0.15	**−0.29**	**−0.38**	**−0.36**
Mining activity	−0.13	−0.08	−0.13	−0.19
Domestic industry	**−0.51**	**−0.53**	**−0.22**	**−0.40**
Organised industry	0.12	0.17	0.05	0.05
Construction work	**0.26**	**0.22**	0.08	0.14
Trade	−0.17	−0.12	−0.20	**−0.26**
Transport	−0.07	−0.04	**0.22**	0.11
Services	−0.01	0.00	**0.28**	0.09

Figures in bold indicate correlation coefficients significant at 1 per cent level.
Critical value for 1971; **r** = **0.21**; df = 150
(Note: df = N−2 = 144, but nearest value in the table has been taken)
Note: * Transformations for the occupation variables in this table have been given in Table 3.3b.
Source: Based on data from Census of India.

between Durgapur and the three other public sector steel towns can hardly be explained in terms of occupation, at least at this level of occupational details.

A plausible explanation (as elaborated in the previous section on High Migration Towns and Poverty Levels), is that Durgapur developed in an

Table 3.13

Decadal Variation of Occupation Proportions in Durgapur

Occupation	*1971*	*1981*
Primary	8.40	5.10
Mining	0.20	0.40
Domestic industry	1.60	1.90
Organised industry	54.50	53.90
Construction	4.20	2.30
Trade	8.20	8.50
Transport	4.20	3.80
Services	18.70	24.00

Note: All figures represent percentage of total working population.
Source: Census of India 1971 and 1981.

area of lower levels of rural poverty so that it received more migrants from other urban areas. On the other hand the three other steel towns were located in areas with higher levels of rural poverty and have been recipients of rural migrants pushed out of the hinterland.

Concluding Remarks

In the entire urban system higher levels of rural poverty are associated with towns with above average rural migrants indicating either these are the recipients of push migration or rural migration to these towns have had the impact of increasing the poverty levels in the rural hinterland. Though it is difficult to decide whether a particular phenomenon is the cause or the effect, since the migration characteristics pertain to 1971 and the poverty levels pertain to 1972–73, it is more likely that rural poverty causes the development of towns with higher levels of rural migrants.

The Older Migrant Centres or type C towns, the Stagnating Recipients of Migration or type D towns seem to be associated with the highest level of rural poverty followed by the Low Migration or type B towns. However, since the Low Migration Towns constitute 43 per cent of the Class 1 towns (compared to 8 per cent for type C and 11 per cent for type D towns), they are by far the most important in the urban economy in terms of spatial distribution. Hence planning policies should turn their attention to the regional enclaves characterised by the development of this type of town. Specially when combined with lower levels of urban-rural population potentials (Figure 3.2) indicating the lack of smaller towns these areas identify regions where towns are not playing a significant role in the labour transfer mechanism. Within these low migration group of towns significant occupation changes are taking place and attention seems to have been diverted to organised industry and construction, while services and transport appear to be lagging behind.

At the same time it has to be taken into consideration that the per capita cost of municipal services begin to rise after a city has reached a population of 250,000–300,000 (according to a research made in Stanford University, Oberai and Bilsborrow 1984); which calls for diverting and inducing migration to smaller sized towns. It has been pointed out with reference to Indian planning:

> First there was an attempt at the physical planning of metropolitan regions and secondly there was an investigation of the possibility of creating market towns. In both the cases the schemes met with success in those areas which this exercise depicts as having a higher level of urban population potentials (Chapman and Wanmali 1981: 39–40).

It has also been pointed out that the assumption of NCAER that all towns could influence the surrounding economy over a radius of 40 miles will not hold true in areas of high rural population and poor transport. Therefore in eastern Uttar Pradesh, Bihar, eastern Madhya Pradesh and Orissa such market towns may not be a success (cited in Chapman and Wanmali 1981).

Though the point regarding transport is highly tenable Chapman and Wanmali have not clarified the specific functions that these market towns are expected to develop. By market towns do they mean higher levels of trading activity? 'The small towns even now are more the outgrowth of a rural background living off extracted surplus rather than the lowest tentacles of an urban hierarchy which should be diffusing modernisation' (Chapman and Wanmali 1981). The occupation data for 1971 shows that among the class 1 towns categorised as 0-3 in Uttar Pradesh and Bihar, 12 per cent have above average construction and 31 per cent have above average organised industry; while 46 per cent have trade and transport above average; 46 per cent are above average in primary activity and 65 per cent are above average in domestic industry. These towns in Bihar are mostly above average in primary activity (100 per cent), trade (86 per cent) and domestic industry (86 per cent). Hence trade, primary activity and domestic industry are above average in half the towns. Trade can hardly be expected to increase further without analogous increase in production or purchasing power of the people.

Towns like Agra, Firozabad, Moradabad, Muzaffarnagar, Rampur and Saharanpur failed to incorporate migrants in spite of the growth of organised industry and construction possibly because they represented old established towns with indigenous unemployed resident population.

The authors of the population potential studies have also pointed out that 'manipulation of farm inputs' and 'commodity prices' from the urban sector are unlikely to be effective in these backward areas which lack access to urban centres. Rural development, though essential, invariably raises the question about the type of rural development. On the one hand rural development has the ultimate objective of increasing the purchasing power of the rural population, on the other hand it requires increased purchasing power to gather its own momentum.

It has been pointed out earlier that increase in purchasing power and access to markets and services can be effected by:

1. Increasing access to rural credit which is bound to increase indebtedness amidst the rural poor.
2. Increasing non-primary or urban employment leading to sectoral transfer of labour; migration potentiality can probably be calculated for a place i with figures of percentage employed at all other places and their distances from place i, the assumption being that migration is a function of employment opportunities in the vicinity. This may imply increase of small-sized production-oriented towns rather than market-oriented towns only. As will be shown in Chapter 5 some of these states tend to consume more than they produce. Perhaps emphasis should be laid on the production of low-priced consumer commodities which will be readily consumed by final demand from the local population. It may hike up migration and remittance to rural areas which in turn will increase the purchasing power of the rural people.
3. Manipulating the rural-urban terms of trade which may be difficult and complicated as internal terms of trade tend to be closely linked with external i.e., international terms of trade.

In areas where remittance link development are likely to be weaker all the above-mentioned possibilities have to be investigated on a priority basis. Rural poverty can hardly be reduced without sectoral transfer, especially when urban products are high-priced compared to the rural ones. That in turn depends, to a large extent, on international terms of trade as pointed out earlier.

In areas with Older Migrant or D type of towns and low urban-rural potential it is necessary to divert migration to new smaller sized centres as is being done in West Bengal. Primary activity and to some extent domestic industry may be the cause as well as the effect of high levels of poverty (Table 3.10). This may signify an interesting, but unwelcome trend in the economy of West Bengal. Instead of continuing to be an instrument in the sectoral labour transfer mechanism a reverse mechanism may be setting in. On the other hand the economic impact may depend on the constituent elements of primary activity and the possibility of a change in these elements. Afforestation in the form of green belts and development of market gardening may provide low paid employment to the urban poor so that the opportunity cost incurred by such employment in reality be zero. The increase in domestic industry in all the types of towns may just indicate spontaneous response of the urban economy to cope with urban poverty and not a factor to induce sectoral labour transfer. Therefore, in both this intermediate and the high migration categories the current trend seem to be an increasing proportion of domestic industries, possibly in response to increasing urban unemployment. This latter trend is evident in Durgapur and all the Class 1 towns of West Bengal.

Within the High Migration Towns as pointed out earlier those with higher proportion of rural migrants are associated with higher levels of rural poverty. As migration is already taking place a rural-oriented policy will be more effective to reduce migration. However such a policy will not be effective in the hinterland of towns receiving more urban migrants. In such areas alternative urban centres are required.

While formulating employment policy in the High Migration Towns, attention should be given to the development of domestic industry, transport and trade to the faster growing group 1 towns in which organised industry and construction have already been initiated. It has been pointed out:

> the fact that trade and transport are emphatically and *negatively* correlated with growth is possibly alarming. In a spatially extensive economy in which agriculture is the dominant employer, and which is dependent on agriculture for much of its capital generation, the implication that there is no stimulation to the linkage and articulation of the economy is unwelcome. Does it suggest that the growing centres of organised industry are going off into orbit on their own? (Chapman 1983: 152).

However it must be noted that the negative correlation and the resultant occupational differentiation between the two types of towns mentioned above have resulted from two factors:

1. The faster growth in the migrant absorbing towns have resulted from inducement of alternative occupations like organised industry, construction and other services. Such employment centres activating occupations alternative to trade and transport are generally initiated by public sector plans or by private sector profit oriented investments. Hence no simultaneous planning is done for growth of trade and transport unless it caters directly to the operation of the new investment nodes of employment. Trade and transport are treated as subsidiary occupations which are expected to gather its own momentum as the urban centre grows. Thus a time lag is inevitable before employment proportions can increase in trade and transport. Therefore by 1981 growth rate ceases to have a significant negative relationship with transport at 1 per cent level of significance by both the methods. However the negative relationship between growth and trade continues to be significant after one decade.

2. In a closed percentage number system, an increase in proportions of trade and transport must result in a decrease in some other occupation. Therefore, proportional figures do not necessarily indicate the level of external or internal linkage of a town nor is it indicative of articulation of an economy. Injection of an organised industry would spontaneously demand both internal and external linkages to assimilate raw materials and distribute the products. It is difficult to determine the critical ratio between organised industry and transport-employment to justify the increased performance of the town in both extra- and intra-city context.

4

Migration to Durgapur

Post-Independence Planning in India and Inception of Durgapur

Second Five Year Plan and its Implications

The Second Plan in post-Independence India was based on the model presented by Mahalonobis in 1953 which emphasised investment in heavy goods industry. This model was based on the following principle:

> higher the allocation of investment to investment goods industries, lower will be the rate of growth of income in the short run, but higher will it be in the long run . . . if one wants a high rate of growth of consumption in the long run, then the best policy is to give priority to the development of investment goods over consumer goods (Chand and Puri 1983: 67).

The strategy of industrialisation as it finally emerged in the Second Plan had the three basic elements:

1. Stepping up the rate of investment;
2. rapid expansion of productive power of the economy by increasing appreciably the proportion of investment in heavy and capital goods sector; and,
3. increasing the scope and importance of the public sector.

The implementation of 'heavy investment goods' sector strategy required heavy resources both domestic (monetary and real) and external (in the form of capital goods, machinery, industrial raw materials and technical knowhow). Though the best method of raising external resources is through expansion of exports, no export strategy was adopted as an integral part of the overall planning. The only recourse was deficit financing resulting in the unleashing of inflationary forces (Chand and Puri 1983). The ultimate objective was import-substitution resulting in emphasis on import restrictions.

Thus independence from the colonial status under British rule combined with the policy stated above had two implications in the short run as pointed out in Chapter 1:

1. Weakening of demand linkages for Indian commodities with the RoW;
2. weak development of demand linkages between RH and UC for UC's goods and services in spite of high investment in the UC; and,
3. strengthening of inter-urban demand linkages between a number of UCs.

However dependence on external resources for industrialisation results in dependence on international terms of trade. The subsequent industries dependent on the high priced products of the initial industries start producing high priced consumer goods, the demand for which remains confined to a small proportion of the population. Hence the required increase in demand to hike up non-agricultural production to absorb the surplus labour does not materialise. Therefore, without the strengthening of demand linkages for UC's goods and services from the RH, transfer of labour force from the rural to the urban sector becomes limited and problematic, resulting in stagnation or even decline of purchasing power (under the influence of inflationary forces) amongst the majority of the people and the emergence of a dual economy with increasing income disparity.

Such an industrial policy led to the inception and growth of the three public sector steel towns at Durgapur in West Bengal, Rourkela in Orissa and Bhilai in Madhya Pradesh during the Second Plan period.[1] Injection of heavy investment in these new centres resulted in in-migration of labour force and as pointed out in the last chapter, by 1971 these three centres have emerged as High Migration Towns. However the regional and sectoral significance of such industrial expansion and the accompanying development of the town through in-migration of its labour force, depends upon the characteristics of the migrants in terms of their areas of origin, past occupation, levels of education at the time of migration, sex as well as the types of occupation in which they have been absorbed. The temporal variation in the number of migrants since the inception of the town can be expected to reflect the temporal variation in the role of the town in the rural-urban labour transfer mechanism and its future potential in that respect.

As pointed out in the Harris-Todaro model, described in Chapter 1, it is closely linked with the migrant's expected probability to find a job in the town which in turn is likely to increase with the years of the migrant's

[1] The Second Plan period in India extended from 1956–57 to 1960–61.

residence in the town. The Harris-Todaro model highlights the significance of the migrants with high job uncertainty in creating a glut in the urban labour market resulting in low wages and slum growth. However this expected probability to find a job at a particular place will also depend upon the local labour force of particular skills available in the town itself i.e., the indigenous labour force of the town. This indigenous labour supply can be expected to increase as the resident population of the town grows, especially for unskilled and semi-skilled labour force.

Hence, at different phases of town growth the proportion of migrants migrating with the expectation of finding a job will vary and may follow a definite pattern. Representation of such a pattern in a functional form may prove to be very important not only in understanding the phases of labour transfer mechanism in operation during the growth of a town, but also in the physical planning and allocation of space within the town. This component of population growth in a town is usually not given adequate consideration while planning allocation of space in the town. Hence predicted values of this component in different phases of the growth of a town can have significant bearing in regulating the growth of squatters. With the aim of addressing these issues this chapter concentrates on analysing the trend of migration and characteristics of the migrants to Durgapur as revealed by the first phase survey described in the next section.

Inception and Phases of Growth of Durgapur

Durgapur is one of the new industrial towns of India which are believed to have been conceived as components of the above-mentioned long range policy of 'national development'. Its inception dates back to the Second Plan period and it was created with the objective that it would evolve into a successful industrial complex in West Bengal with a heterogeneous industrial structure. Consequently Durgapur experienced a flow of manufacturing industries between 1955–66 in accordance with Dr. B.C. Roy's dream of creating an industrial complex. This period can be roughly divided into three phases of growth as described below (Figure 4.1).

The first phase of growth (1955–1961): This phase was characterised by the following investment strategies:

1. Construction of the DVC barrage across the river Damodar.
2. Establishment of a coke oven and by-products plant and a thermal power station by Durgapur Projects Ltd., a Government of West Bengal undertaking.
3. Establishment of the third public sector steel plant (a Government of India undertaking) in accordance with the Second Five Year Plan which laid emphasis on the development of heavy and basic industry.

PHASES OF INDUSTRIAL GROWTH IN DURGAPUR

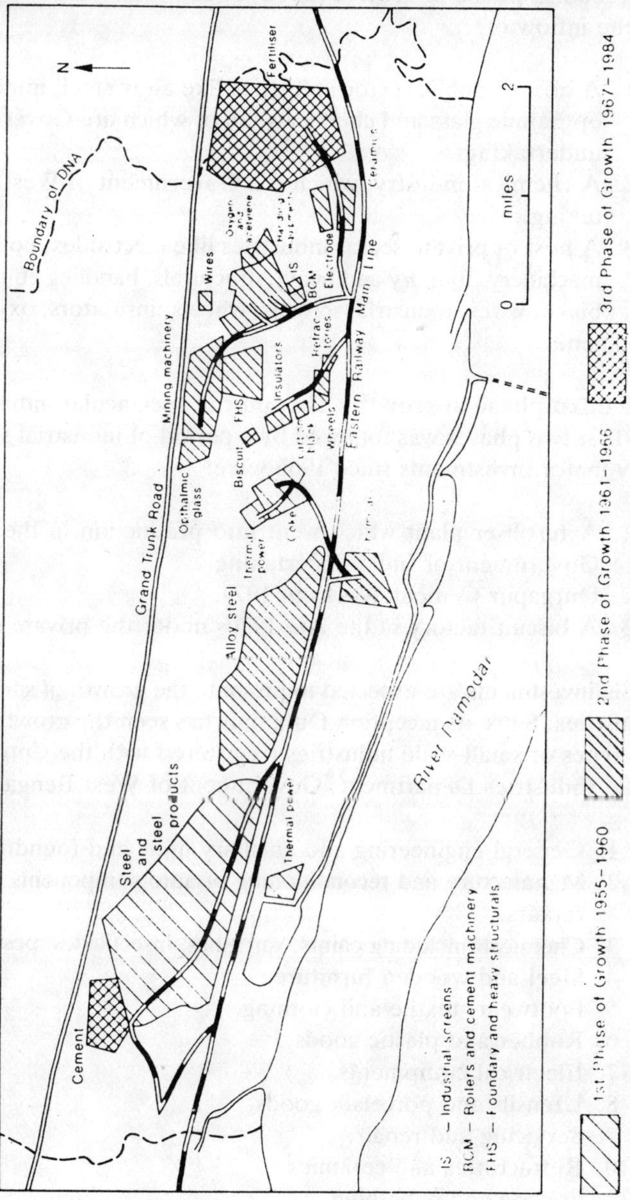

Source: Based on map from ADDA

Fig No 4.01

The second phase of growth (1961–1966): This phase was characterised by the inflow of:

1. A host of public sector industries like alloy steel, mining machinery, opthalmic glass and chemicals, all of which are Government of India undertakings.
2. A chemical industry, which is a Government of West Bengal undertaking.
3. A host of private sector industries like electrodes, boiler and cement machinery, foundry and heavy structurals, handling equipment, carbon black, wires, industrial screens, wheels, insulators, oxygen and acetylene.

The third phase of growth: The spurt of spectacular industrial growth in the first two phases was followed by a period of industrial stagnation. The only major investments since 1966 were:

1. A fertiliser plant which went into production in the early 1970s, a Government of India undertaking.
2. Durgapur Cement Works in 1974.
3. A biscuit factory in the late 1970s under the private sector.

Big investments are expected to promote the growth of small and ancillary industries. Since its inception Durgapur has seen the growth of the following types of small-scale industries (registered with the Cottage and Small-Scale Industries Department, Government of West Bengal):

1. General engineering and ancillary units and foundries.
2. Manufacture and reconditioning of auto components and automobile repairs.
3. Chemicals including paints, varnishes, insecticides, pesticides, candles.
4. Steel and wooden furniture.
5. Footwear, textile and clothing.
6. Rubber and plastic goods.
7. Electrical equipments.
8. Utensils and porcelain goods.
9. Servicing and repair.
10. Refractories and ceramics.
11. Printing and publishing.
12. Food products including rice processing, flour milling, biscuit manufacture, icecream production etc.

The large and medium scale industries mentioned above account for approximately 99 per cent of the total investment and 98 per cent of the total employment in registered large, medium and small-scale industries.[2] The large and medium scale industries developed in the first phase account for 61 per cent of the investments and 64 per cent of all employed in registered large and medium scale industries, those in the second phase account 33 per cent of the investments and 31.92 per cent of employment, while those in the third phase account for only 5.77 per cent of the investment and 3.77 per cent of employment in large and medium scale industries. It has not been possible to procure yearly estimates of total investment in all industries including large, medium and small-scale industries in Durgapur and hence it is difficult to form an estimate of the current value of total investment in Durgapur. The figures available were initial investment figures for small-scale industries without details of the year in which the investment was made. However the above percentages are approximate guides to the amount of investment that has taken place since the inception of the town and the total figure of Rs. 5222 million as total initial investment for the town in 37 years is possibly an underestimation.

Approximately 93 per cent of the total investment in the registered industries has been contributed by the Union and State governments and 90.85 per cent of the employees are in either Government of India or West Bengal government undertakings, thus highlighting the role played by government investment in generating employment in Durgapur. According to the 1981 census 53.9 per cent of the workers in Durgapur are employed in organised industries. Moreover according to the 1971 census while 48.41 per cent of the population are migrants, 80 per cent of the total workers consist of migrants, thus indicating the important role played by government investment in generating income to people who have migrated from areas outside Durgapur.

Data Collection and Field Survey

As detailed data on migration and remittances are not available, this research involved collection of primary data by running a two-phased questionnaire survey in Durgapur. This section deals with the methodology of collection of primary data during the first phase survey which was designed to identify migrants and some of their characteristics.

[2] Source of data on investment and employment: Asansol Durgapur Development Authority, Administrative Report of Durgapur Notified Area Authority (1988) and Small-Scale Industries Board, Government of West Bengal provided the data on investment and employment. It must be noted that the data for small-scale industries gave total initial investment figures and not the year when this investment was made. Similar problems arose with the investment figures given by Asansol Durgapur Development Authority. The employment figures are approximate figures of employees in different large and medium scale units in 1987–88, whereas the figures for small-scale units are based on a survey completed in 1986. Hence a lot of ambiguity exists in the data, though it does give an approximate idea about the structure of investment and employment in Durgapur.

Durgapur is classified as a Class 1 town by the Census of India, according to which the population in 1981 was 3.06 lakhs.[3] Hence the study had to rely on sampling in which the important decisions were:

1. A large sample size was chosen to make the subsamples as representative as possible in both the phases.
2. A sample design was constructed which could be expected to give fairly reliable estimates of the chosen variables, as explained below.
3. An appropriate questionnaire design was developed to elicit as reliable responses as possible.

Sample Size

The first phase of the survey conducted from August to November 1987 involved a questionnaire survey of 1500 households giving a dataset for 6888 people. The purpose of the survey was to identify migrants and analyse the migration characteristics of this type of town on the basis of 14 selected variables; the ultimate aim being to group the migrants and select a smaller subsample for a second phase of questionnaire survey which was expected to concentrate on the collection of information regarding remittances, family links and employment characteristics of the migrants. It must be pointed out that in India it is difficult to get a readymade sample frame, thus necessitating a two-phased survey. A sample design was prepared for 7000 people with the view of obtaining 3000 migrants so that resampling of 10 per cent of the migrants would involve filling up of 300 questionnaires in the second phase. The probability of getting 3000 migrants out of 7000 questionnaires was based on the assumption that the proportion of migrants to total population remained more or less the same as the 1971 Census. The questionnaires did identify 2943 migrants out of 6888 people in the first phase.

Sample Design

During the first phase 1500 households were distributed throughout Durgapur by initially stratifying the residential areas into following categories or strata:

Planned residential areas: this group consists of (*a*) Industrial townships, (*b*) Planned areas outside company towns developed by the government housing department, cooperatives and planning organisation;

Unplanned residential areas: (*a*) Former villages which have expanded to

[3] 1 lakh = 100,000.

form mixed settlements, (*b*) Authorised squatters reflecting the influence of political forces, (*c*) Unauthorised squatters.

Figure 4.2 shows the stratification of residential areas in Durgapur used for sampling and Figure 4.3a shows the spatial distribution of the different types of residential areas in Durgapur and the location of the sample areas.

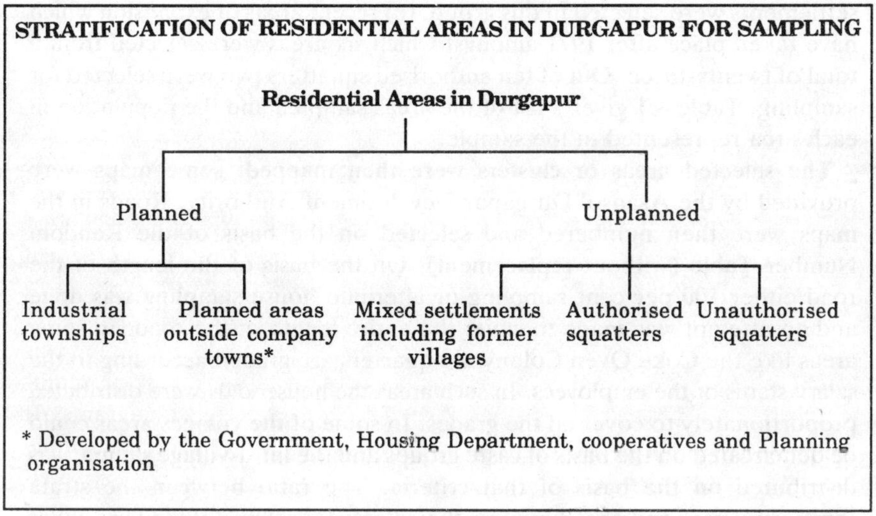

Fig. No. 4.02

The total population in each of these categories of residential areas or strata was available from the unpublished data from the Census Office of Calcutta, thus enabling a proportionate distribution of the sample population between the strata on the assumption that the average household consists of five members. Each stratum was divided into clusters of areas of known population. A list of the clusters weighted by their population size was made. A number of clusters within each stratum were selected randomly from this list on the basis of the Random Number Table by Fisher. However the number of clusters selected in each stratum was determined on the basis of three considerations: (*a*) local information about the homogeneity of population; (*b*) the time available to cover dispersed areas; and, (*c*) the number of areas that could be covered at a given cost.

Out of eight industrial townships four were selected which included one with private sector industrial employees (total of three private sector industrial townships) and three with public sector industrial employees (total of five public sector industrial townships). Out of seven areas designated as planned areas outside industrial townships, four were selected. The mixed settlements were divided into three groups—(*a*) old settlements where 90 per cent of the landholdings have grown before 1964 approximately and four out of ten areas were selected in this group, (*b*) more recent settlements where 75 per cent of the landholdings have grown before 1964, while 25 per cent have grown between 1964–71 and six out of fifteen settlements were selected in this group, (*c*) recent areas of expansion which have taken place after 1971 amongst which six areas were selected from a total of twenty-three. Out of ten authorised squatters two were selected for sampling. Table 4.1 gives a list of the areas sampled and the population in each area represented in the sample.

The selected areas or clusters were then mapped; some maps were provided by the Asansol Durgapur Development Authority. Roads in the maps were then numbered and selected on the basis of the Random Number Table (without replacement). On the basis of the length of the road either 100 per cent sampling or alternate house sampling was done and an attempt was made to cover the entire length of the road. In some areas like the Coke Oven Colony the quarters are graded according to the salary status of the employees. In such areas the households were distributed proportionately to cover all the grades. In some of the villages areas could be demarcated on the basis of caste groups and the intra-village sample was distributed on the basis of that criteria. The ratio between the strata (primary units) and that between the selected clusters (secondary units) were maintained. Figures 4.3b, 4.3c and 4.3d highlight some of the areas sampled.

The sample design thus adopted can be referred to as 'unequal size cluster sampling with stratification'. Consequently a separate ratio estimator approach had to be used for estimation of overall population mean of the different variables. This approach involves the separate estimation of a per element mean for each stratum. These separate mean estimates are then combined with population weights to produce the estimate of the mean for the entire population (Rossi, Wright, Anderson 1983: 57).

Questionnaire Design

The questionnaire in the first phase provided a dataset of two major variables for the sample population of 6871 while 17 cases were recorded as 'no responses'. These two variables were: (*a*) a categorical variable of migration status to divide the population into two subsets viz. migrants and non-migrants, and, (*b*) sex composition of the population.

The subset of 2943 migrants were further questioned to yield a dataset of 14 variables for the migrants, as listed in Table 4.2. The year of migration, as represented later in the time series graphs refer to the period

Table 4.1

Sampled Areas in Durgapur in the First Phase (1987)

Names of Areas	*No. of People in the Survey*
Planned Industrial Townships	
Durgapur Steel Plant's township (public sector)	2538
Coke Oven Colony of Durgapur Projects Ltd. (public sector)	773
MAMC township (public sector)	184
ABL township (private sector)	218
Planned Areas outside Industrial Townships	
City Centre	36
Bidhannagar Housing Colony	133
Areas Developed by ADDA	151
Sagarbhanga Housing Colony	234
Mixed Settlements	
Old Settlements before 1963	
Gopalmath	205
Kamalpur	77
Bijra	68
Shyampur village	311
More Recent Settlements 1964–1973	
Ambagan	152
Bhiringi	263
Karangapara	160
Peala	124
Palasdiha	163
Sagarbhanga village	137
New Areas after 1974	
Vidyasagarpalli	88
Tamla	291
Natunpalli	87
Aurobindopalli	32
Nabapalli	82
Hemantapalli	37
Authorised Squatters	
Shyampur Colony	141
Netaji Colony	204

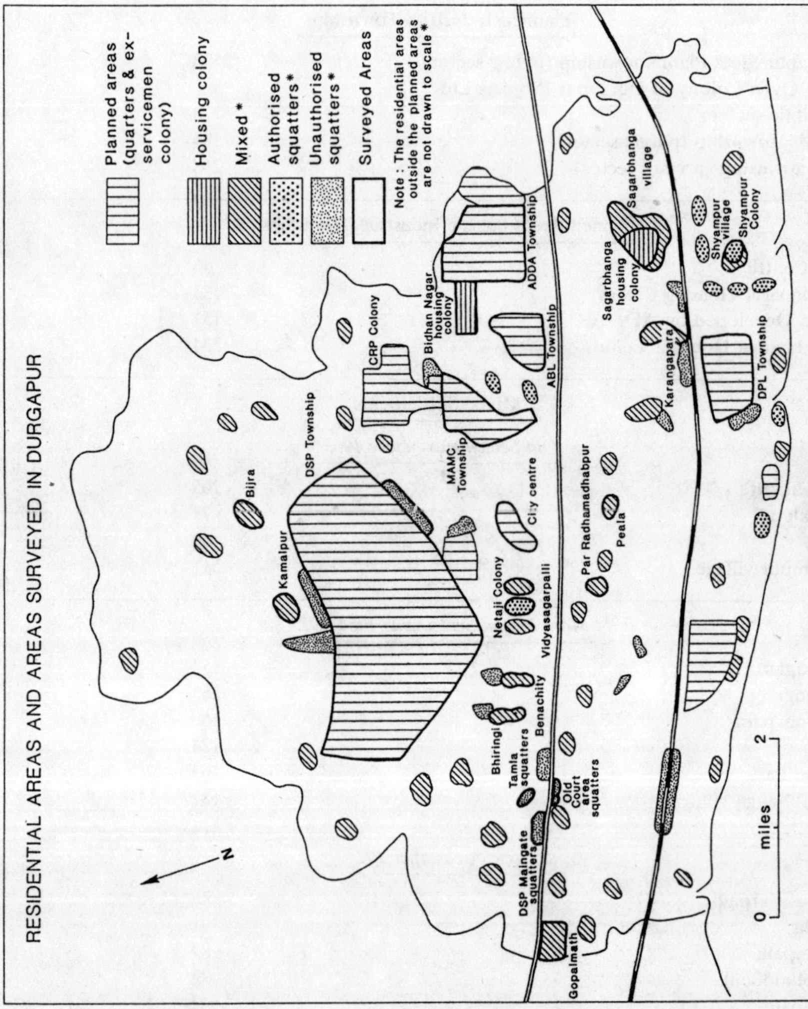

Source: Based on map from ADDA and fieldwork
Fig. No. 4.03a

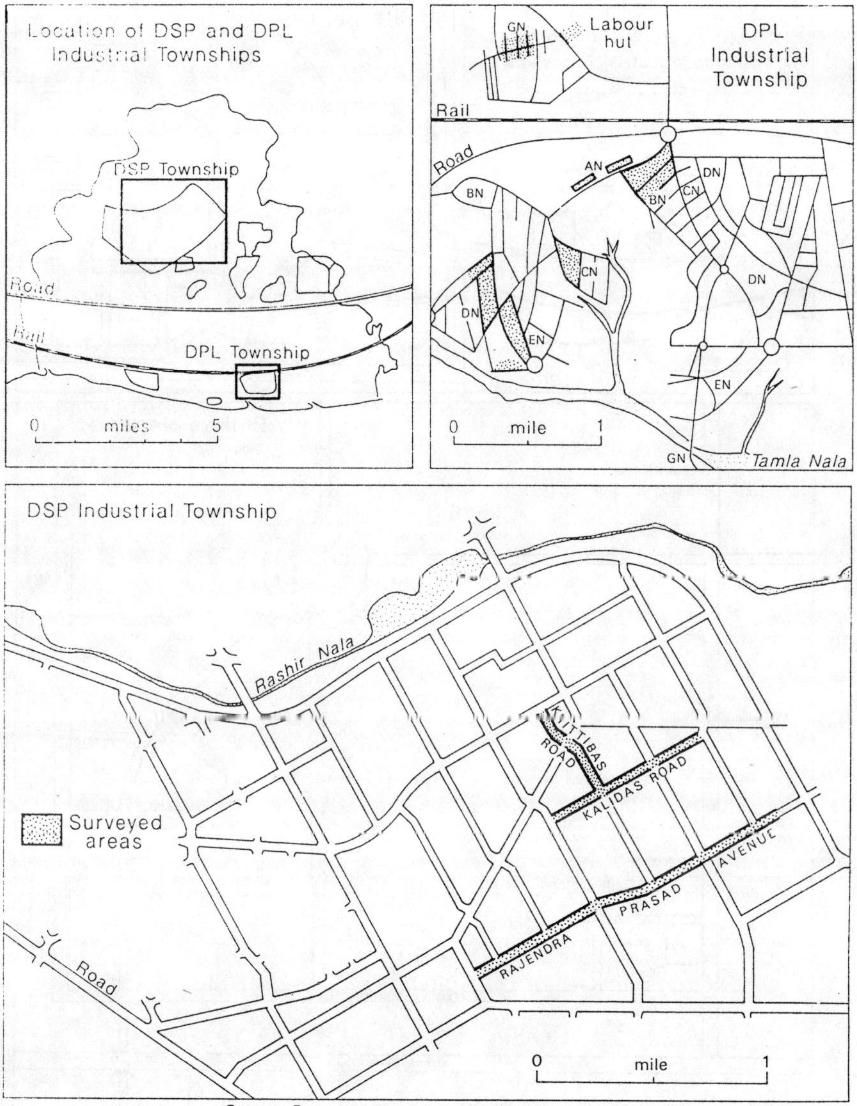

Source: Based on maps from ADDA, DSP and DPL

Fig.No.4.03b

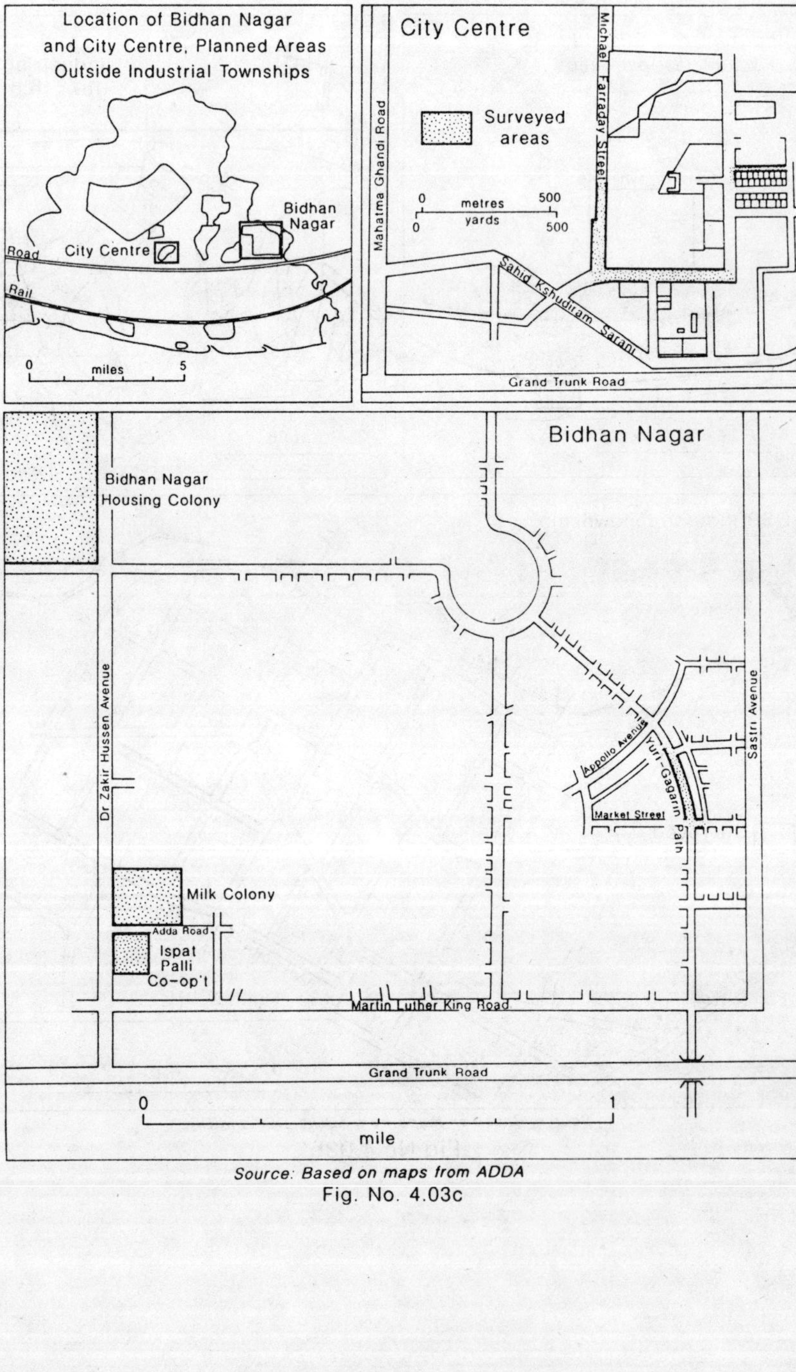

Source: Based on maps from ADDA

Fig. No. 4.03c

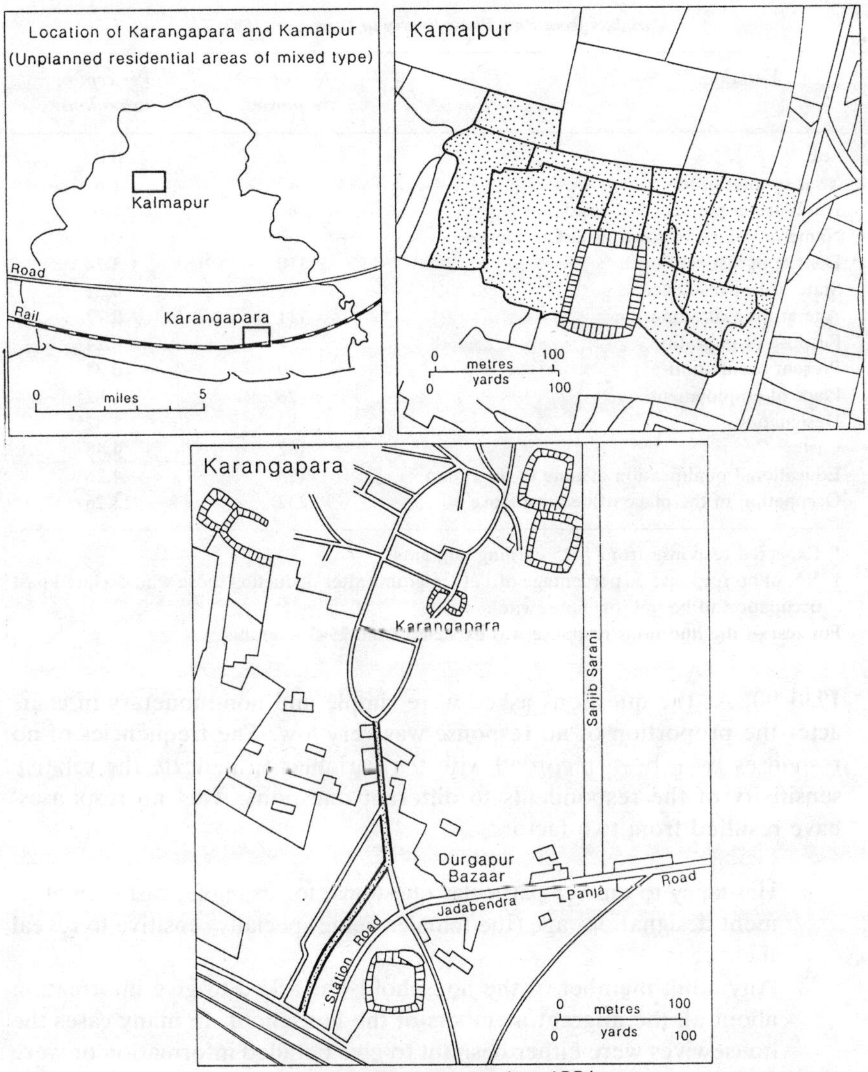

Source: Based on maps from ADDA

Fig. No. 4.03d

Table 4.2

Variables from First Phase Survey in Durgapur (1987)

Variables	*No. of no responses*	*Per cent of no response*
Sex	0	0.0
Year of migration	47	1.6
Rural/urban place of last residence	47	1.6
Name of village or town of last residence	0	0.0
District of last residence	110	3.74
State of last residence	9	0.31
Age at time of migration	111	3.77
Purpose of migration	7	0.24
Present occupation	10	0.34
Place of employment	26	1.82*
Designation	83	5.82*
Caste	132	4.48
Educational qualification at time of migration	125	4.25
Occupation in the place of last residence	232	13.26†

* Expected response from 1425 earning migrants.

† No. of no response as percentage of 1749 migrants after deducting those who declared past occupation to be 'nil' or 'housewife'.

For rest of the questions response was expected from 2943 migrants.

1930–90. As the questions asked were simple and non-monetary in character the proportion of no response was very low. The frequencies of no responses have been recorded with the variables to indicate the relative sensitivity of the respondents to different questions. The 'no responses' have resulted from two factors:

1. Hesitancy to answer particular questions, for example, caste, employment designation, age (the females being specially sensitive to reveal their age).
2. Any adult member of the household was asked to give information about all the migrant members of the household. In many cases the housewives were either hesitant to give detailed information or were ignorant of the details resulting in 'no responses' especially regarding questions on husband's occupation (present and past) and educational qualification.

Definition

From the first phase questionnaire (Appendix 2) it is evident that a person was deemed a 'migrant' if: (*a*) he was born outside Durgapur and has moved to Durgapur after the age of eight (*b*) anyone who has been born in

Durgapur, but has lived outside Durgapur upto the age of eight. Eight is the age after which children start migrating for education or employment. In the study in Ludhiana the age of twelve has been the criterion.

Verification of Two Sample Variables with Census Data

Two variables in the sample population collected in the first phase have been used to test the bias of the sample by comparing them with known or estimated figures from the census. They are:(*a*) proportion of migrants to total population; (*b*) proportion of male to the total population. As the 1987 figures of population and migrants were not available estimates were made on the assumption that the 1971–81 population growth rate for India and urban growth rate for Durgapur remained the same between 1981–87. The decadal population growth rate of 25.2 per cent meant an annual rate of increase of 2.27 per cent. At that rate of increase the population in Durgapur was expected to be 2,96,084. On the other hand the 1971–81 urban growth rate of 50.5 per cent meant an annual growth rate 4.2 per cent. At this rate Durgapur could be expected to have a population of 3,99,098 in 1987. The difference between the two figures viz. (*a*) population based on the growth rate of population of India, and, (*b*) population based on the urban growth rate of Durgapur gave a hypothetical figure for migrants who have migrated between 1971–87 to Durgapur. The figure amounted to 1,03,014 or 25.81 per cent of the expected population of 1987. The sample proportion of migrants arriving in Durgapur after 1971 to the total sample population was 17.27 per cent. However the population growth rate of Durgapur can be expected to have declined having dropped from 131.96 per cent (1961–71) to 50.5 per cent (1971–81), thereby accounting partly for a lower proportion of migrants. In addition the sample considered those who have migrated to Durgapur after the age of 8 years as 'migrants' so that it can be expected to be an underestimation of the total migrants. Moreover the proportion of migrants in 1971 (1971 Census) to the total expected population of 1987 (on the basis of the urban growth rate) worked out to be 25.06 per cent. The proportion of migrants uptil 1971 as percentage of the sample population worked out to be 24.79 per cent. Thus it seemed that the sample proportion of the migration variable seemed to be within a reasonable range.

The sex variable has been tested with the null hypothesis to indicate that there was no significant difference between the proportion of male to total population in the sample (53.38 per cent) and the proportion of male to the total population of 1981 census figure (54.43 per cent). The conclusion was valid at 1 per cent level of significance. Moreover according to the 1971 Census figure females accounted for 43.37 per cent of the migrants compared to 56.63 per cent for the male. The sample showed similar proportions (female—43.82 per cent; male—56.18 per cent) for migrants who have migrated to Durgapur until 1971.

Population Growth and the Trend of Migration to Durgapur

Prior to the growth of the industrial town of Durgapur, the area now designated as Durgapur Notified Area was occupied by 40 villages with a population of 26,101 in 1951. The 1961 Census for the first time records the growth of the steel town and the coke oven colony. These two formed the nucleus of growth pushing up the total population figure to 89,080 in 1961. During this decade characterised by the first phase of industrial growth (1955–61), the town experienced a maximum population growth rate of 241 per cent. In the subsequent decades the growth rate has declined to 132 per cent between 1961–71 and 51 per cent between 1971–81. The last and the latest figure is below the national average for all Class 1 towns of India (70 per cent). Hence Durgapur can no longer be categorised as a fast growing dynamic town. This decline of growth rate could have been caused by the following events: (*a*) Decline in birth rate which could reduce natural growth of the population of the town; (*b*) decline in the rate of in-migration; and, (*c*) increase of out-migration.

The last two points may result from lack of space within the areal extent of the town, though that is not the case in Durgapur. The second point is well reflected in the sample data of migrants. Figure 4.4a shows how the number of migrants have increased since the inception of the town in 1955, as the graph depicts the number of migrants per year, as represented in the first phase sample survey. It has been fitted with a trendline represented by a five point moving average (Figure 4.4b). Hence the resultant time series figures highlight two components of migration: (*a*) Short-term yearly fluctuations or random variations in the short run; (*b*) average or longer-term fluctuation in the number of migrants.

The short-term component reveals that the number of migrants per year has increased after 1955 to reach a peak in 1962 (i.e., the first phase of industrial growth). A second peak was in 1967 which marked the closing years of the second phase of industrial growth. Smaller spurts of increase occurred in 1970, 1972 and 1977. However the general trend has been a decline especially after 1977.

The long-term trend represented by the predicted values of the smoothed curve highlights a decline in the number of migrants after 1965 and a gradual decrease in the rate of change so that the curve levels off at a constant value in the subsequent years between 1975 and 1985 i.e., 20–30 years since the inception of the town. Three other similar curves represented by five point moving averages, depicting a longer-term trend of labour absorption role of Durgapur, are:

Time Series Showing Migration To Durgapur

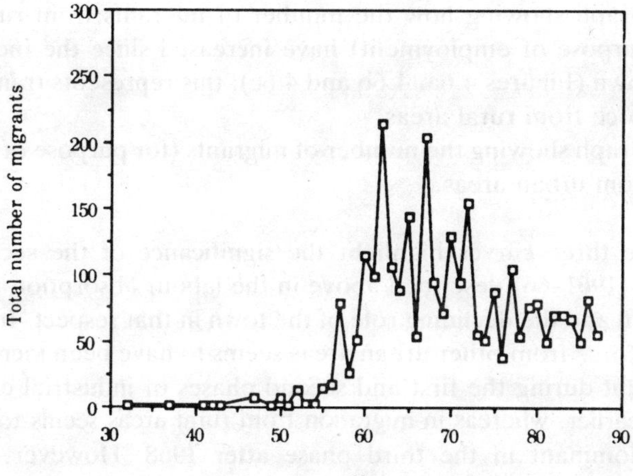

Fig. No. 4.04a

Yearly Rate Of Change Of Migration To Durgapur

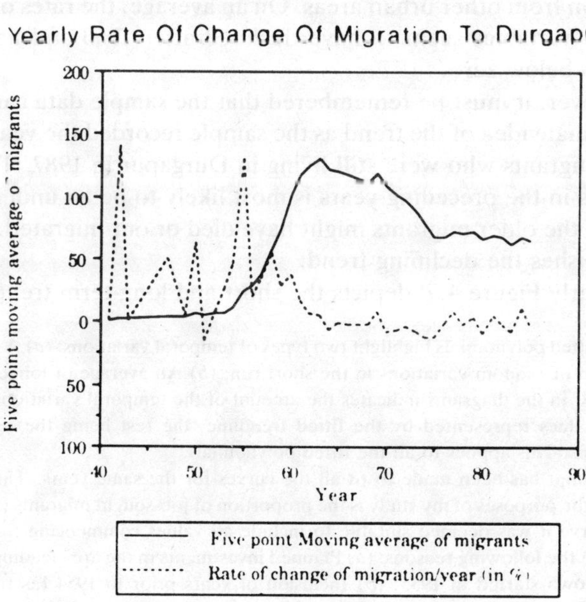

Fig. No. 4.04b

Note: All time series figures refer to the period 1930–1990

1. Graph showing how the number of migrants migrating with the purpose of employment has increased since the inception of the town (Figures 4.5a and 4.5b).
2. Graph showing how the number of migrants from rural areas (for purpose of employment) have increased since the inception of the town (Figures 4.6a, 4.6b and 4.6c); this represents transfer of labour force from rural areas.
3. Graph showing the number of migrants (for purpose of employment) from urban areas.

These three curves highlight the significance of the second phase of growth (1961–66) described above in the labour absorption mechanism of the town and the declining role of the town in that respect. In-migration of labour force from other urban areas seems to have been increasingly more important during the first and second phases of industrial expansion described earlier, whereas in-migration from rural areas seems to have become more dominant in the third phase after 1968. However, by 1987, in-migration from both rural and urban areas seems to have reached the same level, though the annual growth rate of migration from urban areas seems to have increased since 1983, possibly forecasting an increase in in-migration from other urban areas. On an average, the rates of growth of all the four variables seem to have declined after 1960 and have ultimately fallen to below zero.

However, it must be remembered that the sample data can give only an approximate idea of the trend as the sample recorded the year of migration of the migrants who were still living in Durgapur in 1987. The number of migrants in the preceding years is most likely to be an underestimation as some of the older migrants might have died or out-migrated. Nevertheless it establishes the declining trend.

Similarly Figure 4.7[4] depicts the short and long-term trend of migration

[4] The fitted polynomials highlight two types of temporal variations: (*a*) A short-term yearly fluctuation or random variations in the short run; (*b*) An average or longer-term trend; the value of R^2 in the diagrams indicates the amount of the temporal variation explained by the average values represented by the fitted trendline, the rest being the result of short-run fluctuations. This applies to all the fitted polynomials.

An attempt has been made to fit all the curves for the same years. The most important curve for the purposes of my study is the proportion of job-sought migrants (Figure 4.10a) and in this curve it was deemed suitable to include all values commencing from the year 1954 because of the following reasons: (*a*) Planned investments in the area leading to the growth of the new town started in 1955; (*b*) Inclusion of years prior to 1954 (as represented in the sample) led to a rapid decrease of the value of the R^2 possibly indicating that the short-run fluctuations before that year were more random in nature, perhaps due to unrepresentative subsample sizes for the preceding years.

However, in the case of proportion of migrants from rural areas to the total migrants (Figure 4.7), inclusion of 1954 resulted in a sharp decline of the R^2 value; hence in this case 1955 has been used as the starting year.

Time Series Of Migration Of Labour To Durgapur

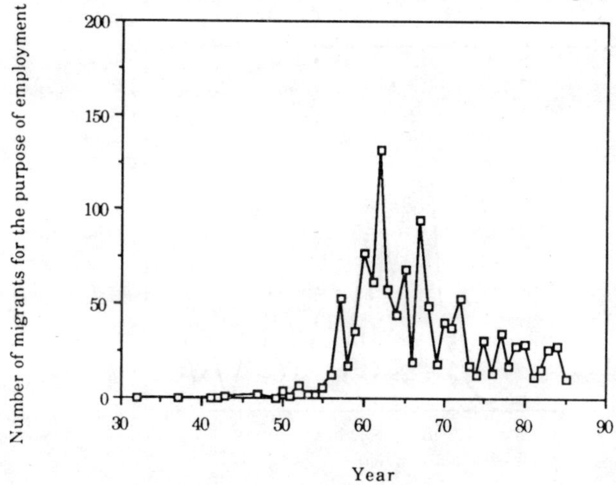

Fig. No. 4.05a

Average Trend Of Migration Of Labour To Durgapur

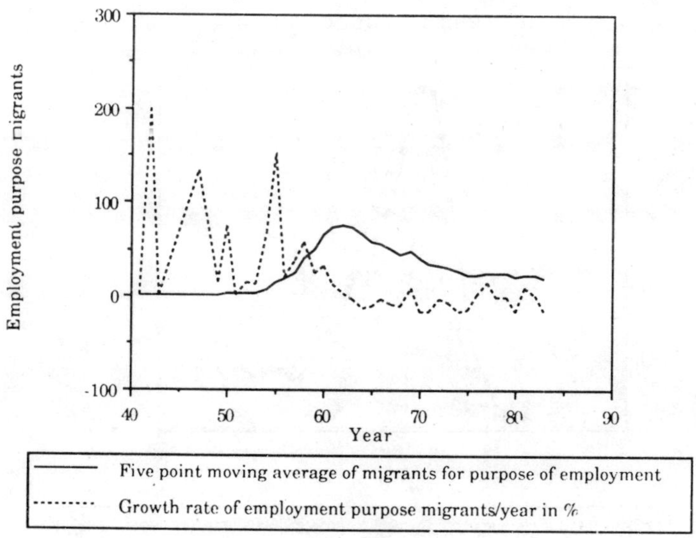

Fig. No. 4.05b

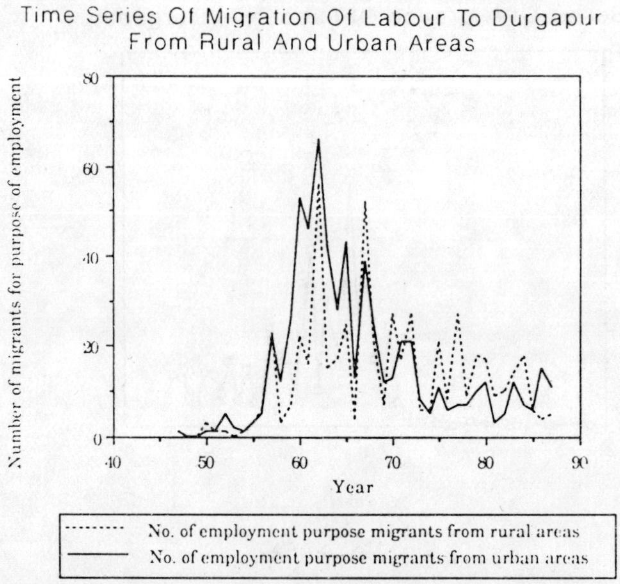

Fig. No. 4.06a

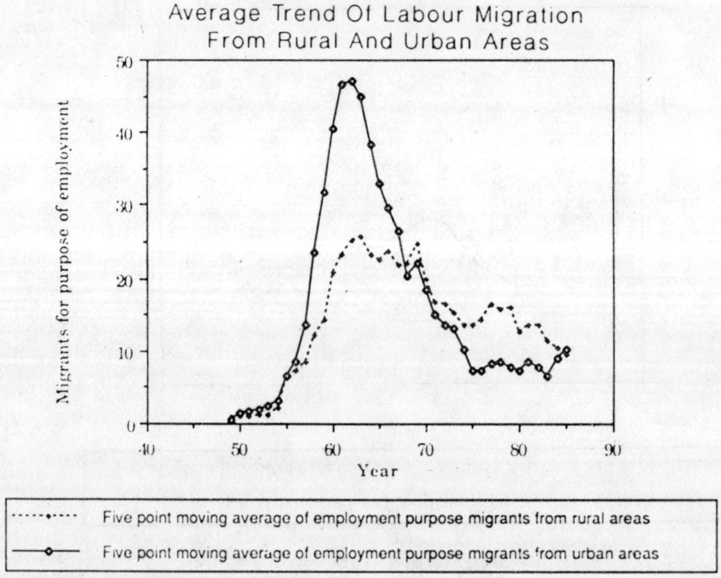

Fig. No. 4.06b

Yearly Rate Of Change Of Migration Of Labour To Durgapur

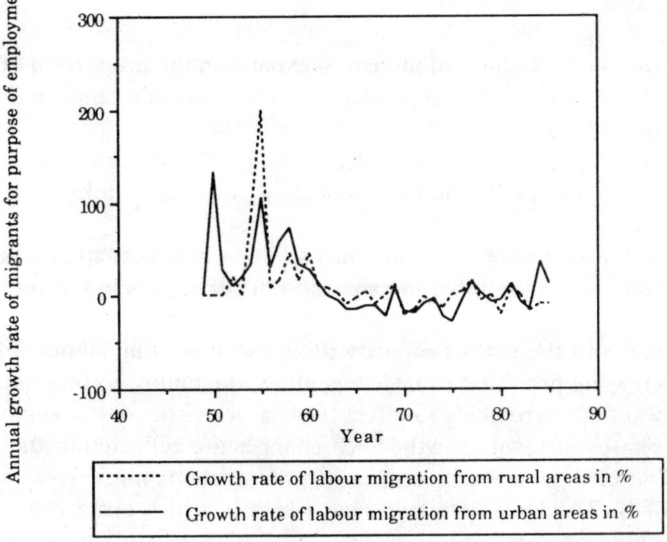

Fig. No. 4.06c

Time Series Of Proportion Of Migrants From Rural Areas

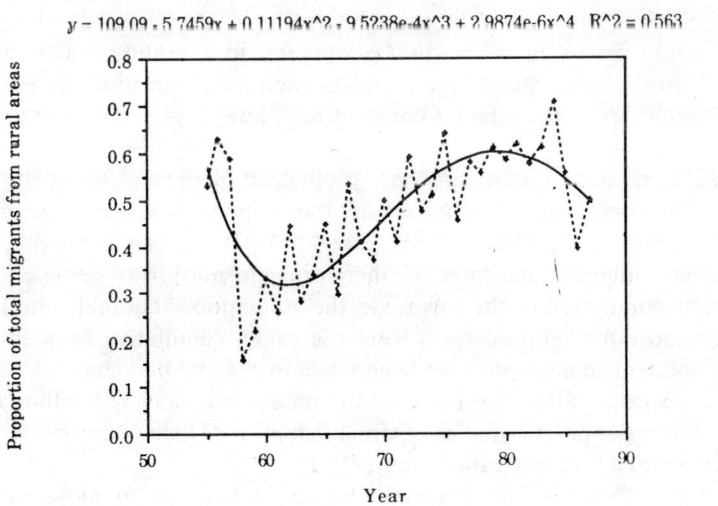

Fig. No. 4.07

to Durgapur from rural areas as percentage of total migrants. Though the short-term trend consists of alternate phases of migration from rural and urban areas, the long-term trendline depicted by fourth order polynomial highlights the following points:

1. During the first phase of industrial expansion the proportion of rural migrants to the total migrants has declined, thus indicating an increasing link of the town with other urban centres.
2. From the second phase onwards, the proportion of rural migrants has increased till 1980, thereby indicating increasing links with rural areas.
3. Since 1980 a phase of decline has set in, which perhaps indicates a limited role of the town in expansion of rural links in the future.

The changes in the town's capacity to absorb migrating labour force as well as increasing provision of civic amenities like family accommodation, shops, schools etc., are likely to affect the characteristics of the migrants in different phases of town growth. Such changes are reflected in the curve showing the change in the proportion of dependent migrants with time (Figure 4.8a). The long-term trendline which is a fifth order polynomial identifies three phases:

1. First phase extending roughly from 1955 to 1960 characterised by rapid rise in the proportion of migrants for the purpose of employment.
2. Second phase extending roughly from 1960 to 1970 characterised by rapid rise in the proportion of migrants in-migrating as dependents.
3. Third phase extending after 1970 when the proportion of dependent migrants has reached a constant high level.

The trend-line representing the proportion of dependents seems to be almost identical with that representing the proportion of female migrants to total migrants of the same order (Figure 4.8b). The increase in the proportion of female migrants indicates an increasing proportion of females in the migrant population of the town. On the assumption that male and female death and out-migration rates were the same, cumulative frequencies of male and female migrants have been taken to indicate the temporal variation in the sex ratio of the migrants over the time period depicted in the sample. The fifth order polynomial in Figure 4.9 depicts a U-shaped curve with two major reversals of sex ratio since 1950.

After 1955 when the sex ratio began to fall due to more male in-migration possibly in response to the growth of industries in the first phase (1955–61). Since 1961 the sex ratio started to rise, though the proportion of male remained more. The absolute difference exhibited a break after 1968

Time Series Of Migration Of Dependents To Durgapur

$y = 558.28 - 38.482x + 1.0512x^2 - 1.4226e{-2}x^3 + 9.5494e{-5}x^4 - 2.5454e{-7}x^5 \quad R^2 = 0.802$

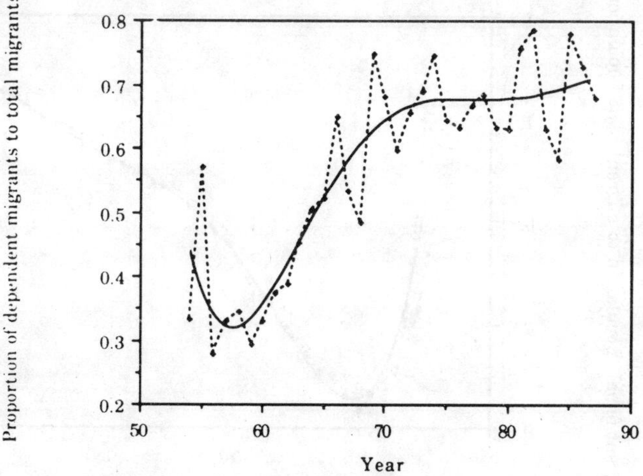

Fig. No. 4.08a

Time Series Of Migration Of Females To Durgapur

$y = 894.97 - 63.023x + 1.7615x^2 - 2.4435e{-2}x^3 + 1.6833e{-4}x^4 - 4.6096e{-7}x^5 \quad R^2 = 0.779$

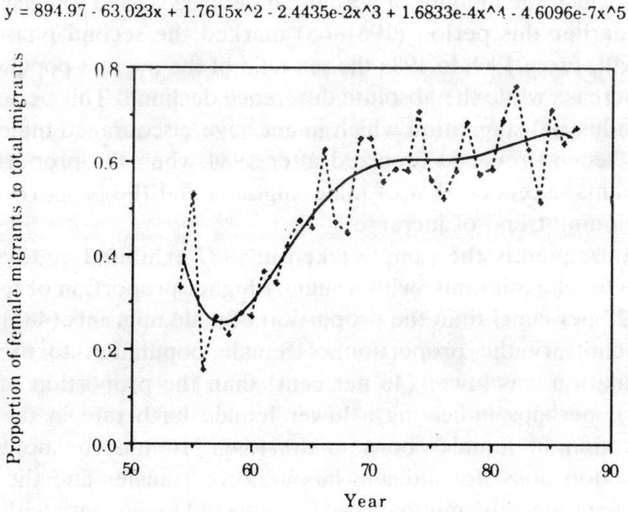

Fig. No. 4.08b

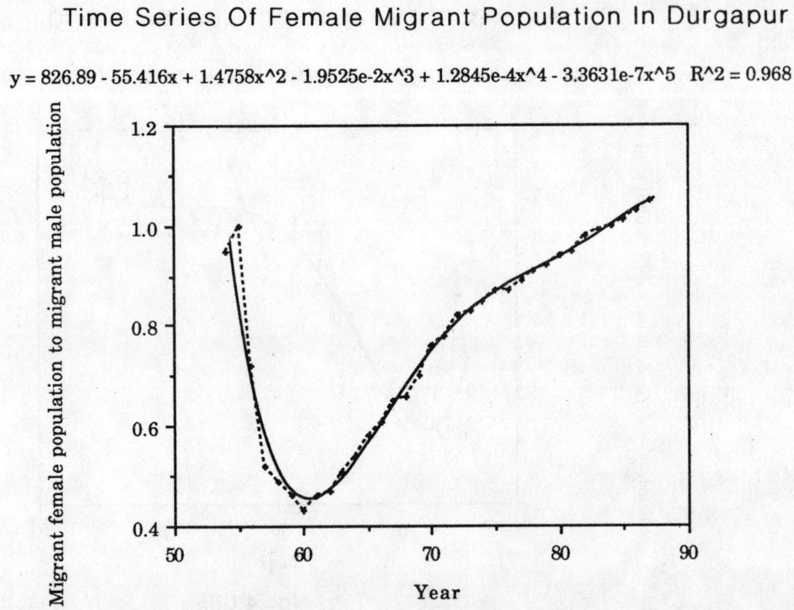

Fig. No. 4.09

after which the amount of absolute difference started to decline. As pointed out earlier this period (1961–68) marked the second phase of industrial growth. From 1968 to 1984 the sex ratio of the migrant population continued to increase while the absolute difference declined. This period was marked by industrial stagnation which might have discouraged male in-migration.

A second reversal occurred after 1984 when the proportion of female migrants exceeded that of male migrants and the proportions indicated a continuing trend of increase.

Consequently the sample taken in 1987 exhibited quite a balanced sex ratio for the migrants, with a slightly higher proportion of female migrants (51.27 per cent) than the proportion of male migrants (48.8 per cent). On the contrary the proportion of female population to the total sample population was lower (46 per cent) than the proportion of male (53 per cent), perhaps indicating a lower female birth rate in the town or out-migration of females born in the town. It must be noted that female migration does not indicate labour force transfer and the propensity to remit amongst the migrants can be expected to decrease with increasing sex ratio because of the following reasons:

1. Only 9.8 per cent of the total earning population in the sample are female. According to a survey in Ludhiana in Punjab in 1977 the proportion was only 3.13 per cent (Oberai and Singh 1981).

2. The propensity to work for an earning[5] seems to be very low amongst female migrants (9.46 per cent) compared to male migrants (92.24 per cent). The propensity to migrate for the purpose of employment[6] is also very low for female migrants (3.53 per cent) compared to male migrants (79.83 per cent).

Migration for Purpose of Employment (Employment Purpose Migration)

Temporal Trend of Labour Force Migration

About 40.8 per cent of the migrants have migrated for the purpose of employment (employment purpose migrants) and this constitutes labour force migration. An analysis of the employment purposes of migration reveals that 57 per cent have migrated to Durgapur with the expectation of finding a job (or job-sought migrants) while only 43 per cent have come with definite-job appointment (or definite-job migrants). This provides empirical confirmation to some of the concepts of Harris–Todaro model referred to above. The job-sought migrants possibly represent surplus labour transfer from one area to another and consist of migrants whose probability of getting a job in the urban destination area is less than 1. In contrast, for the definite-job migrants the probability of getting a job in the urban destination area is 1. Thus these two groups of migrating labour force are characterised by two types of employment certainty.

Figure 4.10a shows the estimated proportions of job-sought migrants to the total employment purpose migrants in different phases of town growth. It approximately represents the variation in surplus labour absorption capacity of the town since its inception. The trend-line depicted by a fifth order polynomial (which explains 54 per cent of the variation), highlights the following points:

1. The first phase of town growth, characterised by the highest amount of investment, experienced a decline in the proportion of job-sought migrants due to increasing in-migration of definite-job migrants.
2. After five years of town growth the proportion of job-sought migrants seems to have increased for the next 15 years to reach a peak around 1975, though investment in registered industries seems to have declined.

[5] Propensity to work for an earning has been calculated as per cent of females/males presently employed or searching for an employment to the total female/male migrants respectively.

[6] Propensity to migrate for the purpose of employment has been calculated as per cent of female/male migrants who migrated for the purpose of finding a job or with definite job appointment to the total female/male migrants respectively in the sample.

3. Thereafter, the trend-line shows a steady decline.

The time lag in the occurrence of high expected job migration might have resulted from the following factors: (*a*) Time taken for the diffusion of job information over space, and, (*b*) the types of job capable of absorbing unskilled or semi-skilled migrants with high job uncertainty come into existence as the resident population of the town increases as discussed later on. Therefore, a spurt of definite-job migration is required to create a demand for services that can be provided by the people in-migrating in search of jobs, for example, shops, barbers, servants or the non-basic activities.

It is interesting to note that the trend-line (Figure 4.10b) giving predicted values of the proportion of employment purpose migrants from rural areas to the total migrating labour force (who have migrated for the purpose of employment) shows an identical pattern of temporal variation as the trend-line for job-sought migrants. This indicates the strong correlation between job-sought migration and rural labour force migration.

Since more than 75 per cent of employment purpose migration from rural areas consists of migrants in search of a job (Figure 4.11a) Durgapur is unlikely to attract rural labour force in future. Figure 4.10c shows that migration with definite-job to Durgapur from rural areas is also declining. As the potential for absorbing rural labour force declines, its links with that sector are likely to become weaker compared to the urban sector, though the remittance linkage may continue for sometime as the old migrants continue to remit.

Some amount of definite-job migration is likely to continue as people in formal employment retire, but expected job migration is likely to cease or remain very low as the indigenous population start providing the labour force required specially for semi-skilled and unskilled jobs. The increase in definite-job migration from urban areas since 1981 (Figure 4.10d) indicates a continuing stronger link of the city with the urban sector. Thus, within thirty-two years of its inception the new town has exhausted its potential to act as a wage equilibrating mechanism through labour force transfer from the rural to the urban sector.

Relative Characteristics of Job-Sought and Definite-Job Migrants

Level of education: In order to analyse the relation between the level of education and employment certainty of the migrating labour force a chi square test has been done between eight education categories and the two employment certainty categories. The chi square value is significant at $p=0.0001$ leading to the acceptance of the alternative hypothesis that there is an association between the level of education and job certainty of the migrants (Table 4.3).

Time Series Of Migration Of Job-Sought Migrants To Durgapur

y = 673.61 - 45.556x + 1.2289x^2 - 1.6546e-2x^3 + 1.1139e-4x^4 - 3.0052e-7x^5 R^2 = 0.542

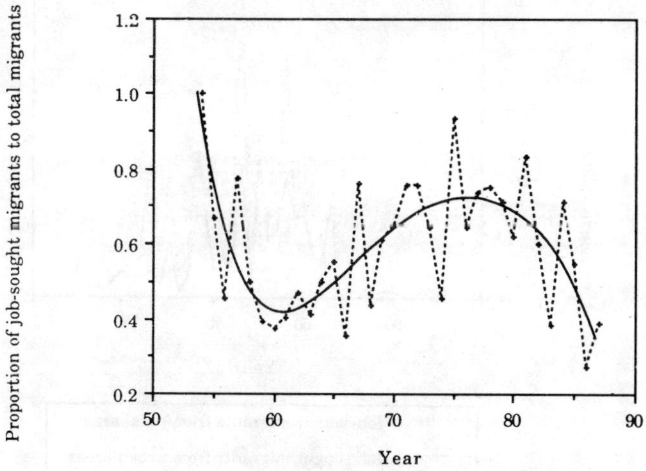

Fig. No. 4.10a

Proportion Of Employment Purpose Migrants From Rural Areas

y = 597.67 - 42.655x + 1.2190x^2 - 1.7440e-2x^3 + 1.2497e-4x^4 - 3.5877e-7x^5 R^2 = 0.624

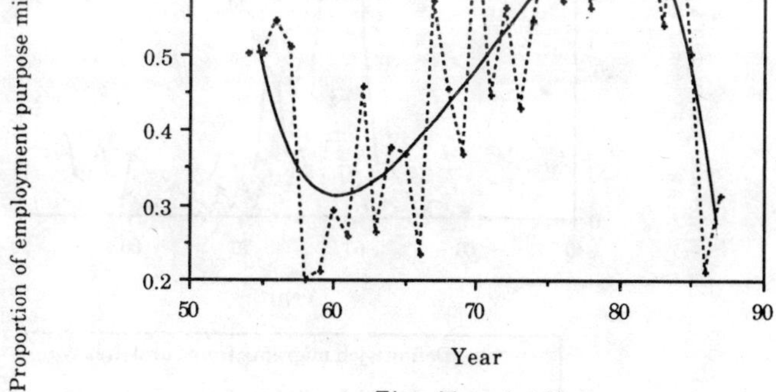

Fig. No. 4.10b

Time Series Of Job-Sought Migrants
From Rural And Urban Areas To Durgapur

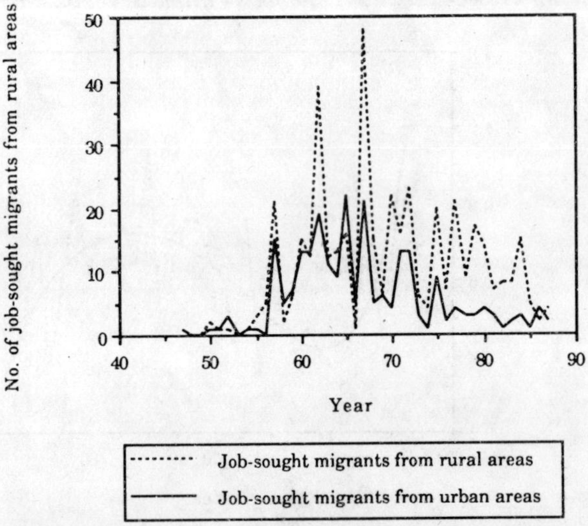

Fig. No. 4.10c

Time Series Of Definite-Job Migrants
From Rural And Urban Areas To Durgapur

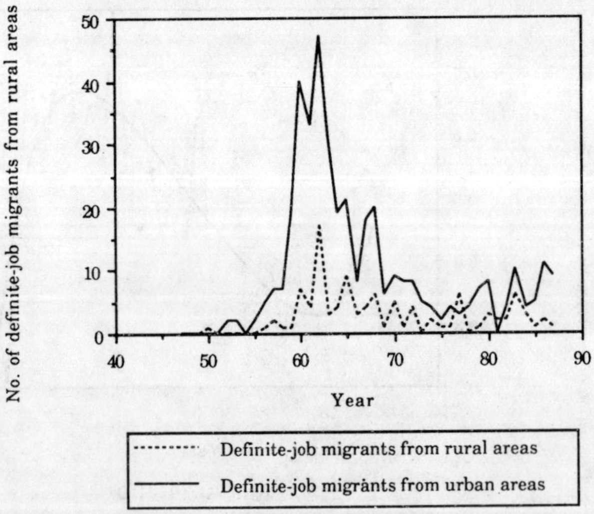

Fig. No. 4.10d

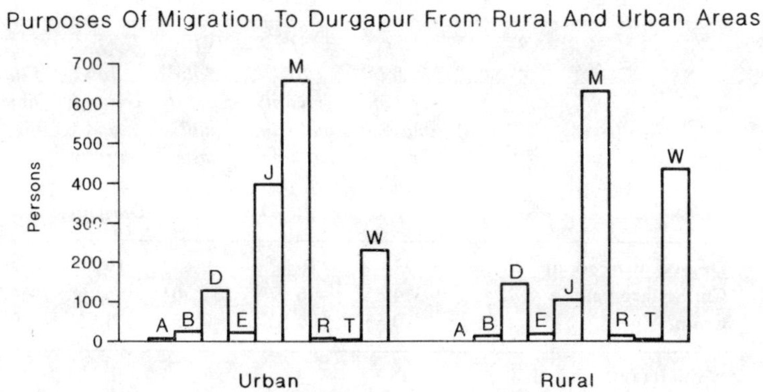

Fig. No. 4.11a

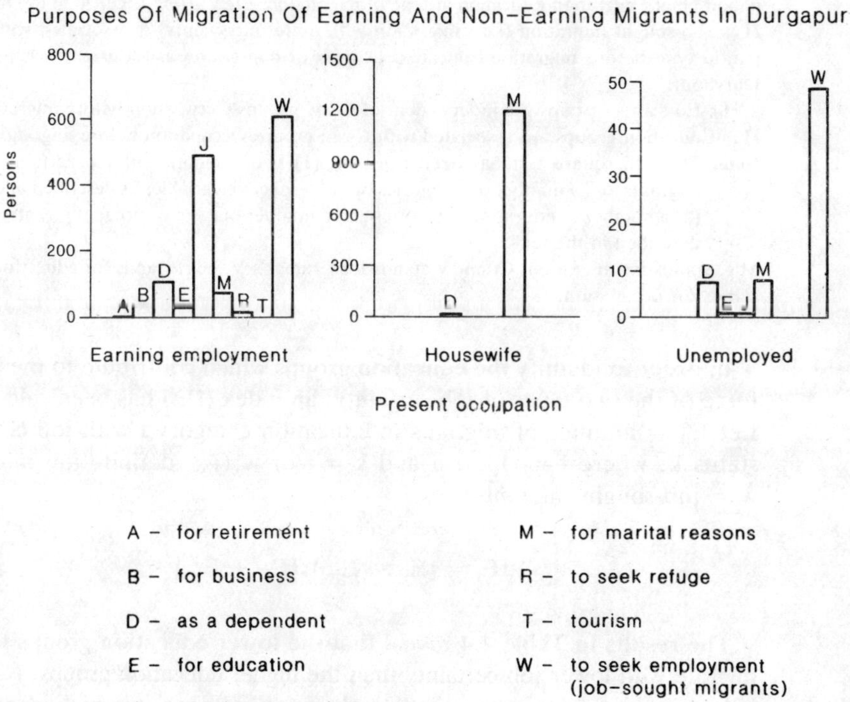

Fig. No. 4.11b

Table 4.3

Results from Chi Square Test Describing the Relationships between Selected Characteristics of the Migrants in Durgapur

	1 *Job certainty and occu. before mig.*	*1* *Job certainty and edu. at time of mig.*	*1* *Job certainty and caste*	*1* *Job certainty and current occu. in Durgapur*	2 *Edu. at time of mig. and caste*	2 *Edu. at time of mig. and occu. before mig.*
Degree of freedom	22	10	9	19	27	8
Chi Square value	314.85*	426.72*	231.30*	446.16*	864.04*	439.39*
Cram. V	0.55	0.52	0.48	0.65	0.34	0.40

* $p = 0.0001$

1 H_0: Job-sought migration (i.e., migration with more uncertainty) is independent of Occupation before migration/Education at time of migration/Caste/Current occupation in Durgapur.
H_A: Job-sought migration (i.e., migration with more uncertainty) is associated with Occupation type before migration/Education at time of migration/Caste/Current occupation in Durgapur.

2 H_0: Education groups are independent of Caste groups/Occupation before migration.
H_A: Education groups are associated with Caste groups/Occupation before migration.

Note: The Chi square test has been run with (1) two categories of job certainty of the migrants and a number of categories of the respective variables as described in the text; (2) a number of education categories and a number of caste or occupation categories as described in the text.

Mig. stands for migration, Cram. V stands for Cramer's V, edu. stands for education, occu. stands for occupation.

In order to identify the education groups which contribute to the labour force of the two types of job certainty, an index (IE_i) has been calculated. Let E_{ik} = number of migrants in education category i with job certainty status k, where i = 1 ....n and k = j or w (j = definite-job migrants; w = job-sought migrants).

$$IE_i = (E_{ij} - E_{iw})/(E_{ij} + E_{iw})$$

The results in Table 4.4 reveal that the lower education groups tend to migrate with lower job certainty than the higher education groups. Negative values in the table indicate the education categories which contribute migrants with low level of job certainty in the destination. Table 4.5a further establishes the fact that the propensity to migrate with the expectation of finding a job (amongst the migrants) is highest in the lower education groups i.e., illiterate to intermediate. About 91 per cent of those who migrate with the expectation of finding a job belong to the lower education groups from illiterate to intermediate. The maximum is the group which

Table 4.4

Identification of Education Categories Contributing Labour Force with Different Types of Job Certainty

Education categories	*Total No. of migrants*	*No. of definite-job migrants*	*No. of job-sought migrants*	*Index values**
Illiterate	536.0	6.0	127.0	−0.91
Literate	189.0	6.0	66.0	−0.83
Primary	921.5	59.0	272.0	−0.64
Matric	355.5	85.5	92.0	−0.04
Higher Secondary	123.5	21.0	23.5	−0.06
Intermediate	114.5	35.5	21.0	0.26
Graduates	336.0	136.5	35.0	0.59
Post-graduate	53.5	18.0	8.5	0.36
Technical training	75.0	49.5	13.0	0.58
Law, medical etc. (Professional)	17.5	13	1.5	0.79

Note: Total migrants consist of those who have responded to the question on educational qualification (at time of migration) and purpose of migration.

* Concentration Index of job-sought and definite-job migrants in different education categories.

Table 4.5a

Job-sought Migrants from Different Education Categories

Education categories	*Total migrants*	*No. of job-sought migrants*	*% job-sought migrants to total migrants*	*% job-sought migrants to total job-sought migrants*
Illiterate and literate	725.0	193.0	26.62	29.11[1]
Class 1-Class 10	921.5	272.0	29.52	41.03[2]
Matric, Higher Secondary and Intermediate	593.5	136.5	23.00	20.59[3]
Graduates	336.0	35.0	10.40	5.28
Technical training	75.0	13.0	17.33	1.96
Engineering	70.5	3.5	4.96	0.53
Post-graduate	53.5	8.5	15.88	1.28
Miscellaneous	17.5	1.5	8.57	0.23

Note: (a) [1+2+3] =90.73 per cent.

(b) Migrants include those who have responded to the question on purpose of migration and level of education.

does not have any formal degree but have attended schools (41 per cent) followed by illiterate and literates (29 per cent) and matric, higher secondary and intermediate (21 per cent). This is possibly because of the following reasons:

1. Lower education groups are more likely to be employed in the less remunerative occupations (before migration) which are characterised by the different types of uncertainties which tend to act as push factors. The relation between education levels of the migrating labour force and their past occupation before migration is discussed in the next section.
2. The lower education groups viz. illiterate, literate capable of signing names, those who had some amount of school education between Class 1 and Class 10, matric and higher secondary together constitute 78 per cent of the migrants to Durgapur (Table 4.5b). Due to the large influx of people who are capable of being absorbed on flexible conditions for varying lengths of time in all types of unskilled and semi-skilled jobs, the employment institutions do not require to give formal appointments with prior complicated appointment procedures. They tend to employ them through contractors and trade unions in the town.

Table 4.5b

Absorption of Migrants with Different Education Qualifications in Earning Occupations in Durgapur

Education categories	*Total migrants*	*Currently earning migrants in Durgapur*	*% earning migrants to total earning migrants in each education category*	*% earning migrants to total earning migrants*
Illiterate, literate	727.0	277.0	38.0	20.04
Class 1–Class 10	922.5	389.5	42.22	28.18
Matric + H.S + I.A	598.5	327.5	54.70	23.70
Graduates	350.5	205.0	58.49	14.83
Technical training	76.5	67.0	87.58	4.80
Engineering	70.5	64.5	91.49	4.70
Post-graduate	53.5	34.5	64.48	2.50
Miscellaneous	19.0	17.0	89.47	1.20
Total		**1382.0**		

Note: H.S stands for Higher Secondary; I.A stands for Intermediate (Arts).

3. This large group of migrants with job uncertainty (amounting to 23 per cent of all migrants) and low skill or education levels are usually prepared to accept jobs at very low wage rates and on uncertain, informal and unwritten employment conditions. This in turn boosts up the demand for unskilled and semi-skilled labour at very low wage rates.

While the first one is a push factor, the last two are pull factors which contribute a certain degree of job certainty to those who migrate in search of a job. Hence phases of high level of job-sought migration can be expected to be associated with influx of unskilled labour force.

Occupation prior to migration: A study of the occupation in the place of last residence of the migrants reveals that only 30.93 per cent of the total respondent migrants were earning an income before migrating to Durgapur (Table 4.6). Of the total earning migrants in Durgapur 54.24 per cent had to forego some form of income in order to migrate to Durgapur.

Table 4.6

Earning Status before Migration of Working and Non-working Migrants in Durgapur

Occupations of migrants in Durgapur	*No. of migrants with earning occu. before migration*	*No. of migrants without earning occu. before migration*	*Total migrants*	*% migrants without earning occu. before migration to total migrants*
Earning	742	626	1368	54.24
Unemployed and student	11	49	60	18.33
Non-working and housewife	113	1259	1372	8.24
Total	**866**	**1934**	**2800**	

Note: occu. stands for occupation.

It is not surprising that the maximum propensity to forego income was amongst those who were able to procure employment in Durgapur before migrating i.e., the definite-job migrants (Table 4.7). In such cases the employment opportunities procured in Durgapur were obviously superior compared to the past ones in the perception of the migrant concerned. Thus the pull factor was an important element in the migration decision.

The propensity was lower, but quite high amongst those who ventured to migrate with the expectation of finding a job in Durgapur. The uncertainty involved in such a move may have failed to deter them from foregoing income because of the following reasons:

1. The probability of finding a job in Durgapur was very high in the perception of the migrant. This may have resulted from already established contacts in Durgapur in the form of relations or friends.
2. The occupation in the last residence was not very remunerative with the possibility that the remuneration received failed to cover the consumption expenditure.

Table 4.7

Earning Status of Migrants with Different Purposes of Migration

Purposes of migration to Durgapur	*No. of migrants with earning occupation before migration*	*Total migrants with different purposes of migration*	*% earning migrants to total migrants with different purposes of migration*
Definite-job migrants	302	488	61.88
Job-sought migrants	403	697	57.82
Retired, refugee, housewife migrants	93	404	23.02
Other dependent migrants	44	268	16.42
Student migrants	3	43	6.98

The former cause is a 'pull factor' while the latter is a 'push factor'.

In order to identify the occupations which generate more push effect relative to the others an index (IP_i) has been computed on the basis of job-sought migration and definite-job migration to Durgapur. The former has more inherent employment uncertainty in the destination which can be expected to be a retarding factor. A chi square test has been used to show that job-sought migration is dependent upon or correlated with particular occupation groups. The value of chi square is significant at $p = 0.0001$ indicating the rejection of the null hypothesis (Table 4.3) and acceptance of the alternative hypothesis that migration with uncertainty in employment correlates with occupation types in the place of last residence at 99.99 per cent level of significance. The Cramer's V of 0.55 indicating the strength of the correlation is less than that for education level.

To identify the specific occupation types which are more susceptible to losing its labour force in spite of high uncertainty involved the following index has been computed:

Let P_{ik} = number of migrants in past occupation category i with job certainty status k, where $i = 1 \ldots. n$ and $k = j$ or w (j = definite-job migrants; w = job-sought migrants).

$$IP_i = (P_{ij} - P_{iw}) / (P_{ij} + P_{iw})$$

The results have been given in Table 4.8. The values with negative signs are the occupations from which labour force has migrated with a high degree of uncertainty in finding employment in the destination. They include the following types of occupations:

Table 4.8

Identification of Occupation Categories Contributing Labour Force with Different Types of Job Certainty

Occupation of migrants before migration	*Total No. of migrants*	*No. of Definite-job migrants*	*No. of job-sought migrants*	*Index values**
1. Domestic & personal services	36.5	3.0	27.0	−0.80
2. Petty manufacture	22.5	2.0	18.5	−0.80
4. Casual & contractor labour	30.5	11.0	17.5	−0.23
5. Petty traders	39.5	2.0	21.0	−0.83
6. Shopowner, wholesaler, hotel owner, 21. contractor	44.5	4.5	20.0	−0.63
7. Rickshaw/van puller, 8. driver, conductor	10.0	2.0	8.0	−0.60
9. Owner cultivator	161.0	6.0	121.0	−0.90
10. Agricultural labour & 31. sharecropper	77.0	2.0	60.5	−0.93
11. Professionals—doctor, lawyer	9.0	7.0	0.0	1.00
12. Office staff—clerk, personal assistant	24.0	17.0	3.0	0.70
13. Chargeman, chargehand, foreman (industrial)	15.0	12.0	2 0	0.71
14. Chemist, physicist, 15. engineer	25.0	25.0	0.0	1.00
16. Director, chairman, manager, superintendent, officer, administrator	22.5	17.5	1.0	0.89
17. Non-technical industrial employee	23.0	13.0	6.0	0.36
19. Unskilled employees	26.0	7.0	14.0	−0.33
20. Safety and rescue service	22.0	16.0	2.0	0.78
22–23. Semi-skilled and skilled technicians	39.5	23.5	15.0	0.22
24, 28, 29, 32. Midwife, nurse, misc.	15.5	7.0	6.5	0.04
25. Teacher, lecturer	75.0	24.0	9.0	0.45
26. Trainee, apprentice	27.0	22.0	4.0	0.69
30. Student	736.0	136.0	177.0	−0.13
91. Nil	305.0	45.0	90.0	−0.33
92. Unemployed	21.0	5.0	16.0	−0.52

Note: Total migrants consist of those who have responded to the question on occupation in the place of last residence and purpose of migration. Details of occupations included in each number category is given in the Appendix 4.

* Concentration Index of job sought and definite job migrants in different occupation categories in the place of last residence.

1. Beggar.
2. Domestic employees like gardeners, cooks, helpers, animal-keepers, servants and maidservants, caretaker, houseguard, driver.

3. Self-employed petty manufacturers like mason, blacksmith, painter, plumber, coachman, tailor, carpenter, bandplayer and seller of personal services like washerman, sweetmaker, porter.
4. Petty trader like seller, dealer, supply agent with no fixed outlet for their trading commodities.
5. Shopowners.
6. Rickshaw puller, van puller, bus conductors.
7. Casual labourers.
8. Shop helpers, peon, sweeper, messenger.
9. Contractor.
10. Those in agricultural production employment including landowners, agricultural wage labour and sharecroppers.

Some of these above-mentioned occupation categories may be characterised by one or more of the following features which encourage loss of labour force: (*a*) Uncertainty of tenure; (*b*) uncertainty of the amount of remuneration; (*c*) uncertainty of the regularity of remuneration; (*d*) low amount of remuneration. The resulting degree of uncertainty must exceed the uncertainty of finding a job with equal or less degree of uncertainty. Moreover unemployed labour searching for an earning occupation, students and those who did not have any earning occupation also contribute job-sought migrants.

On the other hand the other occupation categories which mainly consist of formal employment by registered units probably have more certainty in terms of tenure and remuneration and the labour force migrates only when the alternative employment opportunity and attributes are guaranteed through prior appointment.

The relation between past occupation and education levels is evident from Table 4.9. The lower the level of education, the higher is the proportion employed in past occupations which have given negative values in Table 4.8. A chi square test with Table 4.9 gave a high chi square value, thereby establishing the fact that past occupations with negative values is associated with the level of education and consequently as pointed out earlier they have a higher propensity to encourage out-migration with high level of employment uncertainty.

Table 4.10 shows that a higher proportion of migrants from negative past occupations (indicating those occupations which have contributed job-sought migrants to Durgapur) have migrated from rural areas compared to the urban areas. This may be a function of the following factors:

1. The negative past occupations which tend to push away its labour force tend to dominate the rural occupation structure.
2. The employment conditions in such occupations are worse in the rural areas compared to similar occupations in the urban areas so

Table 4.9

Relation between Education Categories and Past Occupations which have Contributed Labour Force with Two Types of Job Certainty

(1) Education categories to which the migrant belonged at time of migration	*(2)* No. of migrants in past occupation which sent more job-sought migrants	*(3)* No. of migrants in past occupation which sent more definite-job migrants	*(4)* Total migrants (2) + (3)	*(5)* % of (2) to (4)
Illiterate + literate	184.0	2.0	186.0	98.92
Class 1–Class 10	205.0	33.0	238.0	86.13
Matric	47.0	53.5	100.5	46.77
Higher Secondary + Intermediate	18.5	41.5	60.0	30.83
Graduates	12.0	86.0	98.0	12.24
Technical training	2.0	24.0	26.0	7.69
Engineering	2.0	27.5	29.5	6.78
Post-graduate	1.0	17.5	18.5	5.40
Miscellaneous	1.0	11.5	12.5	8.00

Note: Those who have declared their past occupation as student or nil have been excluded as they were in non earning occupations.

Table 4.10

Rural-Urban Origin of Migrants with Past Occupations which have Contributed Migrants with Two Types of Job Certainty

Place of last residence	*No. of migrants in past occupation which sent more job-sought migrants*	*No. of migrants in past occupation which sent more definite-job migrants*
Rural	141.5	242.0
Urban	329.5	55.0

that the labour force in the rural areas are more aware of the rural urban differential in remuneration and job certainty. However they are likely to be unaware of rural-urban differential in the cost of living which may, in real terms, fail to improve the income or level of living after migration to the urban area. In contrast the urban labour force may be exposed to more alternative occupations in the same or positive occupation categories which lowers their propensity to migrate to other urban centres with the expectation of finding a job.

In contrast, the migrants from urban areas tend to move from positive employment categories with definite-job appointment in Durgapur.

Caste: Like education level and pre-migration occupation, the chi square value (Table 4.3) exhibits significant association between job-sought migrants and lower castes, though the strength of the correlation is less than those with education levels or past occupation. A similar concentration index calculated from the number of job-sought and definite-job migrants from different castes migrating to Durgapur shows that there is a general tendency for job-sought migrants to come from lower caste groups (Table 4.11).

Table 4.11

Identification of Castes Contributing Labour Force with Different Types of Job Certainty

Castes	*Total No. of migrants*	*No. of definite-job migrants*	*No. of job-sought migrants*	*Index values**
Brahmin	663	188	99	0.31
Baidya	25	7	73	0.56
Kayasthya	697	169	118	0.18
Goyala	322	10	122	−0.85
Bania	127	11	24	−0.37
Vaisya	38	10	4	0.43
Mahesya	41	6	13	−0.37
Ugro-khatriyo	33	3	4	−0.14
Teli	62	13	12	0.04
Kumore	19	1	2	−0.33
Scheduled tribe	37	2	18	−0.80
Scheduled caste	360	25	133	−0.68

Note: Total migrants consist of those who have responded to the question on caste and purpose of migration.

* Concentration Index of job sought and definite job migrants in different types of castes.

Let C_{ik} = number of migrants in caste group i with job certainty status k, where i = 1....n and K = j or w (j = definite-job migrants; w = job-sought migrants).

$$IC_i = (C_{ij} - C_{iw})/(C_{ij} + C_{iw})$$

The association between caste and job certainty of the migrants is probably the result of a positive correlation between lower caste groups and a low level of education amongst the migrants. Whereas 7.95 per cent of the *brahmin*, *baidya*, *kayasthya*, and *ugro khatriyo* migrants belong to the lowest educational level (literates who can sign their names and illiterates) the figure rises progressively to 66.75 per cent of the scheduled caste and scheduled tribes group of migrants (Table 4.12). On the other hand in the higher education groups like (*a*) engineering, technical and vocational training and (*b*) graduates and post-graduates, the proportion of *brahmins*, *baidyas*, *kayasthyas*, and *ugro khatriyos* is the highest (8.08 per cent and 22.3 per cent respectively) compared to 0.51 per cent and 2.66 per cent for scheduled caste and scheduled tribes (Table 4.12). The chi square value (Table 4.3) also points towards similar conclusions.

Table 4.12

Relation between Caste Groups and Education Level of Migrants

Caste Groups	*1*	2	3	4	5
Brahmin, Baidya, Kayasthya, Ugro-khatriyo	7.95	30.73	30.94	8.08	22.30
Bania, Vaisya	26.79	42.99	13.70	4.05	12.46
Goyala, Mahesya, Teli, Kumore	35.24	45.12	11.11	2.47	6.06
Scheduled tribe, Scheduled caste	66.75	24.11	5.97	0.51	2.66

1 Illiterate and literate migrants as percentage of total migrants who have responded to the question on caste and education level.

2 Migrants who have attended school between Class 1 and Class 10, but have no formal degree as percentage of total migrants who have responded to the question on caste and education level.

3 Migrants who have formal school leaving certificate (matric or secondary or madhyamik), Higher secondary and Intermediate certificates as percentage of total migrants who have responded to the question on caste and education level.

4 Migrants who have diploma or degree in technical training or vocational training and engineering as percentage of total migrants who have responded to the question on caste and education level.

5 Migrants who have graduate or post-graduate degree in the general stream subject as percentage of total migrants who have responded to the question on caste and education level.

Table 4.12 shows that a comparatively larger proportion of this upper caste belongs to both the higher education groups like graduates, post-graduates, engineering and technical educationists as well as middle education groups like primary education in schools, matric, higher secondary and intermediate. Therefore, they are susceptible to both push and pull factors. Though a larger proportion have migrated with definite-jobs (62.81 per cent), 37.19 per cent have migrated in search of jobs. Therefore, they are likely to constitute the largest proportion amongst the migrants.

In contrast the third caste group (consisting of the *mahesya*, *goyala*, *teli* and *kumore*) has the next highest proportion of migrants and has been subjected to more push factor as 83.24 per cent have migrated for the purpose of finding a job in Durgapur. The lowest category (consisting of scheduled caste and scheduled tribes) have similar but lower proportion of migrants with greater emphasis on push factors only, as 84.23 per cent have migrated in search of jobs. The concentration index in job certainty in these three caste groups shows that as it decreases from 0.256 for the upper caste, to −0.665 for the second last caste to −0.697 for the lowest caste group the proportion of migrants in each caste group also decreases (Table 4.12). Hence the upper castes may tend to be more mobile than the lower ones, though this cannot be established for certain as the figure for their propensity to migrate cannot be calculated.The second caste group of *bania* and *vaisya* is an anomaly. Though it contributes labour force to both the groups of job certainty its proportion in total migrants is low.

Table 4.13 shows that 59.3 per cent of the migrants belong to the upper castes consisting of *brahmins*, *baidyas*, *kayasthyas* and *ugro khatriyos*, followed by the third caste group of *mahesya*, *goyala*, *teli* and *kumore* (17.96 per cent), scheduled caste and scheduled tribe (16.06 per cent) and *vaisya* and *bania* (6.68 per cent). However in order to understand their relative importance in the propensity to migrate, their total numbers are required for the source areas to act as a deflator to get the proportions; but they are not available.

Table 4.13

Proportion of Migrants in Different Caste Groups

Caste groups	*Total migrants*	*% migrants in each caste group to total migrants*
Brahmin, Baidya, Kayasthya, Ugro-khatriyo	1466	59.30
Bania, Vaisya	165	6.68
Goyala, Mahesya, Teli, Kumore	444	17.96
Scheduled tribe, Scheduled caste	397	16.06
Total	**2472**	**100.00**

Note: Total migrants include all migrants who have responded to the question on caste.

Occupation in Durgapur: It is interesting to note that 90 per cent of those who have migrated with the expectation of finding a job were recorded to have an earning occupation in the sample (Table 4.14a). Table 4.14b shows that the maximum proportion has been absorbed in trading activities (26.4 per cent), followed by industrial semi-skilled labour (20.4 per cent), casual and contractor labour (9 per cent) and those engaged in domestic services, for example, servants, cook, gardener etc. Figure 4.11b shows that the highest proportion of earning migrants have migrated in search of jobs.

Table 4.15 indicates that 37 per cent of the rural migrants who earned a remuneration in the place of last residence were owner-cultivators while 16 per cent were landless labourers and 3 per cent sharecroppers. While 40.6 per cent of the owner-cultivators have been formally employed in registered

Table 4.14a

Propensity of Job-sought Migrants to Procure an Earning Occupation

Purpose of migration	*No. of migrants in earning occupation in Durgapur*	*No. of unemployed migrants searching for a job*	*Total no. of job-sought migrants*	*% of job-sought migrants who have an earning occupation in Durgapur*
Job-sought migrants	612	48	679	90.13

Table 4.14b

Absorption of Job-sought Migrants in Different Types of Earning Occupations in Durgapur

Types of present earning occupations of the migrants in Durgapur	*No. of job-sought migrants*	*% of job-sought migrants in different earning occupations to total job-sought migrants*
1 Domestic and personal services	42.5	7.2
2 Petty manufacturing	21.0	3.6
3 Beggar	0.5	0.1
4 Casual and contractor labour	53.0	9.0
5 Petty trader	111.0	18.8
6 Shopowner, wholesaler, petty trader	45.0	7.6
7 Rickshaw/van puller	37.0	6.3
8 Driver and conductor of vehicles	16.0	2.7
9 Owner cultivator	4.0	0.7
10 Landless agricultural labourer	2.0	0.3
11 Professionals—doctor, lawyer	3.5	0.6
12 Office staff—clerk, cashier, accountant	12.0	2.0
13 Chargeman, chargehand, foreman	24.0	4.1
14 Chemist, physicist, pharmacist, scientist and statistician	2.0	0.3
15 Engineer	4.0	0.7
16 Director, chairman, officer, administrator	12.0	2.0
17 Inspector, verificator, surveyor, timekeeper	29.0	4.9
18 Personal assistant, steno-typist, telephone assistant	2.0	0.3
20 Safety and rescue work	6.0	1.0
21 Contractor	6.5	1.1
22 Draftsman, designer, programmer	1.0	0.2
23 Semi-skilled and skilled technicians	120.5	20.4

Table 4.14b (Continued)

Types of present earning occupations of the migrants in Durgapur	*No. of job-sought migrants*	*% of job-sought migrants in different earning occupations to total job-sought migrants*
24 Midwife, nurse	1.0	0.2
25 Teacher	8.0	1.4
28 Priest/pir/astrologer	3.0	0.5
Total	**590.5**	**100.00**

Table 4.15

Occupation of Migrants before Migration by Rural and Urban Place of Last Residence

Occupation before migration	*No. of migrants from rural areas*	*No. of migrants from urban areas*	*% of earning rural migrants to total migrants with earning occupation in rural areas before migration*
1 Domestic and personal services	25.5	9.0	7.01
2 Petty manufacturing	13.5	7.0	3.71
4 Casual and contractor labour	16.0	14.0	4.40
5 Petty trader	17.0	23.0	4.68
6 Shopowner, wholesaler, petty trader	19.0	22.0	5.23
7 Rickshaw/van puller	2.0	1.5	0.55
8 Driver and conductor of vehicles	3.0	3.5	0.82
9 Owner cultivator	133.0	25.0	36.59
10 Landless agricultural labourer	57.0	6.5	15.68
11 Professionals—doctor, lawyer	2.0	7.0	0.55
12 Office staff—clerk, cashier, accountant	3.0	21.0	0.82
13 Chargeman, chargehand, foreman	1.0	14.0	0.27
14 Chemist, physicist, pharmacist, scientist and statistician	1.0	3.0	0.27
15 Engineer	1.0	19.0	0.27
16 Director, chairman, officer, administrator	5.5	18.0	1.51
18 Personal assistant, steno-typist, telephone assistant	0.0	2.0	0.00
19 Unskilled employee in non-domestic work—attendant, peon, messenger	10.0	16.0	2.75
20 Safety and rescue work	4.0	18.0	1.10
21 Contractor	1.5	2.0	0.41

Table 4.15 (Continued)

Occupation before migration	*No. of migrants from rural areas*	*No. of migrants from urban areas*	*% of earning rural migrants to total migrants with earning occupation in rural areas before migration*
22 Draftsman, designer, programmer	0.0	1.0	0.00
23 Semi-skilled and skilled technicians	8.5	28.0	2.34
24 Midwife, nurse	1.0	2.0	0.27
25 Teacher	13.0	61.0	3.58
26 Trainee, apprentice	5.0	22.0	1.37
28 Priest/pir/astrologer	2.0	2.0	0.55
31 Sharecropper	11.0	0.0	3.03
32 Misc.—football player, volunteer force worker, subeditor, vaccinator	3.0	5.0	0.82
90 Migrants with earning occupation before migration	363.5	–	100.00
30 Student	242.0	481.0	–
91 Nil	689.0	484.0	–
92 Umemployed	9.5	5.0	–

units as clerical and office workers or in industries as skilled and semi-skilled personnels or in defence occupations like police or in schools as teachers, only 15.8 per cent of the agricultural labourers have found employment in these occupations. The employees of these formal occupations can be expected to have better remuneration and protected terms and conditions of employment as most of them are in industries and offices. On the other hand the agricultural labourers are mainly employed as petty traders (24.5 per cent), rickshaw and van pullers (18.6 per cent), servants, cook, gardener (12.7 per cent), driver and bus conductors (9.8 per cent). Hence the owner cultivators can be expected to remit back more than the agricultural labourers.

Amongst the non-industrial and non-official occupations (consisting of domestic employees and those providing personal services, petty manufacturers, petty traders, shop and hotel owners, 'rickshaw' and 'van' pullers, self-employed workers who drive hired or own vehicles for public transport or hire out vehicles for commodity transport, casual and 'contractor labourers' in industries), proprietorship of shops or trading establishments and contractor labourers in industries can be expected to yield higher remuneration. In both the groups the proportion of owner cultivators is greater than agricultural labourers (Table 4.16).

About 55 per cent of the migrants or 57 per cent of the earning migrants

Table 4.16

Absorption of Migrating Owner Cultivators and Agricultural Labourers in Different Types of Earning Occupations in Durgapur

Current earning occupations of migrants in Durgapur	*Occupation before migration*	
	% of owner cultivators in different earning occupations in Durgapur	*% of agricultural labourers in different earning occupations in Durgapur*
1 Domestic and personal services	5.7	12.7
2 Petty manufacturing	1.9	4.9
4 Casual and contractor labour	13.3	8.8
5 Petty trader	22.7	24.5
6 Shopowner, wholesaler, petty trader	9.1	2.0
7 Richshaw/van puller	3.0	18.6
8 Driver and conductor of vehicles	2.3	9.8
9 Owner cultivator	1.5	1.0
10 Landless agricultural labourer	0.0	2.0
12 Office staff—clerk, cashier, accountant	1.9	0.0
13 Chargeman, chargehand, foreman	1.9	0.0
15 Engineer	0.0	2.0
16 Director, chairman, officer, administrator	0.8	0.0
17 Inspector, verificator, surveyor, timekeeper	3.4	0.0
19 Unskilled employee in non-domestic work—attendant, peon, messenger	4.2	2.0
20 Safty and rescue work	1.9	2.0
23 Semi-skilled and skilled industrial workers	24.6	9.7
29 Landlord	0.8	0.0
Total migrants	**100.0**	**100.0**

are employed in organised industries listed in Table 4.17. The table highlights the role of Durgapur Steel Plant, Durgapur Project Ltd. and Alloy Steel plant in providing industrial employment to the migrating labour force. The occupation structure as revealed by Table 4.18 shows that industrial and office employment is followed by sellers and shop owners (20 per cent) and domestic services (9 per cent) in absorption of the migrant labour.

The occupations at the destination area constitute the pull factor. The chi square test (Table 4.3) again establishes the correlation between job-sought migration and types of occupation in Durgapur which have exhibited a greater propensity to absorb them. The Cramer's V indicates that the strength of association of this variable with job uncertainty is maximum when compared with those of the other variables like education, past occupation and caste.

Table 4.17

Absorption of Migrant Labour Force by the Major Large and Medium Scale Industries in Durgapur

Names of industries	*No. of migrants employed as represented in first phase sample survey*
ABL	50
Asiatic Oxygen	1
Alloy Steel Plant	158
Bengal Tools	3
Bharat Opthalmic Glass Ltd.	3
Burn Standard	2
Burnshed Co. Ltd.	1
Durgapur Chemical Ltd.	7
Durgapur Projects Ltd.	189
Durgapur Steel Plant	267
Durgapur Cement Works	1
Eastern Biscuit	2
Fertiliser Corporation of India	5
Graphite India Ltd.	4
Hein Lehmann	2
Indo American Electricals	3
LPG	1
MAMC	33
Mecon	5
Phillips Carbon Black	1
Sankey Wheels	26
Saxby	2
Total	**766**

Table 4.18

Occupation of Migrants in Durgapur

Occupation Categories	*No. of migrants*
Beggar	1
Domestic services	119
Casual labour	76
Shop owners and sellers	264
Rickshaw/van pullers	39
Driver, bus conductors	19
Agriculture, priest, landlord	12
Doctor, lawyer, teacher, nurse, midwife	75
Contractor	10
Industrial, official	717
Apprentice	9
Nil including housewife	1601
Total	**2942**

A concentration index of job certainty has been calculated (Table 4.19) with the following equation:

Table 4.19

Identification of Earning Occupations in Durgapur which Absorb Labour Force Migrating with Different Types of Job Certainty

Earning occupations	*Total no. of migrants*	*No. of definite-job migrants*	*No. of job-sought migrants*	*Index values**
1 Domestic, personal services	91.0	14.5	42.5	−0.49
2 Petty manufacturer	26.5	0.0	21.0	−1.00
3 Beggar,	77.5	0.0	53.5	−1.00
4 casual & contractor labour				
5 Petty trader	150.0	3.0	111.0	−0.9
6 Shopowner, wholesaler, hotelowner,	123.5	6.0	51.5	−0.79
21 Contractor				
7 Rickshaw/van puller	39.0	0.0	37.0	−1.00
8 Driver, conductor	19.0	2.0	16.0	−0.78
9+10 Owner cultivator, agricultural labour	8.0	0.0	6.0	−1.00
11 Professionals—doctor, lawyer	15.0	2.5	3.5	0.36
12+18 Office staff—clerks, personal assistant	52.0	29.0	14.0	0.35
13 Chargeman, chargehand, foreman (industry)	79.0	53.0	24.0	0.38
14 Chemist, physicist, scientist, statistician	19.0	16.0	2.0	0.78
15 Engineer	48.0	42.0	4.0	0.83
16 Director, chairman, manager, officer, administrator	144.0	122.0	12.0	0.82
17 Non-technical industrial employee	74.0	40.0	29.0	0.16
19 Unskilled employee in non-domestic units	42.5	5.5	24.0	−0.63
20 Safety, rescue service	24.5	18.0	6.0	0.50
22+23 Draftsman, designer, programmer, semi-skilled and skilled industrial employee	230.0	86.5	121.5	−0.17
24+26+28 Midwife, nurse, trainee, apprentice miscellaneous	16.0	1.0	4.0	−0.60
25 Teacher	56.0	12.0	8.0	0.20

Note: Total migrants consist of those who have responded to the question on current earning occupation in Durgapur and purpose of migration. Details of occupations in each number category is given in the Appendix 4.

* Concentration Index of job-sought and definite-job migrants in different earning occupations in Durgapur.

Let O_{ik} = number of migrants in occupation group i with job certainty status k, where $i = 1....n$ and $k = j$ or w (j = definite-job migrants; w = job-sought migrants).

$$IO_i = (O_{ij} - O_{iw})/(O_{ij} + O_{iw})$$

Certain employment or earning categories like (*a*) beggar, (*b*) domestic employees, (*c*) personal services, (*d*) petty manufacturers, (*e*) petty traders, (*f*) shopowners, (*g*) casual and contractor labour, (*h*) 'rickshaw' and 'van' puller, bus 'conductor', driver of hired or owned vehicles, hiring out of vehicles for commodity transport, (*i*) agricultural production occupations, (*j*) contractor supplying various commodities to the formal units of employment, (*k*) unskilled and (*l*) semi-skilled industrial employment, (*m*) midwife and nurse, (*n*) teachers in schools, (*o*) priest and astrologer show higher propensity to absorb labour force who have migrated with high job uncertainty. The demand for labour force in occupation categories (*a*)–(*h*) above is likely to increase with the resident population of the town and can be expected to be characterised by a high degree of uncertainty in remuneration and tenure. However with a larger population, the probability of procuring a job in this group is likely to be higher than in a smaller place with less people. On the other hand jobs numbered (*j*)–(*n*) can be expected to have greater degree of certainty in terms of tenure and remuneration. Of these (*k*) and (*l*) are mostly office and industrial employments which in turn trigger off demand for services provided by occupations (*a*)–(*h*).

Thus from the above discussion it is evident that migration in search of job is a function of:

1. Three push factors viz. past occupation, education level and caste; these three are in turn interdependent, caste to some extent being the determinant of the education level of the migrant, while that acts as a determinant of the past occupation.
2. Pull factors like type of present occupation which in turn is to some extent dependent upon the size and purchasing power of the resident population in the destination area which in turn is determined by the ability of other occupations to pull people with definite-job having fixed terms and conditions.

Table 4.20 shows the relative importance of employment centres in absorbing migrants with different types of job certainty. The higher the positive value, the greater is the propensity to trigger off definite-job migration. The higher the negative value, the greater is the propensity to absorb migrants with high job uncertainty. However the size of the employment centre is important as it affects the size of the population in the town. Though DSP (Durgapur Steel Plant) ranks lower compared to ABL (ACC-Babcock Limited), in terms of absolute number of employees it is larger and therefore has greater impact on the absorption of migrants with both types of job certainty.

Significance of Job-sought Migration in Planning

In Durgapur a concerted effort has been made since the first phase of development by the individual industries to provide accommodation to the

Table 4.20

Identification of Places of Employment in Durgapur which Absorb Labour Force Migrating with Different Types of Job Certainty

Place of employment	*Total no. of migrants*	*No. of definite-job migrants*	*No. of job-sought migrants*	*Index values**
ACC-Babcock Limited	50	32	12	0.45
Alloy Steel Plant	157	83	64	0.13
Durgapur Projects Limited	189	100	76	0.14
Durgapur Steel Plant	267	134	96	0.16
Educational institute	57	11	8	0.16
Mining and Allied Machinery	33	19	10	0.31
Milk vending	96	0	84	−1.00
Not fixed	146	5	95	−0.90
Nil	1509	19	54	−0.47
Trade, transport	186	25	92	−0.57

Note: Total migrants consist of those who have responded to the question on place of employment in Durgapur and purpose of migration.

* Concentration Index of job-sought and definite-job migrants in different places of employment in Durgapur.

industrial employees with permanent jobs. Since a very small proportion of the job-sought migrants have been absorbed in permanent industrial employment the majority of them could not be eligible for company accommodation. Consequently 40.55 per cent of the earning migrants from rural areas (surveyed in the second phase) seem to be residing as squatters on unregistered landholdings occupied without permission from the landholder. In contrast only 18.33 per cent of the earning migrants from urban areas seem to have settled down as squatters. Table 4.21 shows that amongst the earning male migrants from both rural and urban areas the propensity to squat has been the highest among those who have migrated between 1971 and 1980. As pointed out earlier both proportion of rural migrants and job-sought migration reached its peak around 1975–76. These figures establish the hypothesis that rural migrants migrating with the expectation of finding a job tend to settle down in unplanned squatter colonies.

As pointed out in the last chapter the per capita cost of providing municipal services rises after a town has reached a population of 2,50,000–3,00,000. By 1975 the population of Durgapur has crossed the 2,50,000 threshold. Table 4.22 shows that the per capita expenditure (excluding general administration) by the Durgapur Notified Area Authority declined between 1964–65 and 1970–71. However by 1980–81 it has risen sharply resulting in a deficit budget of Rs. 10.72 per capita. This reversal to deficit financing on expenses excluding general administration seems to have

Table 4.21

Propensity to Squat amongst Earning Migrants of Both Sexes from Rural and Urban Areas

Migrants stratified on the basis of sex and year of arrival in Durgapur	*Total no. of migrants in the second phase sample*	*% migrants who are squatters to total in each stratum*
Male migrants from urban areas		
Arrived in Durgapur before 1961	55	9.09
Arrived in Durgapur 1961–1970	81	19.75
Arrived in Durgapur 1971–1980	53	26.41
Arrived in Durgapur after 1980	21	4.76
Male migrants from rural areas		
Arrived in Durgapur before 1961	44	38.64
Arrived in Durgapur 1961–1970	68	32.35
Arrived in Durgapur 1971–1980	73	50.68
Arrived in Durgapur after 1980	25	44.00
Female migrants from urban areas		
Arrived in Durgapur before 1961	3	0.00*
Arrived in Durgapur 1961–1970	21	14.29
Arrived in Durgapur 1971–1980	10	0.00
Arrived in Durgapur after 1980	2	0.00*
Female migrants from rural areas		
Arrived in Durgapur before 1961	1	100.00*
Arrived in Durgapur 1961–1970	13	69.23
Arrived in Durgapur 1971–1980	10	60.00
Arrived in Durgapur after 1980	5	20.00*

* Subsample is too small for proper representation; however if all the female earning migrants from urban areas are compared with those from rural areas, then the total observations in each group is large enough to show that those migrating from rural areas have a higher propensity to settle as squatters.

taken place in the period corresponding with high job-sought migration. By 1981 the population of Durgapur has exceeded the 3,00,000 threshold. This emphasises the necessity to estimate the level of influx of job-sought migrants and allocate income, expenditures and space for them as well.

The Zonal Development Plan for Benachity and Bhiringi area in Durgapur drawn up by the Asansol-Durgapur Development Authority in 1983 has recognised, for the first time, the necessity to reserve certain areas for the residences of the service sector people in order to prevent scattered growth of slums (Asansol-Durgapur Development Authority 1983: 3–16). Not only is it a belated decision, as growth of squatter colonies have preceded

Table 4.22

Per Capita Income and Expenditure of Durgapur Notified Area Authority

Year	*Per capita income of Durgapur Notified Area Authority (DNAA) in Rs.*	*Per capita expenditure of DNAA (excluding general administration) in Rs.*	*Difference between per capita income and expenditure in Rs.*	*Total population of Durgapur Notified Area*
1964–65	9.14	7.73	1.41	89080*
1970–71	5.99	5.01	0.98	206638
1980–81	31.52	42.24	−10.72	311798

Note: Income and expenditure of DNAA for 1964–65 and 1970–71 have been taken from Sivaramakrishnan, 1976–77, appendix 7.2.3; and the figures for 1980–81 has been obtained from Durgapur Notified Area Authority, 1983–84, p. XIII and p. 2.

* Total population of the 40 villages which occupied the area covered by Durgapur Notified Area in 1971 and 1981 obtained from the census.

planning, but also there does not seem to be any estimates on which the allocation of residential space may be based. Therefore the trendline showing the proportion of job-sought migrants may be used as a guideline for such estimates for allocation of space, perhaps provision of low cost housing and other civic amenities, from the inception, in a new town of similar character.

Geographical Extent of Migration Linkage of Durgapur

State Level Migration

Seventy per cent of the migrants and 67 per cent of the earning migrants represent intra-state migration. In contrast amongst the earning migrants 19 per cent have migrated from Bihar, while Uttar Pradesh and Orissa account for 4 per cent and 2 per cent of the labour force respectively; these three states together accounting for only 24 per cent of the earning labour force in Durgapur (Table 4.23). Hence the impact of the town and the remittance links to be discussed in the next chapter can be expected to be mostly confined within the state of West Bengal with minor leakages to Bihar, Uttar Pradesh and Orissa.

In terms of job certainty the propensity to migrate with high job uncertainty is highest in Bihar followed by Uttar Pradesh, Orissa and West Bengal (Table 4.24). The state of Bihar is characterised by the highest level of rural and average poverty followed by Uttar Pradesh, Orissa and

Table 4.23

State Level Migration Hinterland of Durgapur

State	*No. of earning migrants*	*% earning migrants from different states to total earning migrants*
Andhra Pradesh	6	0.42
Assam	15	1.06
Bihar	268	18.90
Gujarat	5	0.35
Haryana	1	0.07
Karnataka	2	0.14
Kerala	4	0.28
Maharashtra	5	0.35
Madhya Pradesh	7	0.49
Orissa	28	1.97
Punjab	9	0.63
Rajasthan	12	0.85
Tamil Nadu	1	0.07
Tripura	3	0.21
Uttar Pradesh	50	3.53
West Bengal	948	66.85
Union Territory	5	0.35
Sikkim	1	0.07
	International migrants	
Bangladesh	43	3.03
Nepal	3	0.21
United Kingdom	1	0.07
Total	**1418**	**100.00**

Table 4.24

Identification of States Contributing Labour Force with Different Types of Job Certainty

States	*Total No. of migrants*	*No. of definite-job migrants*	*No. of job-sought migrants*	*Index values**
Andhra Pradesh	9	5	0	1.00
Assam	28	4	5	−0.11
Bihar	500	74	158	−0.36
Maharashtra	11	3	2	0.2
Madhya Pradesh	10	6	1	0.71
Orissa	51	10	16	−0.23
Punjab	15	1	6	−0.71
Rajasthan	29	2	2	0.00
Uttar Pradesh	89	13	27	−0.35
West Bengal	2045	377	441	−0.08

Table 4.24 (Continued)

Note: Total migrants consist of those who have responded to the question on state of last residence and purpose of migration. States represented by less than nine migrants in the first phase sample have been excluded.

* Concentration Index of job-sought and definite-job migrants from different states.

West Bengal. The inception of a new town with low level of indigenous labour supply can be expected to attract labour force from poverty stricken areas as the probability of finding a job can be expected to be higher during the initial stages of town growth compared to old towns with a large indigenous resident population as discussed in Chapter 3. It has been pointed out that Bihar and Uttar Pradesh are characterised by low migration towns where the probability of finding a job on the part of a migrant can be expected to be lower. Hence these states have tended to contribute job-sought migrants to the new town outside the respective states.

On an average 52 per cent of the migrants and 54 per cent of the earning migrants in Durgapur have migrated from urban areas (Table 4.25). However, Bihar is one of the two states which shows a greater bias towards the rural sector link than the urban sector; about 58 per cent of the earning migrants have come from rural areas (Table 4.26). Uttar Pradesh can be expected to have more urban bias in its links with Durgapur compared to Bihar, but more rural bias compared to West Bengal. Consequently it ranks after Bihar in migration with job uncertainty, but higher compared to West Bengal. Orissa has more urban bias in terms of the last residence of the earning migrants than Uttar Pradesh. Consequently it ranks lower to Uttar Pradesh in uncertain job migration. However it has less urban bias and definite-job migration than West Bengal.

Table 4.25

Rural-Urban Origin of Earning Migrants in Durgapur

Currently earning migrants in Durgapur	*Place of last residence*		*Total earning migrants in Durgapur*	*% urban to total earning migrants*	*% rural to total earning migrants*
	Urban	*Rural*			
Female	66	68	134	49.25	50.75
Male	673	564	1237	54.40	45.59

Since the sample has shown that the highest proportion of rural migrants who had an income in the place of last residence is accounted for by owner-cultivators or landowners followed by landless agricultural labourers a comparison has been made of these two variables between the four states shown in Table 4.27. Owner-cultivators account for 77 per cent of the

Table 4.26

Rural-Urban Origin of Earning Migrants to Durgapur from Different States

State	*Place of last residence*		*Total*	*% rural to total of each state*
	Urban	*Rural*		
Andhra Pradesh	5	1	6	16.66
Assam	11	4	15	26.67
Bihar	109	149	258	57.75
Orissa	15	13	28	46.42
Punjab	2	7	9	77.78
Rajasthan	7	4	11	36.36
Uttar Pradesh	26	24	50	48.00
West Bengal	518	418	936	44.66
Others	16	4	20	80.00

Note: All observations having less than nine total have been excluded. International migration has also been excluded from this table.

Table 4.27

Relative Importance of Owner Cultivators amongst Migrants from Different States/Districts

States	*Owner cultivator*	*Agricultural labourer*	*Total*	*% owner cultivator to total in each state*
Bihar	35.5	30.5	66	53.78
West Bengal	99.0	30.0	129	76.74
Orissa	6.0	1.0	7	85.71
Uttar Pradesh	10.0	2.0	12	83.33
Districts				
West Bengal				
Barddhaman	14.0	5.0	19	73.68
Bankura	56.5	22.5	79	71.50
Bihar				
Darbhanga	5.0	17.0	22	22.72

All observations having a total of less than nine have been excluded except Orissa.

cultivating class who have migrated to Durgapur from different parts of West Bengal compared to 54 per cent of the cultivating class who have migrated from Bihar. The higher level of migration of landless labourers from Bihar again reflects the push factor operating amongst the poverty stricken areas so that people are more prepared to take the risk of migrating with employment uncertainty to a newly developing town with higher expected probability to earn an income. The subsample sizes of the other two states are too small though both emphasise the mobility of the land-owning class.

District Level Migration

West Bengal: Table 4.28 highlights the districts in West Bengal which have contributed migrants to Durgapur in order of proportion of migrants from different parts of West Bengal. The district in which the town is located viz. Barddhaman[7] accounts for the highest proportion followed by the neighbouring district of Bankura and Calcutta Metropolitan District. In terms of the earning migrants, Calcutta Metropolitan District has contributed the maximum proportion of the labour force followed by Barddhaman and Bankura (Table 4.29 and Figure 4.12a). Smaller proportions have been contributed by the other districts as shown in Figure 4.12a. Amongst these districts Barddhaman has been noted for remarkable agricultural development in the past few decades, though the incidence of landless labour has increased.

Table 4.29 shows that the rural sector of Bankura, Birbhum and Purulia can be expected to have stronger links with Durgapur than their urban sectors. In the five districts viz. Bankura, Purulia, Midnapur, Nadia and Howrah the propensity to migrate to Durgapur with employment uncertainty is higher than that of definite-job migration as revealed in Table 4.30 and Figure 4.12b. In contrast the urban sector is likely to have stronger link with Durgapur compared to the rural sector in Calcutta Metropolitan District, 24 Parganas, Nadia, Howrah, Barddhaman and Hugli. Amongst these districts the propensity to migrate with job uncertainty is high only in Nadia and Howrah (Table 4.30). The districts which contribute more than 50 per cent of their migrating labour force from rural areas are associated with low levels of urbanisation (below 10 per cent of the population) as revealed by the table.

In absolute terms the rural sector contribution to the labour force mainly comes from Bankura followed by Barddhaman, Purulia, 24 Parganas, Midnapur, Nadia, Howrah and Hugli. From the above discussion it follows that in most of the districts like Midnapur, Barddhaman, Hugli, Howrah, Nadia and 24 Parganas the urban sector can be expected to

[7] The English spellings of the Indian names of the districts have been changed several times leading to a lot of confusion in the academic and real world. All institutes and books do not adopt the new spellings instantaneously so that at a particular point of time both the versions may be used in the real world. At the time of the survey the railway stations have implemented the new spelling 'Barddhaman' instead of 'Burdwan' and 'Hugli' instead of 'Hooghly' while up to October 1989 the spelling of 'Howrah' has remained the same, though it was supposed to be changed to 'Haora'. Hence this book uses the following spellings: Barddhaman (old spelling Burdwan), Hugli (old spelling Hooghly), Midnapur (old spelling Midnapore, to be further changed to Medinipur) and Howrah (to be changed to Haora). It is an inevitable problem of trying to have a standardised version of spellings in a different language.

Table 4.28

District Level Migration from West Bengal to Durgapur

Districts of West Bengal	*No. of migrants in first phase sample*	*% distribution of migrants by district*
Barddhaman	494	24.44
Bankura	459	22.71
Calcutta Metropolitan District	408	20.19
24 Parganas	129	6.38
Birbhum	112	5.54
Nadia	104	5.14
Midnapur	79	3.91
Purulia	63	3.12
Howrah	53	2.62
Hugli	53	2.62
Murshidabad	42	2.08
Jalpaiguri	13	0.64
Malda	6	0.30
Darjeeling	3	0.15
Coochbehar	3	0.15
Total	**2021**	**100.00**

Table 4.29

Rural-Urban Origin of Earning Migrants to Durgapur from Different Districts of West Bengal

Districts	*Place of last residence*		*Total no of migrants*	*% rural to total of each district*	*% urban to total population (1981)**
	Urban	*Rural*			
Bankura	25	159	184	86.41	7.63
Barddhaman	102	83	185	44.86	29.65
Birbhum	17	34	51	66.67	8.33
Calcutta M.D.	207	1	208	0.48	–
24 Parganas	46	20	66	30.30	38.90
Nadia	35	16	51	31.37	21.44
Midnapur	17	19	36	52.78	8.54
Purulia	7	21	28	75.00	9.00
Howrah	16	10	26	38.46	45.22
Hugli	11	9	20	45.00	45.00

Source: * Biplab Dasgupta, 1987, p. 282 except Calcutta Metropolitan District which is an urban settlement.

develop remittance links as well as the rural sector. However a substantially strong link with the urban sector is represented by Calcutta Metropolitan District to which the new town was expected to be a counter magnet.

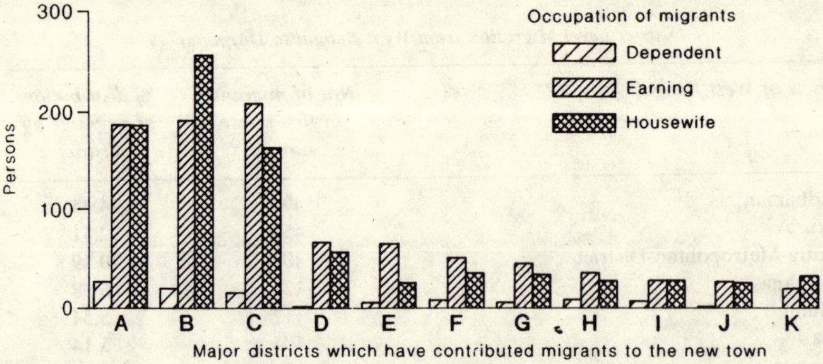

Occupation of Migrants in Durgapur

Fig. No. 4.12a

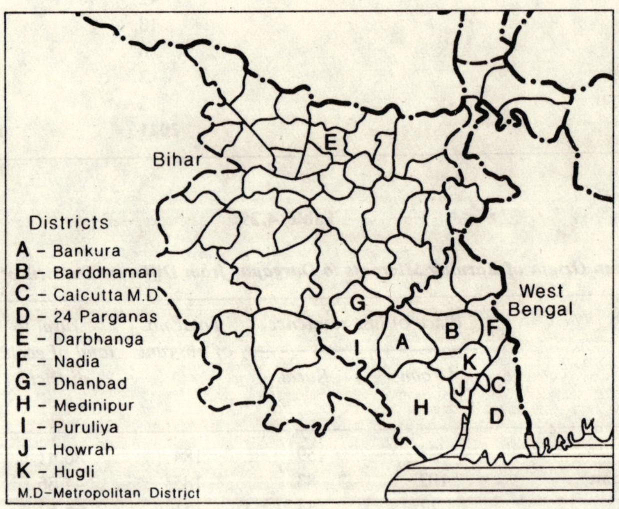

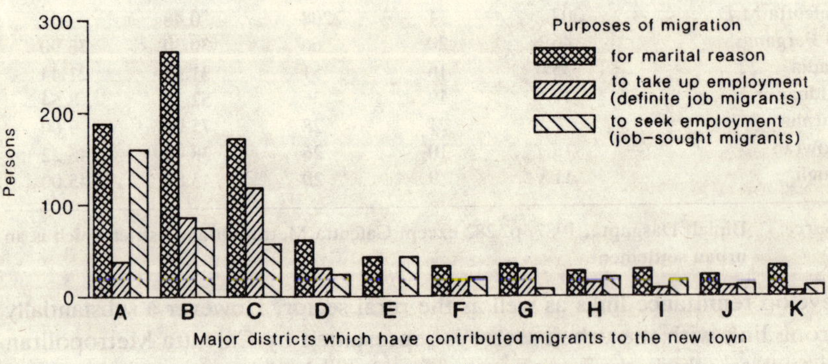

Purposes of Migration to Durgapur

Fig. No. 4.12b

Table 4.30

Identification of Districts of West Bengal Contributing Labour Force with Different Types of Job Certainty

Districts	*Total No. of migrants*	*No. of definite-job migrants*	*No. of job-sought migrants*	*Index values**
Barddhaman	494	86	75	0.07
Bankura	459	38	162	−0.62
Calcutta M.D.	406	119	57	0.35
24 Parganas	129	31	24	0.13
Birbhum	111	23	22	0.02
Nadia	103	18	21	−0.08
Midnapur	79	15	21	−0.17
Purulia	63	9	18	−0.33
Howrah	53	12	13	−0.04
Hugli	52	5	12	0.91
Murshidabad	42	9	7	0.12
Jalpaiguri	13	5	2	0.43

Note: Total migrants consist of those who have responded to the question on district of last residence and purpose of migration. Calcutta M.D. is abbreviation for Calcutta Metropolitan District. Districts having less than nine migrants have been excluded.

* Concentration Index of job-sought and definite-job migrants from different districts.

Bankura and Purulia seem to be the only districts in which the link with the urban sector appears to be weak. The variations in sectoral links between the districts might affect relative development of the districts.

Though the subsamples for the cultivating class for the district level is too small, most of the districts in West Bengal represented in the sample show migration of the landowning class. The only two districts with a fairly larger sample size are Barddhaman and Bankura. Barddhaman shows a higher percentage of landowning migrants than Bankura (Table 4.27).

Bihar: In terms of contribution to the labour force of Durgapur in the sample Bihar ranks second. At the district level Darbhanga ranks highest both in its contribution to the total migrants as well as to the labour force currently employed (Tables 4.31, 4.32 and Figure 4.12a) followed by Dhanbad and Singbhum.

Table 4.32 shows the districts which have a rural bias in their link with Durgapur in terms of earning migrants. 98 per cent of the earning migrants from Darbhanga in Durgapur have migrated from rural areas followed by Muzaffarpur, Monghyr, Madhubani and Dumka. The subsamples of the last four districts are very small to be representatively conclusive. All the five above-mentioned districts have contributed to a higher proportion of migrants with high employment uncertainty compared to the proportion of

Table 4.31

District Level Migration from Bihar/Uttar Pradesh/Orissa to Durgapur

Districts	*No. of migrants in first phase sample*	*% distribution of migrants by district*
Bihar		
Darbhanga	103	28.06
Dhanbad	87	23.70
Singbhum	43	11.72
Ranchi	26	7.08
Dumka	21	5.72
Madhubani	20	5.45
Hazaribagh	16	4.36
Monghyr	14	3.81
Muzaffarpur	14	3.81
Patna	12	3.27
Samastipur	11	3.00
Total	**367**	**100.00**
Uttar Pradesh		
Azamgarh	11	
Ballia	9	
Orissa		
Cuttack	18	
Ganjam	11	

migrants who have migrated with definite-job appointment. It has been pointed out earlier that the rural sector contributes more migrants with job uncertainty. Darbhanga shows a higher proportion of migration of agricultural labourers (78 per cent of the cultivating class who have migrated). In the other districts the subsamples are too small to be conclusive.

In contrast the districts of Singbhum, Ranchi, Dhanbad and Samastipur have contributed more migrants from urban areas than rural areas into the labour force of Durgapur (Table 4.32). Table 4.33 shows that with the exception of Samastipur the first three districts have contributed a higher proportion of migrants with definite-job appointment to the labour force. Only Samastipur shows higher proportion of urban migrants and uncertain job migration.

Uttar Pradesh: Bihar is followed by Uttar Pradesh in its contribution to

Table 4.32

Rural-Urban Origin of Earning Migrants to Durgapur from Different Districts of Bihar/Uttar Pradesh/Orissa

Districts	*Place of last residence*		*Total*	*% rural to total of each district*
	Urban	*Rural*		
Bihar				
Darbhanga	1	70	71	98.59
Dhanbad	41	5	46	10.87
Singbhum	15	0	15	100.00
Ranchi	13	0	13	100.00
Dumka	3	8	11	72.73
Madhubani	2	6	8	75.00
Hazaribagh	3	4	7	57.14
Monghyr	1	5	6	83.33
Muzaffarpur	1	7	8	87.50
Patna	5	1	6	16.67
Samastipur	6	3	9	33.33
Uttar Pradesh				
Azamgarh	1	7	8	87.00
Ballia	3	3	6	50.00
Orissa				
Cuttack	4	6	10	60.00
Ganjam	2	3	5	60.00

the labour force in Durgapur. At the district level Azamgarh and Ballia exhibit slightly higher frequencies of migrants than the other districts. Azamgarh appears to have a slight rural bias though the subsample of all the employment variables at two or three dimensional district levels are too small to be conclusive.

Orissa: Orissa ranks next to Uttar Pradesh in terms of earning migrants. At the district level Cuttack and Ganjam have contributed higher proportion of migrants than the other districts in the sample. Both have contributed 60 per cent of migrants to Durgapur from rural areas and consequently migration with job uncertainty is greater than definite-job migration in both the districts. Though all the migrants from the cultivating class in rural area of last residence appear to be landowners in both the districts the subsample is again very small.

Table 4.33

Identification of Districts of Bihar Contributing Labour Force with Different Types of Job Certainty

Districts	*Total no. of migrants*	*No. of definite-job migrants*	*No. of job-sought migrants*	*Index values**
Darbhanga	103	0	43	−1.00
Dhanbad	89	30	8	0.58
Singbhum	43	11	8	0.16
Ranchi	26	11	1	0.83
Dumka	31	0	9	−1.00
Madhubani	20	0	9	−1.00
Monghyr	14	1	5	−0.67
Muzaffarpur	14	0	9	−1.00
Patna	12	3	3	0.00
Samastipur	11	1	5	−0.67

Note: Total migrants consist of those who have responded to the question on district of last residence and purpose of migration. Districts having less than nine migrants have been excluded.

* Concentration Index of job-sought and definite-job migrants from different districts.

Concluding Remarks

The above discussion provides empirical evidence which tends to support the Harris–Todaro model and introduces the concept of how the age of a town and growth of its indigenous population (or second generation migrants) may affect a potential migrants expccted probability of finding a job. Thus a new town like Durgapur can be expected to experience distinct phases of labour force migration with different proportions of different types of employment certainties which in turn will guide the growth of squatter colonies in the town. Hence this High Migration Town of 1971 has possibly become a Low Migration Town in the late 1980s, thus exhausting its potentiality to play an active role in the labour transfer mechanism and thereby also losing its potentiality to act as a counter magnet to Calcutta by diverting migration away from the old metropolis.

This however does not mean a decline in the migrant population in the town in absolute terms, but a decline in the rate of increase of the migrant population. Its linkage with the urban sector is likely to become stronger relative to the rural one. It has been shown that the phase of high job-sought migration from rural areas seems to be associated with increasing cost of providing civic amenities by the municipality after 20 years of its inception. Hence physical planning of a town should take into account the expected components of (*a*) labour force migration (*b*) proportion of in-migration of dependents in different phases of town growth. However it must be noted that the time series curves predicting the values of these variables are likely to be different in different types of towns. Hence the effect of injecting new investment in a town, on the shape of the curves can be expected to vary according to the type of the town. This study provides the evidence from one type of town and emphasises the necessity for future research in this field for planning purposes.

The survey data has highlighted the in-migration or absorption of a higher proportion of landowners compared to landless labourers and sharecroppers. On the basis of the Census data, it has already been pointed out that:

> in the non-urban area surrounding Durgapur . . . the most significant trend noticeable in the last three decades has been the changing composition of the primary sector employment. While the share of the primary sector in the total workforce has been declining, agricultural labourers have doubled their share in the last three decades. In contrast cultivators have been a declining proportion of the workforce (Jagannathan 1987: 555).

According to the author this changing composition of the primary sector employment has been the result of urbanisation in Durgapur due to the following processes:

1. Cultivators owning land and having a minimum education level secured jobs in the large, newly-created industrial sector in the town. As agricultural land was unproductive many of them moved residence to Durgapur.
2. For agricultural labourers, the lack of educational credentials prevented them from competing for most organised sector jobs.
3. Job opportunities in the growing tertiary sector (such as the construction industry, trade and transport sector) were difficult to gain access because (*a*) large construction contractors brought in their own labour from the other parts of West Bengal and the neighbouring states and (*b*) marginal trading establishments primarily employed entrepreneurs who had well-established links with wholesale traders.
4. The large-scale acquisition of land that has taken place in the first phase of development has affected the agricultural labourers adversely because compensation was paid only to landowners, while the agricultural labourers and sharecroppers were displaced without compensation to find alternative employment in the adjoining villages.

The author further adds: 'The failure of strong linkages between Durgapur and its immediate hinterland is attributable to both natural factors and planning deficiencies' (Jagannathan 1987: 557). He has identified 32 *mouzas*[8] surrounding Durgapur Notified Area as the 'hinterland' which

[8] Smallest administrative unit equivalent to the areal extent of a village.

include villages within five to ten kms of the town which have fairly good road communications. His study therefore has two implications:

1. The failure of the rural areas surrounding Durgapur to be incorporated in the zone of commutation to Durgapur due to lack of infrastructure and the recruitment policy for the labour force in Durgapur.
2. The possibility of greater significance of migration as a linkage.

However it must be noted that the study, (as revealed by the article), is not based on commuting data. He writes:

> The population of an average village has increased from 500 in 1951 to 800 in 1971 . . . . Two interesting inferences that emerge from the data are: (*a*) The percentage of cultivators in the workforce of these villages in 1981 was 16%, or half the rate of rest of the hinterland. As data on secondary sector is not available, one is unable to draw any conclusion as to whether industrial workers in search of land for urban housing have begun moving to these villages. Agricultural labourers however, constitute 32% of the workforce (the same as in the other surrounding villages). (*b*) The area of land not available for cultivation has been less than one half of the village area in all except one village (Jagannathan 1987: 557).

It is obvious that primary activity has declined in the area, indicating sectoral transfer of labour force. The alternative employment sectors which have grown may represent a direct or indirect link with Durgapur. The above quoted statement does acknowledge the possibility that industrial workers might have been moving to the villages, which in reality may represent the development of a commuter linkage. Such a linkage may represent a mechanism, (as pointed out in the first chapter), by which income or finance is being unobtrusively transferred from Durgapur to the *mouzas* taken into consideration. The impact of such a transfer of purchasing power on production and employment, depends upon the consumption patterns of the households, the mechanism of procuring the required goods and the spatial distribution of the places from which they can be procured. Moreover, decline of proportion of cultivators may increase the demand for agricultural labourers who may migrate from other rural areas, perhaps representing increase of employment.

Indicators like lack of electricity or assured water supply, lack of educational facilities beyond primary level, lack of irrigation and incidence of agricultural labourers (in the face of declining proportion of workforce in primary activity), persistence of subsistence agriculture in an area with poor soil conditions do not necessarily indicate the linkages or their strength. No doubt the administrative and planning bodies should look into the physical infrastructure and rural development in these areas, but the development of Durgapur can hardly be blamed entirely for it.

While focusing on the migration linkages it is evident that the maximum impact of the town should be felt within the districts of Calcutta, Barddhaman and Bankura as they have contributed the maximum number of migrants and earning migrants. While Bankura, Birbhum and Purulia have predominantly rural linkage with this new town, Midnapur, Barddhaman, Hugli, Howrah, Nadia and 24 Parganas seem to have contributed labour force from both rural and urban areas; on the other hand Calcutta Metropolitan District represents a strong urban link.

Amongst these districts Calcutta, Barddhaman, Howrah, 24 Parganas and Hugli are highly urbanised and have also experienced higher levels of agricultural progress as revealed by the yield per unit of land in case of rice as well as high growth rate in agricultural production. Bankura, Birbhum and Midnapur, though referred to as a 'backward' district show good yield figures. Midnapur holds good position in terms of agricultural growth (Dasgupta, 14 February 1987a: 282). Amongst the districts of Bihar, rural migration links have developed mainly with Darbhanga, while urban links are stronger with Dhanbad and Singbhum in Bihar, the last two being more urbanised than the first due to development of mining and industry.

Now the interesting questions that arise at this point and are discussed in the next chapter are: Which of these areas gain financially from remittances sent back by the migrant labour force in Durgapur? What type of area is likely to gain from such a link from the new town—rural or urban? Since 54.5 per cent of the male earning migrants have migrated from urban areas, does the town have a similar urban bias in its remittance linkage as well? What are the likely uses of the remittances sent back?

5

Monetary Remittances from Durgapur

Trickle-down Effects

In the context of regional development post-Independence planning in India has been criticised severely for failing to achieve the desired 'spread effect' of growth from the newly-built industrial towns. As pointed out in the previous chapter, public sector investment was also diverted to industrial development of the backward states of Bihar, Madhya Pradesh and Orissa.'However the impact of such large public sector investment on the regional economies of Bihar, Madhya Pradesh and Orissa has not been significant. The anticipated spread effects have not materialised and the economies of these states continue to be backwards as usual' (Chand and Puri 1983: 174). In the case of Durgapur in West Bengal Sivaramakrishnan writes:

> Despite the high investment, technology and skills which have gone into the creation of Durgapur as a major complex of heavy industries, its impact on the region has been limited . . . there was the usual expectation that the benefits of the investment would somehow trickle down to the surrounding region (Sivaramakrishnan 1982: 157).

According to him the 'trickle down' process was slightly manifested, but only in the following ways:

1. Ranigunge traditionally the wholesale commercial centre for the region expanded its business to serve Durgapur 20 km away.
2. The administrative functions were added on to Asansol the sub-district headquarters 35 km away.
3. Immediately west of Durgapur, one of Asia's largest railway marshalling yards was developed at Ondal.
4. To the east a group of three adjoining villages, Panagarh, Debipur and Kanksa attracted several service industries, especially auto repairs. The author adds, 'However to the south across the Damodar

River, the Bankura district has maintained its predominantly rural character.'

From the above points, it is clear that the author highlights the effects of the inception of a town, but does not analyse the mechanisms by which the benefits are expected or can in reality trickle down to areas outside the town. He ignores the alternative ways in which spread effects may still be operating in the agricultural sector of settlements outside Durgapur. However the manifestations of spread effects given above does imply an increase in demand for commodities and services from the adjoining settlements which should result in re-channelling finance from Durgapur to the supplying areas thereby triggering off an employment and income multiplier.

As pointed out in Chapter 1 these empirical observations are based on the theoretical conception that 'trade linkages' are the only channels through which finance is redistributed to cause a 'spread effect'. This chapter investigates the development of remittance linkage between Durgapur and its migration-hinterland as an alternative mechanism.

Remittances through Money Orders

It is interesting to note that the transfer of money through money orders from Durgapur amounted to Rs. 2.9 million per month in 1988 which represents gross outremittance[1] from Durgapur and it was distributed through 13,540 money orders. Figure 5.1 shows that the money value of gross remittance in 1988 is approximately equal to what it was in 1974 (2.8 million), thus indicating a fall of gross remittance in real terms. An analysis of money order records of Pauri Garhwal district in Uttar Pradesh estimated an inflow of Rs. 3.4 million per month (from outside the district) in 1972–73 (Dobhal 1981). The number of money orders issued was 37,000 roughly indicating the number of recipient families. The author writes: 'The district economy depends to a large extent on outside incomes chiefly by way of money order remittances from its migrant population working outside the region' (Dobhal 1981: 80).

Hence it seems that Durgapur alone channels via money orders to other regions, an amount which is equivalent to 85 per cent of the amount received (by the same method) and required for the sustenance of a single district, as represented by Pauri Garhwal. It must be pointed out that only 24 per cent of the remitters from Durgapur send by money orders compared to 71.97 per cent (Dobhal 1981: 96) of the remitters to Pauri Garhwal district. Hence the total money channelled by Durgapur (estimated to be Rs. 253 million in 1988–89) is likely to be approximately two times the

[1] Gross remittance as defined in Chapter 2.

Monetary Remittances From Durgapur Via Money Orders

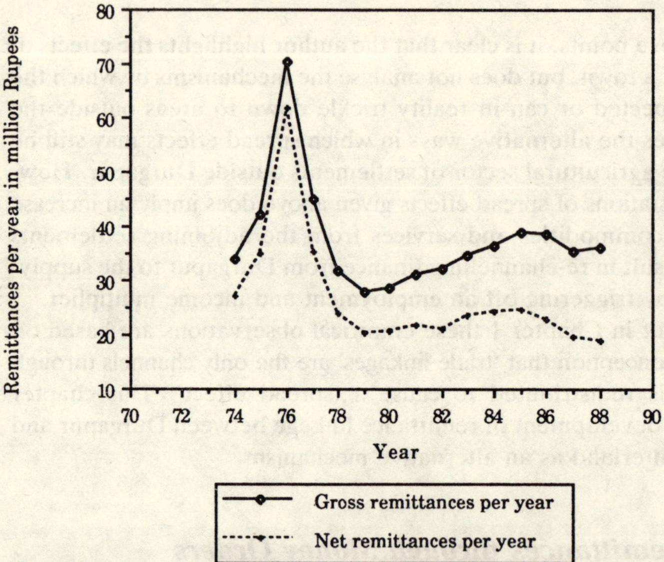

Source: Based on unpublished yearly data from Main Post Office of Durgapur

Fig. No. 5.01

estimated amount of receipts in Pauri Garhwal district in 1988–89.[2] This indicates the significance of the role of the new town to areas outside its municipal boundary as a source of income.

The total net remittance[3] from Durgapur through money orders amounted to Rs. 1.5 million per month in 1988. Figure 5.1 showing the temporal variation of yearly money transfer through money orders highlights the following points:

1. Both gross and net remittance seem to have been maximum in the year 1976 after which there has been a sharp decline till 1979. This period was followed by a slight increase till 1985 followed by a minor trend towards a decline. While 1976 experienced a transfer of Rs. 70 million, since 1979 gross remittance has varied between Rs. 30–40 million per year, thereby maintaining a relatively constant level. Net

[2] The estimated values for Pauri Garhwal district is based on the figures given for 1972-73 (Dobhal 1981: 80, 96) and the assumptions are: (*a*) 8.95 per cent growth rate of money order receipts between 1965–66 and 1969–70 have continued till 1988, (*b*) per migrant value of remittance to Pauri Garhwal by those who do not send by money orders is same as those who send by money orders (*c*) the proportion of migrants sending via money orders has not changed between 1972–73 and 1988.

[3] Net remittances as defined in Chapter 2.

remittance follows an identical pattern of a high value of Rs. 60 million in 1976 and Rs. 17–25 million between 1977 and 1988. Since the absolute number of resident migrants is unlikely to decrease, as pointed out in the last chapter, the gross remittance is also unlikely to decline. It is more likely to maintain a constant level in absolute amount.

2. The difference between gross and net remittance values represents the amount of monetary inflow to Durgapur from other areas. It is interesting to note that the minimum inflow was in the year 1976 and since then it has increased steadily till 1988. Such an increase can be explained by the fact that in 30 years time, since inception, people have out-migrated and have started remitting to Durgapur. However the inflow has at no point exceeded the outflow thereby emphasising the net gain of areas outside Durgapur in monetary terms. At the same time it must be noted that net remittance seems to be experiencing a declining trend after 1985, perhaps signifying a gradual decline in the role of the new town in rechannelling finance.

Thus the money order transfers indicate a possible decline of gross remittances in real terms and a decline in the net remittances in money value as well as in real terms. Though money order records give an idea about the significance of the town in channelling finance in absolute terms, the scope of an analysis through money orders is limited due to the following reasons:

1. Prevalence of alternative means of transfer by bank or by hand through friends, relatives or personal visits.
2. Data of money order issue (which indicates outflow from the area under the jurisdiction of the issuing office) are recorded in 'M.O. journals' and 'M.O. receipt books'. It can give the following variables: (*a*) the name of the payee (*b*) the name of the destination offices, indistinctly written by hand with incorrect or shortened spellings with no indication of its location either in terms of the postal circle, state or district(*c*) the amount sent in rupees and paisa.

   Money order vouchers of payment at the delivery office (which indicates inflow to the area under the jurisdiction of the particular delivery office) can give the following variables only: (*a*) name of the issuing post office available from the stamp which is often indistinct, (*b*) amount received in rupees and paisa, (*c*) name and address of the payee; name and address of the sender is unavailable.
3. Money orders mostly represent personal income transfers, the maximum amount of money that can be sent via money order in India is Rs. 1000.00. However such transfers from Durgapur seems to include payment of wage to school teachers by the district administrative

authorities in Barddhaman or payments of insurance premium. Hence it is not necessarily personal income transferred by a migrant.

A survey of postal records can give no detailed spatial, familial or socio-economic information about the sender or the receiver. Therefore, though money order records were surveyed, only a small portion of it has been used in this book. For an understanding of the strength and characteristics of the remittance linkage the running of a two-phased questionnaire survey in Durgapur was necessary. The sample survey shows that only a very small proportion of the migrants use money orders as a means of transfer. Most of the transfer seems to be taking place by hand through friends, relatives or personal visits. Moreover the remitters via money orders do not necessarily consist of migrants. Hence this study will concentrate on the estimates of remittances made on the basis of the second phase sample survey in Durgapur as described in this chapter.

Primary Data on Remittances Collected in the Second Phase Sample Survey

The second phase questionnaire survey was conducted from January to April 1989. It represented a continuation of the survey done in 1987 (described in the last chapter) which provided a sample frame of migrants who were reinterviewed for information on family links, remittances and employment characteristics.

Sample Size

The second phase survey involved interviewing 552 migrants which represented 18 per cent of the migrant population recorded in the first phase survey. This survey included the interview of 34 per cent of the earning migrants and only 4 per cent of the non-earning migrants identified in the first phase. The purpose of the second phase survey was to measure qualitatively and quantitatively the characteristics of the remittance linkage which has evolved since the inception of the town.

Sample Design

For the second phase a stratified random sampling was done from the 2943 migrants identified in the first phase. The migrants identified in the first phase were regrouped as shown in Figure 5.2. Within each category or stratum the names of the migrants were numbered and then selected for resurvey in the second phase on the basis of the random number table. Due to the constraints of time and money a 100

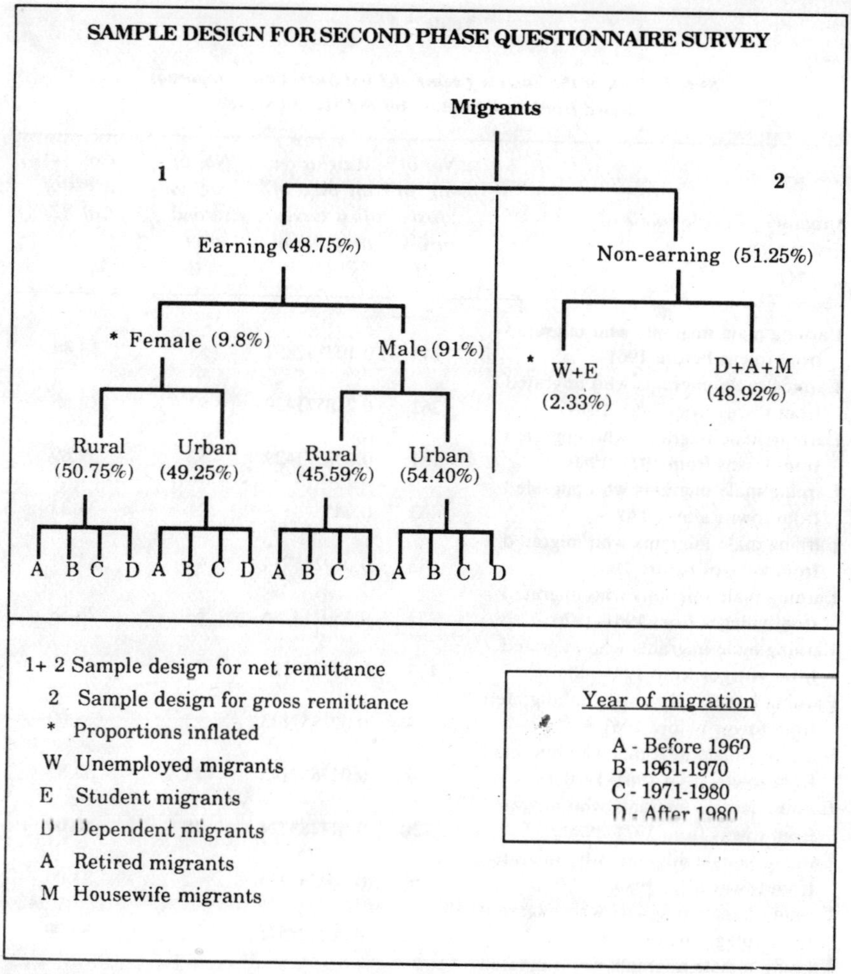

Fig. No. 5.02

per cent sample was not possible during the second phase. In order to get fairly representative subsamples of each group for intra- and inter-group analyses, the proportion of respondents in each group was not made constant. The number of migrants interviewed in some of the smaller groups was inflated thus giving higher proportion as shown in Table 5.1. However in some of the categories as shown in the table, the number of migrants interviewed is very small giving unrepresentative subsamples. The main reason for such under-representation of certain categories is the non-availability of more migrants in that group for the second phase as they have left the place of residence recorded in the first survey and could not be traced. However the incorporation of

Table 5.1

Stratification of the Sample Frame of First Survey and Proportion Selected from each Stratum for the Second Survey

Stratum of sample frame of first survey *(1)*	*No. of mig. in first survey* *(2)*	*Weights on the basis of first survey proportions* *(3)*	*No. of mig. in second survey* *(4)*	*Col. (4) as % of Col. (2)*
Earning male migrants who migrated from towns before 1961	143	0.102142857	55	38.46
Earning male migrants who migrated from towns from 1961–1970	362	0.258571429	82	22.65
Earning male migrants who migrated from towns from 1971–1980	131	0.093571429	52	39.69
Earning male migrants who migrated from towns after 1980	63	0.045	21	33.33
Earning male migrants who migrated from villages before 1961	83	0.059285714	44	53.01
Earning male migrants who migrated from villages from 1961–1970	253	0.180714286	68	26.88
Earning male migrants who migrated from villages from 1971–1980	174	0.124285714	72	41.38
Earning female migrants who migrated from towns before 1961	4	0.002857143	3	75.00
Earning female migrants who migrated from towns from 1961–1970	39	0.027857143	21	53.85
Earning female migrants who migrated from towns from 1971–1980	20	0.014285714	10	50.00
Earning female migrants who migrated from towns after 1980	6	0.004285714	2	33.00
Earning female migrants who migrated from villages before 1961	2	0.001428571	1	50.00
Earning female migrants who migrated from villages from 1961–1970	27	0.019285714	13	48.15
Earning female migrants who migrated from villages from 1971–1980	27	0.019285714	10	37.04
Earning female migrants who migrated from villages after 1980	10	0.007142857	5	50.00
Total earning migrants	**1400**	**1.000000000**	**484**	**34.57**
Unemployed and student migrants	53	–	22	41.51

these categories was important to form aggregate estimates, though inter-group comparisons of these under-represented categories were not possible.

Since the relative proportions were not maintained, each variable collected from the second phase of survey had to be weighted by the proportions of each group to the total represented in the first phase.

Questionnaire Design

The second phase questionnaire was divided into seven sections and had to be carefully designed to provide 109 variables with emphasis on monetary remittance and income. Hence as expected, the respondents were very hesitant requiring considerable amount of persuasion. The interview was designed to start with general questions about the residence, occupation and age of selected relatives, the purpose being to initiate a relaxed conversation and to form a prior idea about possible remittance links, before the migrant was asked about transfer of finance. It was expected to help in cross-checking and even prompting and gently pressurising the respondent to give fairly truthful answers.

This was followed by a detailed section on the type and monetary value of the remittance, place to which it is sent, the socio-economic characteristics of the recipients and amount of in-remittance if applicable. Next were sections on employment and income characteristics, followed by details on the living conditions of the migrants. The income variable was cross-checked by the following method:

1. Some migrants in the formal sector showed their payslips.
2. Some of the responses were randomly cross-checked with the pay register of the industry or employer; most of the responses seemed to have been truthful, though some of them had to be corrected.
3. In the case of self-employed migrants, experienced local people living in the same area were asked to give a rough estimate of the migrant's income status.
4. An approximate value or quantity of the assets or products or sales or consumers were noted with the running costs to form an estimate. An example is to estimate the average production of milk by the total number of cows and buffaloes owned and multiply it by the local price of milk (Rs. 6.50/kg or Rs. 7.00/kg). From that amount the running cost has been deducted to give an estimated earning.
5. Checked whether personal possessions and living conditions matched the income. Errors were detected only if the income given was less than the impression given by the personal possessions and living conditions. The assumption was that people tend to declare less than their earnings for fear of taxation.

The questionnaire provided in the appendix shows a number of variables which have not been used in the analysis. However, they helped in cross-checking the variables used in the analysis and verifying the responses during the interview. The variables extracted from the completed questionnaires were computerised directly on the same day. In case of any discrepancy between the variables the person was re-interviewed. The questionnaire is given in Appendix 3.

Definitions

Important definitions used in the second phase questionnaire are given below as they are essential for understanding the subsequent analyses.

Remittance: From the above discussion of the collected variables and the questionnaire provided in Appendix 3 it is evident that the term 'remittance' has been used in a very broad sense to encompass the following types of flows: (*a*) Personal income transfer to any person outside Durgapur during the year 1988–89 i.e., one year preceding the time of survey via money order, bank and friends, (*b*) Personal income transfer through visit to any relative or property owned by the migrant outside Durgapur during the specified period.

Thus remittance is defined as a sum of money from a migrant's[4] income transferred to any place outside the administrative or census boundary of the town of residence. Any article purchased with the migrant's income in the town and sent or transferred for the personal use of anyone outside it was recorded as remittance of goods. This broad definition was necessary because often the migrants tend to transfer their income by hand when they visit their family or property. It includes fare and consumption expenditure of the migrant in the place of visit, but excludes visits for the purpose of tourism. However since details of the frequency of transfer and intended or actual use of the remitted money or goods have been recorded, personal expenses and fare can be excluded from the analysis, if required.

Among the studies referred to in Chapter 2, the survey conducted by Johnson and Whitelaw in Nairobi tried to measure income remittance with the following questions: '(*a*) Do you ever send any money to other areas in Kenya? (*b*) If so how much? (*c*) What is the purpose of sending the money?' (Johnson and Whitelaw 1974: 474). It is obvious that this definition does not include income transfer through personal visits to relatives or property and is therefore an underestimation of all possible recurring financial links of the migrant with areas outside the town of residence.

As it has not been possible to procure the questionnaires of the other surveys referred to in Chapter 2 it is not possible to gauge the comparability of the results of the present study.

[4] It was not possible to include in the survey the migrants who failed and went back, as well as others who have permanently out-migrated from Durgapur. This is likely to have the following effects on the estimation of remittances: (*a*) If those who have moved out have taken with them large amounts of remittances then there has been an underestimation of the total remittances flowing from Durgapur; (*b*) If those who have moved out have not taken any remittances then the propensity to remit by individual migrants has possibly been given an upward bias. However, such inaccuracies are inevitable in a social science survey of this nature.

Origin: Remittance has been measured in terms of financial flows to 'origin' and 'origin areas' in the studies in Ludhiana (Oberai and Singh 1981) and Delhi (Banerjee 1981). However neither of the papers have defined the term origin. It must be pointed out that the places receiving money or goods from the remitter may not be the origin area in terms of place of birth. The outflow of money to any area will have the initial impact in terms of increase of money supply in the area which may or may not have the expected chain reaction of demand, employment or income multiplier as described in Chapter 2. In case of step migration it becomes very difficult to identify the origin areas as every intermediate move prior to the arrival at the current town of residence represents reduction in consumption expenditure, though the employment and income generated might have been passed on to an unemployed migrant or indigenous person.

In the present study the first phase survey has considered the place of last residence because that place directly experienced the impact from the migrant's motivation to move to Durgapur, though indirect impact may reach to the place of birth of the migrant, residence of relatives and friends and place of property ownership by the migrant. In some cases such transfer may actually be the result of out-migration of a member of the migrant's family from Durgapur, for example, an offspring born in Durgapur and therefore considered to be a non-migrant may have out-migrated and his/her father who is a migrant may be sending money to the offspring. Hence it is a secondary effect of the initial decision to migrate to Durgapur. The current study has opted to consider all types of personal income transfer by a migrant with perhaps more emphasis on the place of last residence as the stratification system of the first phase sample frame considered the rural or urban nature of the place of last residence as a criterion.

Propensity to Remit

Average Propensity for Male and Female Migrants

The propensity to remit may be defined as:

1. Percentage of migrants or earning migrants who remit goods and/or money.
2. Amount of money or value of goods remitted per migrant or earning migrant.

With the definition of remittance for the present study (given above) 43 per cent of the total migrants[5] seem to be remitting goods and/or money from Durgapur while 41 per cent seem to be responsible for channelling a proportion of their cash income from Durgapur to other areas.

A comparison with the figures of Ludhiana reveals that while only 11.1 per cent of the earning migrants from urban areas as last residence remit money to home areas, in Durgapur 85 per cent of the earning migrants from urban areas as last residence transfer money to areas outside Durgapur. For those who have migrated directly from rural areas to Ludhiana, 27.1 per cent has been recorded as remitting money to origin areas; but the proportion of migrants from rural areas responsible for channelling money outside Durgapur is 87 per cent. Hence the difference in the propensity to remit between migrants from urban and rural areas seem to be less conspicuous in the sample from Durgapur compared to that from Ludhiana.

In terms of the value of yearly remittances the migrants from urban areas in Ludhiana have been reported to remit Rs. 167 per earning migrant compared to Rs. 271 remitted per earning migrant who have migrated from rural areas (Oberai and Singh 1981, based on a survey conducted in 1976–77). In the case of Durgapur, earning migrants seem to remit a greater amount, from urban areas i.e., Rs. 3360 per earning migrant and Rs. 3491 per earning migrant from rural areas (based on a survey conducted in 1989). On the other hand in Ludhiana, earning migrants from urban areas remit Rs. 1504 per remitter compared to Rs. 1002 per remitter in the case of earning migrants from rural areas. In Durgapur the earning migrants from urban areas remit Rs. 3950 per remitter compared to Rs. 3983 per remitter in the case of earning migrants from rural areas. Some of the differences between Ludhiana and Durgapur may be attributable to differences in definitions as pointed out earlier.

If expenditures on personal consumption expenses and fare are eliminated in the Durgapur survey, then the earning migrants from urban areas show a lower propensity to remit in terms of size of the yearly remittance since the value per earning migrant from urban areas is Rs. 2879 compared to Rs. 3129 for earning migrants from rural areas. A similar trend is noted for the values per remitter as shown in Table 5.2a.

The above figures indicate the significance of earning migrants from rural areas in channelling finance to areas outside Durgapur in terms of both number and size. It must be noted that the extremely high values of propensity to remit amongst earning migrants (both in terms of number and size), compared to Ludhiana have possibly resulted from a broader definition of remittances in the questionnaire run in Durgapur (as pointed out earlier).

Propensity to Remit for the Earning Male Migrants

Out of the total earning male migrants 92 per cent seem to be remitting

[5] 'Total migrants' include earning and non-earning migrants of both sexes.

Table 5.2a

Average Propensity to Remit of Earning Migrants

Earning migrants from two types of areas	*% of total earning migrants who remit*	*Total amount channelled including expenses during visits (in Rs.)*		*Amount channelled excluding personal expenses during visits (in Rs.)*	
		Rem. per year per earning migrant	*Rem. per year per remitting migrant*	*Rem. per year per earning migrant*	*Remittance per year per remitting migrant*
Urban	85	3359.66	3950.69	2878.60	3885.01
Rural	88	3491.44	3983.39	3129.38	3570.32

Note: Rem. stands for remittance.

money and/or goods while 86 per cent are channelling cash income to areas outside Durgapur. In the survey in Ludhiana only 19 per cent of the earning male migrants were reported as remitters to origin areas (Oberai and Singh 1981). However the significantly smaller proportion in Ludhiana compared to Durgapur possibly indicates a narrower definition of remittance in the Ludhiana study. In the study in Delhi (Banerjee 1981) 77.9 per cent of the earning male migrants reported visits to origin while 66.3 per cent were remitting to origin.

In the present study 56 per cent of the earning male migrants seem to be transferring money during visits for personal consumption expenditures, fare etc. However 42 per cent seem to be channelling money from Durgapur for the purpose of consumption expenditure and maintenance of relatives living outside Durgapur. In terms of regularity of remitting money, 55 per cent of the earning male migrants seem to be remitting at least once a year to the same place and this excludes those who remit solely in terms of personal expenditure and fare during visits. Moreover 32 per cent of the earning male migrants have the propensity to remit money every month.

In terms of transfer to rural and urban areas, 54 per cent of the male earning migrants seem to be transferring money to other rural areas, while 36 per cent seem to be transferring money to other urban areas. In terms of size of remittances, transfer to rural areas per earning male migrant is Rs. 169 per month compared to Rs. 124 per month to the urban areas. However per remitting male earning migrant the transfer to rural areas is Rs. 312 per month compared to Rs. 340 per month to urban areas. This shows that though male earning remitters have a higher propensity to remit to urban areas compared to rural areas in terms of size, they have a lower propensity in terms of number. So the net effect is that remittances to rural areas from Durgapur exceed remittances to urban areas by Rs. 542 per year per earning male migrant.

If the amount spent on personal consumption expenditure and fare is deducted, then the transferred money to rural areas for someone else's use exceeds that to urban areas by Rs. 506 per year per earning male migrant and this lower amount of excess indicates that more money is spent per migrant to rural areas for personal visits compared to urban areas.

Hence in Durgapur, the earning male migrants seem to have a higher propensity to remit to rural areas outside Durgapur (for all purposes including personal expenses and fare) in terms of both number and size compared to migrants from urban areas. However it must be remembered that in the case of Durgapur 'remittance' includes money sent to any area outside Durgapur while in the case of Ludhiana 'remittance' includes money sent to origin areas only; thus the values cannot be directly compared.

Propensity to Remit for the Earning Female Migrants

It is interesting to note that 86 per cent of the earning female migrants seem to be channelling a proportion of their cash income to areas outside Durgapur. This is mainly because in households having both female and male earning migrants as spouses, any remittance is usually contributed jointly from the total income. Hence, though female migrants are expected to be less significant in the development of remittance linkage, the propensity to transfer finance to areas outside Durgapur on the part of the earning female migrants seem to exhibit similar trends as the earning male migrants. In contrast, in the Ludhiana study only 3 per cent of the earning female migrants were recorded as remitters (Oberai and Singh 1981).

However, unlike male earning migrants, a higher proportion of the female earning migrants (63 per cent) transfer finance out of Durgapur for personal expenditure and fare during visits to relatives, friends or property every year, while only 37 per cent contribute money for the maintenance and consumption expenditure of someone else. In terms of regularity 80 per cent transfer finance at least once a year or more, but only 29 per cent seem to remit every month. Thus female earning migrants seem to contribute more towards personal visits, rather than providing income support to a relative or friend.

While 52 per cent of the earning female migrants send their cash income to rural areas, 41 per cent send money to other urban areas. In terms of the size of remittances, though the absolute amounts per earning female migrant and remitting female migrant are less than that of the male migrants, the rural-urban characteristics follow the same trends. The mean remittance transferred to rural areas per month works out to be Rs. 108 per earning female migrant compared to Rs. 99 to the urban areas. However per remitting female migrant the transfer to rural areas amounts to Rs. 206 per month compared to Rs. 241 to urban areas. Hence, though the female migrants have a higher propensity to remit to rural areas in terms of numbers, in terms of size the remitters to the urban areas exhibit a higher propensity. However the net effect is that transfer to rural areas exceeds that to urban areas by Rs. 103 per year per earning female migrant.

After excluding the amounts transferred for the purpose of personal expenditure and fare, the transfer to rural areas exceeds that of urban areas by Rs. 60 per year per earning female migrant.

Hence, transfer through male migrants is more significant both in number and amount, partly reflecting the differences in the income earned between the two sexes to be discussed later. Though there seems to be very little difference in the average propensity to remit by male and female earning migrants, 98 per cent of the total money sent out of Durgapur is sent by male earning migrants because of the low level of participation of female migrants in the labour force (Table 5.2b). On an average the rural sector seem to be gaining more from remittances, in monetary terms, than the urban sector outside Durgapur as 86 per cent of the total value of the remittances from Durgapur is being sent to rural areas.

Table 5.2b

Propensity to Remit for Male and Female Earning Migrants to Rural and Urban Areas

Remittances to:	*Proportion of earning migrants who remit*		*Amount of remittance sent per month (in Rs.)*	
	Male	*Female*	*Male*	*Female*
Urban areas	36.46	41.16	124	99
Rural areas	54.28	52.45	169	108
Total	**86.32**	**86.41**	**288**	**255**

Note: 98.15 per cent of the total money channelled out of Durgapur is sent by male earning migrants.

Table 5.2c

Temporal Variation in Propensity to Remit

Year of arrival in Durgapur	*% of remitter to total earning migrant*	*Value remitted per earning migrant (in Rs.)*	*% of remitter to towns to total earning migrant*	*% of remitter to villages to total earning migrant*	*Value to town per earning migrant (in Rs.)*	*Value to village per earning migrant (in Rs.)*
Before 1961	79.74	5103.84	46.27	43.08	2639	2465
1961–1970	87.13	3441.49	43.88	46.84	1694	1747
1971–1980	88.76	2566.75	19.25	71.93	423	2142
1981–1987	88.73	2998.73	28.87	68.40	1117	1882

Temporal Variations in the Propensity to Remit

Figures 5.3a and 5.3b show the propensity to remit in terms of the number of remitters as percentage of earning migrants and amount remitted per earning migrant to both rural and urban areas. The propensity to remit in terms of number of remitters to rural areas tend to decrease with time, indicating that older migrants have a lower propensity to remit to rural areas. In the case of number of remitters to urban areas the trend is exactly the reverse as the older migrants show a higher propensity to remit. Thus the migrants tend to increase their links with the urban sector with time. On an average while the number of remitters as percentage of earning migrants shows a very gradual decline over time, the value remitted per earning migrant seems to increase over time (Figures 5.3c and 5.3d). Those who have migrated in the first phase of growth seem to be remitting Rs. 5,100 per year compared to the most recent migrants who remit Rs. 3,000 per year. Hence the amount remitted for the town as a whole is more likely to depend on the temporal variation in the size of the migrating labour force.

In terms of size of the remittance the older migrants seem to remit higher amounts both to rural and urban areas, thus indicating that propensity to remit per earning migrant increases over time. The decrease is more conspicuous for remittances to urban areas compared to rural areas.

It has been pointed out earlier that migrants per year have declined over time so that the rate of increase of earning migrants in the town has declined, though the absolute number has possibly increased or remained constant. The total value of remittances can be expected to follow a similar trend characterised by rapid increase of the absolute value channelled out of the town, possibly till the mid-1970s, followed by gradual decrease in the rate of increase until it reaches a constant level with minor fluctuations in the short run. However, such a temporal change can only remain as a hypothesis as time series data on the amount of remittances has not been monitored in any town in India.

Since a very high proportion of the earning migrants from both rural and urban origin seem to be remitting, the temporal variation in the size of the migrating labour force, (as highlighted in the last chapter), is the only indicator of the probable trend of the growth of a remittance linkage from the town. From the trendline depicting migration link of labour force, it seems, as pointed out earlier, that the linkage of the town is likely to strengthen with the urban sector in future. However the remittance linkage will also depend upon the duration of stay in the town by the earning migrant. Though it is difficult to be specific, it is likely that like the migration link the long-term trend will be an increasing link with the urban sector rather than the rural sector.

It is interesting to note that the study in Ludhiana revealed two points:

Propensity To Remit To Rural And Urban Areas In Terms Of Number Of Remitters

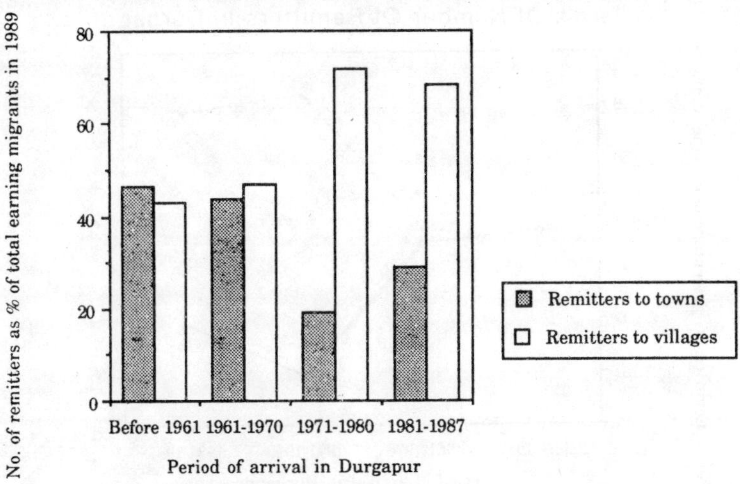

Propensity To Remit To Rural And Urban Areas In Terms Of Amount Remitted

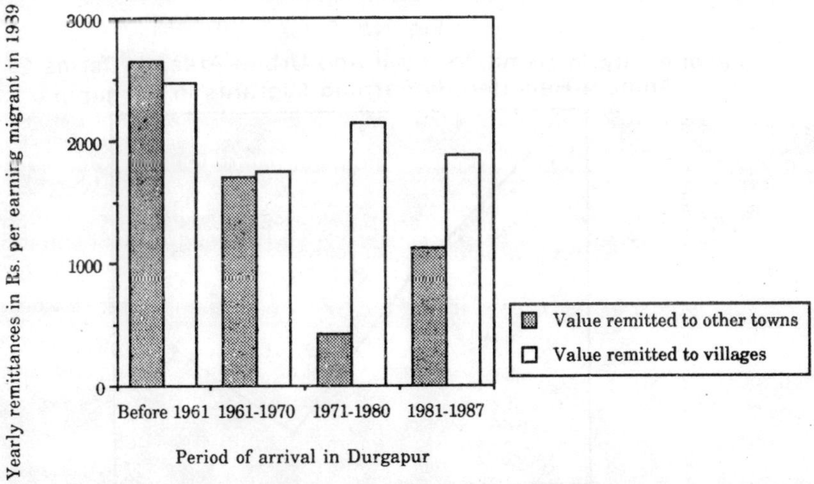

The values represented by the bargraphs imply a change in the propensity to remit over time. The implied temporal difference in the propensity to remit by rural and urban migrants can be better depicted by superimposed frequency polygons derived from these bargraphs as shown by the figures 5.03a and 5.03b.

Propensity To Remit To Rural And Urban Areas In Terms Of Number Of Remitters In Durgapur

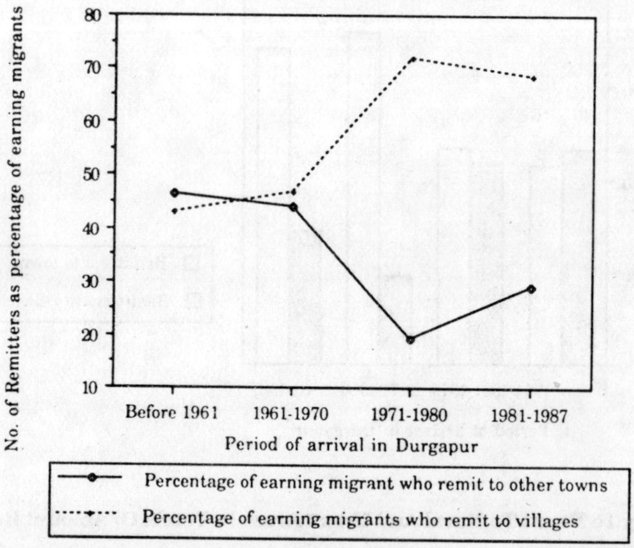

Fig. No. 5.03a

Propensity To Remit To Rural And Urban Areas In Terms Of Amount Remitted By Earning Migrants In Durgapur

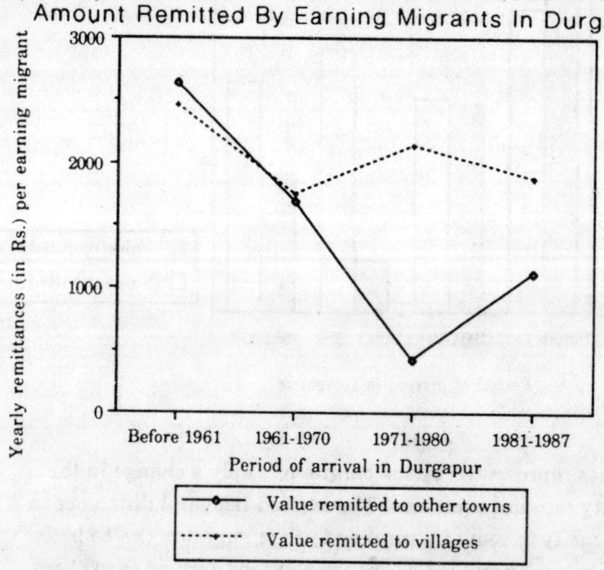

Fig. No. 5.03b

Propensity To Remit In Terms Of Number Of Remitters

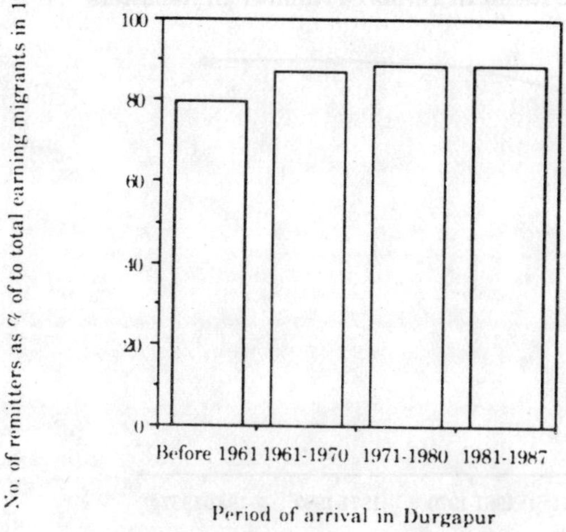

Period of arrival in Durgapur

Propensity To Remit In Terms Of Amount Remitted

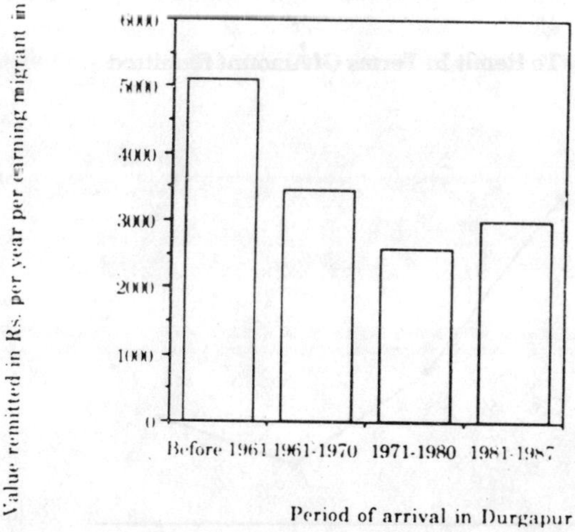

Period of arrival in Durgapur

The values represented by the bargraphs imply a change in the propensity to remit over time which can be better understood from the frequency polygons derived from these bargraphs as shown by the figures 5.03c and 5.03d.

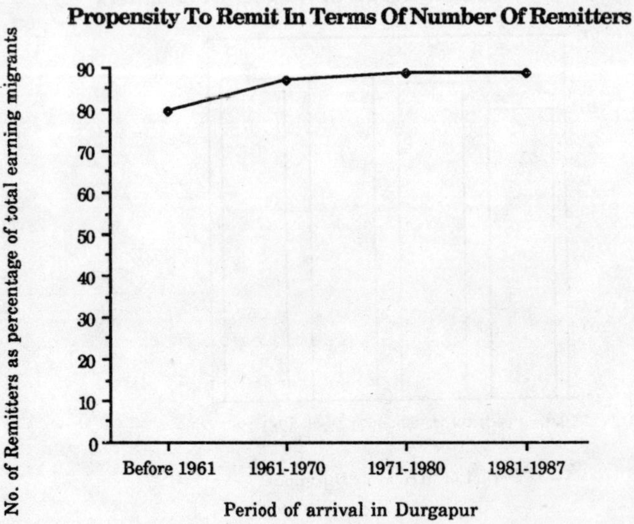

Fig. No. 5.03c

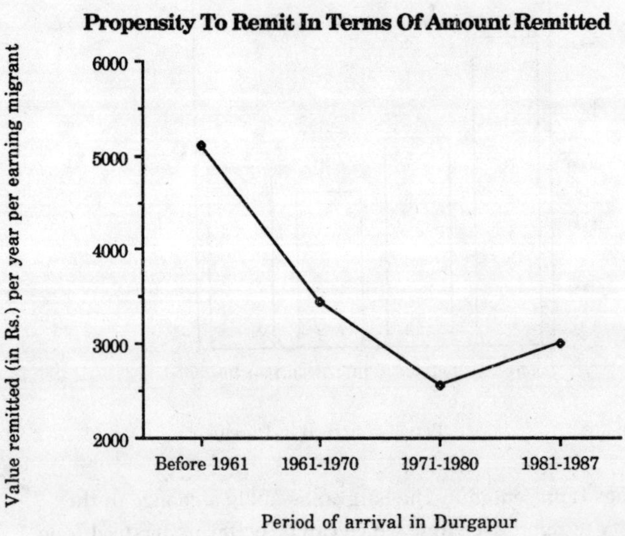

Fig. No. 5.03d

(*a*) rural migrants show a greater propensity to remit; (*b*) rural remittances decline slowly over time. Based on these two points the authors have concluded:

> However, the finding that migrants from rural areas have a higher propensity to remit as well as remit for longer period compared with migrants from the urban areas suggests that given other things rural areas are likely to receive a relatively larger proportion of the outflow of remittances from urban migrants. Thus from the point of view of development of the origin areas, through income transfers rural-urban migration is to be more beneficial to the rural areas than urban-urban migration (Oberai and Singh 1981: 34).

In Durgapur, as pointed out earlier, first the difference between propensity to remit by rural and urban migrants is not so conspicuous either in terms of number or amount, though in absolute terms remittances to rural areas exceed that to urban areas (as a number of migrants who have declared their last residence to be an urban area, remit to relatives or property in rural areas); second, the propensity to remit to urban areas by the earning migrants seems to increase over time, while that to rural areas seem to decline; third, the value remitted per earning migrant to rural and urban areas seems to increase over time; fourth the proportion of migrants from urban areas seems to be increasing. Hence it is very difficult to conclude or predict, only on the basis of the propensity to remit in terms of number of remitters, the temporal trend of the strength of the remittance linkage of a town.

Types of Relationships and Monetary Links

Table 5.3 shows that the household size of the earning in-migrants in the urban destination area in Durgapur in West Bengal is different from that of Ludhiana in Punjab in two ways:

1. In Durgapur, only 7 per cent of the earning in-migrants live in single member units, while, in Ludhiana 13 per cent live in single member units. In the study on Ludhiana it has been pointed out that: 'The household size is inversely related to the percentage of remitters' (Oberai and Singh 1983: 303). Hence a town with a lower proportion of single member units like Durgapur can be expected to have a comparatively lower propensity to remit in terms of number of remitters.
2. A larger proportion of in-migrants in Durgapur live in households with four members compared to Ludhiana where the proportion of households with 5–7 members is higher than that of Durgapur.

Table 5.3

The Size of Household of the Earning In-migrants in Durgapur and Ludhiana

No. of members	*% of earning in-migrants in Durgapur*	*% of earning in-migrants in Ludhiana*
1	6.87	12.86
2	6.87	7.38
3	15.73	15.10
4	25.68	16.89
5–7	35.08	38.70
8 and above	9.76	9.06

The proportion of households with 2, 3 and 8-and-above members are more or less the same in both the towns and the highest proportion of in-migrants live in households of 5–7 members in both the towns. Hence Durgapur can be expected to have an equal or lower propensity to remit than Ludhiana in Punjab, though the surveys do not seem to establish this hypothesis, possibly because of definitional differences.

As a small proportion of earning in-migrants in Durgapur live in single member units, the highest proportion of remitters seem to be remitting money to parents (37 per cent), followed by those remitting to brothers and sisters (25 per cent), son and/or daughter (12 per cent), in-laws (12 per cent), uncle and/or aunt (8 per cent) and wife (only 6 per cent) (Table 5.4a). The importance of parents as receivers of monetary remittance results from two factors: (*a*) the sense of duty in the social system to provide financial support to parents in their old age, especially by earning sons; (*b*) the financial support by adult earning offspring is a type of pension for retired old people in the absence of formal social security measures. Brothers and sisters may receive monetary remittance as gifts during festivals or during visits; while brothers may receive contribution towards maintenance of inherited property. A small proportion may receive for maintenance or education. Remittance to children may be for the following purposes:

1. Gifts to married offspring.
2. Maintenance of children left in the place of last residence or areas of origin.
3. Higher education of children in better universities in other towns.

As the proportion of single member units is small, most of the remittances to children may be a result of out-migration of children for education, jobs or marriage.

Table 5.4a

Types of Relation and Monetary Links

Relation who receives monetary remittance	*% of total remitters**	*% of earning migrants*
Parents	37.47	32.42
Uncle/Aunt	7.86	6.80
Wife	6.32	5.47
In-laws	12.22	10.57
Son/daughter	12.49	10.81
Brother/sister	25.05	21.68
Employee	0.63	0.54
Cousin	2.20	1.90
Son/daughter-in-law	0.20	0.17
Friend	0.51	0.44
Doctor/lawyer	0.32	0.27
Nephew/niece	2.59	2.23
Institute	1.02	0.88
Property[1]	0.09	0.08

* The total does not add up to 100 per cent because some of the remitters send money to more than one relative.

[1] This may be a relation or employee supervising property or any money spent for maintenance of property outside Durgapur.

Table 5.4b shows that the propensity to remit to parents decline with time as parents of older migrants have possibly died. Hence 64 per cent of those who have migrated after 1980 remit to parents compared to 49 per cent of those who have migrated between 1971 and 1980, 34 per cent of those who have migrated between 1961 and 1970 and only 27 per cent of those who have migrated before 1961. However older migrants seem to have a greater propensity to remit to brothers and sisters compared to the recent migrants possibly due to the following reasons:

1. For the recent migrants, the brothers and sisters may still be living with the parents so that money sent to parents may include remittances to the same households as brothers and sisters.
2. For the older migrants, in the absence of parents it may be the responsibility of the earning brother to give the customary gifts to the married and unmarried sister during festivals, whereas for the younger migrants the first responsibility is to remit to the parents.
3. In a closed number system the higher proportion of remitters remitting to parents may automatically mean lower proportion for other relatives.
4. Perhaps the decline in proportions remitting to brothers and sisters

Table 5.4b

Temporal Variations in Proportion of Remitters Sending Money to Different Types of Relation

Relation receiving monetary remittance	*% of remitters who migrated to Durgapur up to 1960*	*% of remitters who migrated to Durgapur 1961–1970*	*% of remitters who migrated to Durgapur 1971–1980*	*% of remitters who migrated to Durgapur 1981–1987*
Parents	27.04	33.52	48.65	63.62
Uncle/Aunt	0.90	9.21	9.07	2.27
Wife	0.00	6.92	8.33	5.34
In-laws	20.32	12.62	7.38	9.63
Son/daughter	25.07	12.11	7.17	9.92
Brother/sister	29.73	26.48	20.01	19.26
Employee	0.90	0.86	0.00	0.00
Cousin	5.57	1.47	2.48	0.00
Son/daughter-in-law	1.56	0.00	0.00	0.00
Friend	0.00	0.86	0.00	0.00
Doctor/lawyer	2.46	0.00	0.00	0.00
Nephew/niece	4.26	3.03	0.99	0.00
Institute	0.00	1.73	0.00	0.00
Property	0.00	0.00	0.00	2.55

Note: The column totals do not add up to 100 per cent because some of the remitters send money to more than one relative.

may indicate reduction in the importance of extended family system over time.

A larger proportion of older in-migrants tend to be remitting to their son or daughter than the recent in-migrants due to the following reasons:

1. Older in-migrants are more likely to have children residing outside Durgapur possibly because daughters have been married and live outside Durgapur or are pursuing higher education in other cities with better education facilities, while sons may be either students or earning members in other towns or villages. Money can be expected to flow as gifts especially during festivals as well as to finance education.
2. The most recent in-migrants are most likely to have left their spouses and children in the place of last residence or areas of origin with the in-migrant's parents.
3. The lowest proportion of remitters remitting to children, are those who have in-migrated in the intermediate period between 1971–80 because: (*a*) possibly they have had time to bring their families to Durgapur, (*b*) the children are not old enough to pursue higher education in other towns, (*c*) the school facilities of Durgapur are

good compared to the facilities of Calcutta, hence not necessitating out-migration of children for education.

The older migrants tend to show a higher propensity to remit to in-laws as they are more likely to be married than the more recent ones. Remittance to in-laws usually takes the form of gifts during festivals or visits. Only a very small proportion of migrants who have migrated after 1960 tend to send monetary remittance to support their spouses who have been left behind.

Standard of Living and Propensity to Remit

Income Levels and Propensity to Remit

The average monthly income per earning migrant works out to be Rs. 2187 and Table 5.5a shows a gradual increase of monthly income with years of residence in the town as the older migrants earn more than Rs. 3000 compared to Rs. 1665 earned by the recent migrants. However the recent migrants tend to remit the highest proportion of their income, possibly because they have not yet settled with their families in the town. The lowest proportion is sent by those who have migrated between 1971 and 1980. Older migrants tend to remit higher proportion possibly because their family links outside the town increases with out-migration of offspring as discussed earlier.

Table 5.5a

Average Monthly Income and Remittance of the Earning Migrants

Year of arrival in Durgapur	*Monthly income per earning migrant*	*Proportion of income remitted per year*
Before 1961	3034.46	0.14
1961–1970	2170.60	0.13
1971–1980	1808.11	0.12
1981–1987	1665.53	0.15

The average income amongst the male earning migrants (with varying duration of residence in Durgapur) from urban areas varies between Rs. 2100–3500 per month and there seems to be no significant difference between the migrants and remitting male migrants in this category. The male earning migrants from rural areas tend to have lower monthly income varying between Rs. 1250–3000 (Table 5.5b). Amongst those who have migrated from rural areas the average income seems to have increased with

Table 5.5b

Income Levels for Earning Migrants of Both Sexes of Rural and Urban Migrants

Migrants stratified on the basis of sex and year of arrival in Durgapur	*Average income per month for all earning migrants (in Rs.)*	*Per capita income per month for all earning migrants (in Rs.)*	*Per capita income per month for remitters (in Rs.)*
	Male migrants from urban areas		
Before 1961	3053	694	778
1961–1970	2330	578	578
1971–1980	2466	598	682
1981–1987	2191	854	819
	Male migrants from rural areas		
Before 1961	2985	596	636
1961–1970	1967	598	589
1971–1980	1443	395	404
1981–1987	1273	444	509
	Female migrants from urban areas		
Before 1961	*	*	*
1961–1970	2472	718	658
1971–1980	1245	442	529
1981–1987	1650	600	600
	Female migrants from rural areas		
Before 1961	175	25	**
1961–1970	675	153	161
1971–1980	710	204	152
1981–1987	166	63	43

* Mistake in recorded data which could not be corrected; however the average monthly income can be expected to be Rs. 2500 approximately; three observations for both earning and remitting migrants.

** No remitter in that category.

years of residence as the older migrants have higher levels of income than the recent ones, varying from Rs. 2985 (amongst the older migrants) to Rs. 1273 (amongst those who have migrated after 1980). This trend is not clear amongst those who have in-migrated from urban areas, though the oldest group receives the highest income. Amongst those who have migrated during the first phase of industrial growth, the remitting migrants seem to have slightly higher level of income than the average for all migrants.

The per capita income per month seems to vary between Rs. 400 and Rs. 800 amongst the earning male migrants. For those who have migrated from rural areas, the amount varies between Rs. 400–650, while for those who have migrated from urban areas the amount varies between Rs. 570–820 (Table 5.5b).

The female earning migrants from rural areas have very low monthly income varying from Rs. 150–750, compared to those who have migrated from urban areas who receive more than Rs. 1000 per month, the older ones receiving more than Rs. 2000 per month (Table 5.5b).

Table 5.6 shows that amongst the male earning migrants the proportion of income remitted is highest amongst the recent migrants and declines

Table 5.6

Monthly Income of the Remitters and Proportion of Income Remitted

Migrants stratified on the basis of sex and year of arrival in Durgapur	*Average income per month of remitters (in Rs.)*	*Proportion of income remitted*
Male migrants from urban areas		
Arrived in Durgapur before 1961	3342	0.16
Arrived in Durgapur 1961–1970	2252	0.17
Arrived in Durgapur 1971–1980	2593	0.15
Arrived in Durgapur after 1980	2120	0.26
Male migrants from rural areas		
Arrived in Durgapur before 1961	3213	0.15
Arrived in Durgapur 1961–1970	1761	0.19
Arrived in Durgapur 1971–1980	1419	0.22
Arrived in Durgapur after 1980	1383	0.22
Female migrants from urban areas		
Arrived in Durgapur before 1961	*	*
Arrived in Durgapur 1961–1970	1946	0.20
Arrived in Durgapur 1971–1980	1389	0.22
Arrived in Durgapur after 1980	1650	0.46
Female migrants from rural areas		
Arrived in Durgapur before 1961	**	0.00
Arrived in Durgapur 1961–1970	701	0.14
Arrived in Durgapur 1971–1980	639	0.12
Arrived in Durgapur after 1980	48	0.97

* Mistake in recorded data which could not be corrected.

** No remitter in that category.

Note: The proportion of income remitted refers to the income of the remitters only and hence the values are higher than the average proportion of 13.41 per cent of the income of all the in-migrants sent outside the town (referred to in the text).

over time, especially amongst those who have in-migrated from rural areas. Amongst the rural in-migrants it varies between 15 per cent and 22 per cent, while amongst the urban migrants it varies between 15 per cent and 26 per cent. Amongst the female earning migrants those who have in-migrated from rural areas remit 0 per cent to 97 per cent of their income, the recent ones remitting the highest proportion. Amongst the female earning migrants who have in-migrated from urban areas the amount varies between 20 per cent and 46 per cent, the recent ones remitting the highest proportion.

Though the amounts remitted seem to have significant positive relation with the total income and per capita income per month amongst the earning male migrants who have migrated before 1981, there do not seem to be significant correlations between the proportion of income remitted and total income or per capita income.

Hence, as expected rural in-migrants seem to have lower income levels for both male and female earning migrants. Though the level of income does affect the absolute value of the remittance, it is interesting to note that the proportion of income remitted has no significant relation with the level of income, whereas for other cities it has been shown that it tends to vary inversely with the level of income. This is possibly due to the fact that most of the in-migrants have migrated with their families irrespective of the level of income (as discussed earlier) and income is not the sole determinant of remittance.

Apart from the female earning migrants who have migrated from urban areas before 1960, the others do not exhibit a lower propensity to remit in terms of proportion of income remitted compared to the male earning migrants. On the other hand the recent ones from rural areas seem to be sending back all of their income and this proportion is also quite high for those who have migrated from urban areas compared to their male counterpart. However, the female earning migrants from rural areas have a markedly lower level of income, which no doubt affects the total value of the remittance sent by the female earning migrants. Moreover, as pointed out earlier, female earning migrants are very few compared to the male earning migrants so that the amount remitted becomes primarily a function of the income and family links of the male in-migrants.

On an average only 13.41 per cent of the income generated by the in-migrants at the time of the second phase survey was being rechannelled to areas outside the town to other rural and urban settlements. However, in absolute terms, this amounts to Rs. 253 million per year, which, as pointed out earlier, is more than the total receipts of remittances in the district of Pauri Garhwal. It must be noted that majority of the migrants have moved in with their families as concerted effort was made to provide family accommodation to the workers as discussed later. Hence it is not surprising that the proportion of income remitted appears to be quite low, though no comparative figures from other towns are available.

Squatting and Propensity to Remit

The sample shows that 28 per cent (Table 5.7) of the earning migrants can be classified as squatters as (*a*) they live in houses for which no landholding tax is paid to the Notified Area Authority; or (*b*) they live in houses built on land owned privately by individuals or industries without the permission of the owner.[6]

Table 5.7

Relative Propensity to Remit by Squatters and Non-squatters

Tax paying status (for residential land)	*% of total remitt.*	*% of total value remitted*	*Value per remitt. (in Rs.)*	*% of total earning mig.*	*Value per earning mig. (in Rs.)*	*% of earning mig. who remit*
Tax paid by the migrant or employee**	65.97	69.52	4192.79	64.43	3664.85	87.41
Private landlord pays**	5.02	7.57	6001.93	4.56	5639.82	93.97
Will pay in future*	0.82	0.42	2023.61	1.30	1090.36	53.88
Do not pay*	25.69	21.26	3293.30	26.67	2708.33	82.24
Do not know	2.50	1.23	1963.67	3.04	1376.77	70.11
Total	**100.00**	**100.00**				
* Current squatters			3253.96		2633.03	80.92
** Current non-squatters			4320.74		3795.42	87.84

Note: Remitt. stands for remitters and mig. stands for migrants.

Eighty-one per cent of the earning migrants who are squatters seem to be sending remittances to areas outside Durgapur and the value of remittances sent per earning migrant who live as squatters amount to Rs. 2633.03 per year; while the amount per remitter is as high as Rs. 3253.96 per year. 26.51 per cent of the total earning remitters live as squatters.

Seventy per cent of the earning migrants live in registered accommodation for which either the migrant or the owner pays tax to the Notified Area Authority and the house is occupied by the migrant with the consent of the landowner. Compared to the squatters this group has a higher propensity to remit as 88 per cent of them remit money to areas outside Durgapur and the amount is Rs. 3795 per year per earning migrant in this group. The value remitted is as high as Rs. 4320 per year per remitter.

Type of Housing and Propensity to Remit

Twenty-two per cent of the earning migrants live in houses which can be classified as temporary or semi-permanent on the basis of the building materials. Roof built with: (*a*) thatch and bamboo have been classified as

[6] The landowner pays the landholding tax.

temporary; (*b*) tile, tin and asbestos have been classified as semi-permanent; (*c*) concrete have been classified as permanent. Similarly walls built with (*a*) mud, bamboo,straw, leaves have been classified as temporary; (*b*) tin have been classified as semi-permanent; (*c*) brick and cement have been classified as permanent.

Eighty-six per cent of earning migrants who live in temporary and semi-permanent dwellings seem to remit to areas outside Durgapur and the amount of remittances sent per earning migrant living in such dwellings is Rs. 2575 per year; the value is as high as Rs. 3011 per year per earning remitter living in temporary and semi-permanent shelter. 21.99 per cent of the total remitters tend to live in temporary and semi-permanent dwellings.

Another 35 per cent of the earning migrants live in dwellings which have a mixture of brick, cement and concrete with the temporary and semi-permanent materials. Table 5.8 shows that they have a much lower propensity to remit as only 48 per cent of them remit to areas outside Durgapur and the amount of remittance per year per earning migrant is Rs. 1852 per year. This group possibly include people who started off with temporary and semi-permanent dwellings, but have tried to improve their shelter. This has either been the cause or the effect of lower propensity to remit. The value per year per earning remitter is however higher than the former group i.e., Rs. 3860.

Table 5.8

Housing and Propensity to Remit

Type of structure of residence based on building materials	*% of total remitt.*	*% of total value remitted*	*Value per remitt. (in Rs.)*	*% of total earning mig.*	*Value per earning mig. (in Rs.)*	*% of earning mig. who remit*
Temporary and semi-temporary	21.99	16.59	3017.94	21.95	2575.09	85.51
Semi-permanent	34.01	32.89	3860.28	35.42	1852.85	48.00
Permanent	65.99	67.11	4059.83	64.58	3540.58	87.21

Note: Remitt. stands for remitters and mig. stands for migrants.

Sixty-six per cent of the earning migrants live in accommodation built with permanent building materials as defined earlier. They exhibit the highest propensity to remit amongst the three groups as 87 per cent seem to be sending money outside Durgapur, the value being 3540 per year per earning migrant in this category. The value per remitter is Rs. 4059 per year.

Sanitation Facility of the Remitters

Twenty-four per cent of the earning migrants live in accommodation which have no sanitary facilities. 87 per cent of the earning migrants living without sanitary facilities tend to send remittances, the value amounting to Rs. 2981 per year per earning migrant in this group (Table 5.9). The amount per remitter is Rs. 3438 per year. 13 per cent of the earning migrants live in accommodation with toilets with low cost dumping facilities.[7] This group shows a lower propensity to remit as 72 per cent of the earning migrants of this group tends to send remittances and the value is only Rs. 672 per earning migrant per year and Rs. 938 per earning remitter. This latter group represents a section of the population who have tried to improve their sanitation; the effort representing either the cause or an effect of the lower propensity to remit.

Fifty-four per cent of the earning migrants have access to private toilets and another 3 per cent have access to common toilets, both types having septic tank for disposal of the waste. Hence, 57 per cent of the earning migrants have access to a sophisticated and hygienic method of waste disposal. This group ranks the highest in the propensity to remit as 88 per cent of them send remittances and the value per earning migrant is Rs. 4301 per year. The value per earning remitter in this group is Rs. 4893 per year.

Since toilets involve private expenditure either for construction or for payment of higher rent for accommodation with adequate toilet facilities, expenses on that account may cause the migrant to remit less. Alternatively, the migrants who remit less due to other factors (like lack of family links outside the town in the case of refugees who have in-migrated from Bangladesh) may spend money for improving the sanitation. The priority given to expenditures for the improvement of sanitation may also depend upon the necessity of such facilities in the perception of the migrant, which may vary according to the regional characteristics of the migrants. Migrants from rural areas of Bihar may not be able to perceive the necessity of formal sanitation facilities as they may be more used to the open air system in the villages. Moreover they tend to be more interested in making expenditures in their place of birth or native villages and perceive their accommodation in Durgapur to be very temporary and not worth improving. On the other hand migrants from Bangladesh seemed to be very conscious about the necessity of having proper toilets and have consequently tried to construct them in the cheapest way, even within the squatter colonies. This difference in attitude and the resulting propensity to remit which depresses the

[7] A small underground chamber is dug and strengthened with bricks and mortar, which is connected to the toilet, so that the waste is dumped into the chamber. The chamber is covered at the top. It is cheaper to construct compared to a septic tank, but has the disadvantage of getting filled up in future, thus requiring the digging of a new chamber.

Table 5.9

Sanitary Facility and Propensity to Remit

Type of sanitation facility available in the residence	*% of total remitt.*	*% of total value remitted*	*Value per remitt. (in Rs.)*	*% of total earning mig.*	*Value per earning mig. (in Rs.)*	*% of earning mig. who remit*
No sanitary facility	24.68	20.73	3438.20	24.23	2981.61	86.72
Low cost dumping facility	11.15	2.56	938.66	13.24	672.56	71.65
Septic tank	55.33	65.37	4837.40	53.81	4233.29	87.51
Septic tank (common)	3.56	5.01	5766.14	3.20	5451.78	94.55
Non-flushable (not specified)	2.26	4.28	7738.52	2.24	6669.83	86.19
Non-flushable (common)	3.02	2.06	2788.75	3.28	2187.97	78.46
Total	**100.00**	**100.00**		**100.00**		

Note: Remitt. stands for remitters and mig. stands for migrants.

expenditure multiplier in the town, also affects the urban environment especially within the squatter colonies.

Implications for Town Planning

Earning migrants in squatter settlements, living in temporary and semi-permanent accommodation with no sanitary facilities show a slightly lower, but quite high propensity to remit both in terms of number and value of the remittance compared to those living in legal settlements, permanent accommodation with sophisticated sanitation. Hence this process of re-channelling finance to other areas not only depresses the multiplier in the urban area, but also perhaps contributes to deterioration of urban environment.

Many studies have referred to the creation of 'urban villages' which replicate the lifestyle of the source area of the migrant. However certain facilities like toilets and sanitation which may not appear to be a necessity in the rural areas become a necessity for hygienic reasons in densely populated urban areas. The migrant may remain unaware of this changing necessity and hence may find it more worthwhile to invest in land, agriculture or building permanent accommodation in the source areas. Moreover as pointed out earlier dowry for marriage of daughters may provide a greater impetus to save rather than to invest in improving the living conditions in the urban area where he/she is residing. Finally a squatter can hardly be expected to improve his accommodation on a piece of land on which he/she has no permanent claim.

However it is interesting to note that within the squatter settlements certain groups of people seem to have made an effort to improve their toilets and have invested in providing a temporary disposal facility for themselves. As has been pointed out earlier this group shows a lower propensity to remit. The question remains whether people from certain regions have greater propensity to live without sanitation than those from other regions? The Notified Area Authority have tried to provide some temporary disposal facility and toilets among the poorest sections of the community within the unauthorised and authorised[8] squatter colonies. Perhaps, as pointed out in the last chapter the planning authorities can make an effort to provide low-cost housing with cheap sanitation or allocate space for squatters and impose some rules and provisions for having cheap sanitation facilities. The low cost dumping system mentioned in the last section can be used to provide raw material for the production of bio-gas.

Intended Use of the Remitted Money

Average Use in Rural and Urban Areas

Table 5.10 shows the relative importance of different uses of the remitted money as expected or known by the remitter. While 66 per cent of the total remitters transfer finance to areas outside Durgapur for personal expenditure and fare during visits, 48 per cent send remittances for the purpose of general maintenance of relatives which can be expected to include mainly purchase of consumption goods—both food and durable commodities. These two major purposes are followed by contributions as gift during festivals, marriage of relatives (other than own offsprings) and funeral by 23 per cent of the remitters. It is interesting to note that 13 per cent of the remitters contribute money for the continuance and development of agriculture in the receiving areas. This is followed by 11 per cent channelling money for purchase of land and 10 per cent channelling money for construction or improvement of residential buildings in the receiving areas.

In terms of proportion of remitted money used for different purposes the maximum proportion is represented by maintenance (mainly consumption expenses) (31 per cent) as shown in Table 5.11, followed by daughter's marriage or dowry (15 per cent), personal expenses during visits (13 per cent), construction and improvement of residential buildings (10 per cent), gifts for festivals, marriage and funeral (8 per cent), education (8 per cent), agriculture (6 per cent) and purchase of land (5 per cent).

Though in terms of number of remitters agriculture ranks higher than construction, dowry and education, its lower position in terms of size, indicates that in the receiving areas the agriculture practised is less capital intensive than any investment in construction and education. Similarly

[8] Authorised squatters are those settlements which started as squatters, but the inhabitants are being given legal rights to the landholdings by the Durgapur Notified Area Authority.

Table 5.10

Relative Importance of the Expected Use of the Remittance in Terms of Proportion of Remitters Contributing to a Particular Use

Use	*Percentage of total remitters*		
	Male earning migrants	*Female earning migrants*	*Total earning migrants*
1. Agriculture	12.64	14.37	12.81
2. Education	8.16	7.37	8.08
3. Gift—festival, funeral	23.33	14.70	22.50
4. To finance self-employment	1.89	0.00	1.71
5. Construction/improvement of residential buildings	10.99	1.14	10.04
6. Salary to employees	0.81	0.00	0.73
7. Litigation	0.58	0.00	0.52
8. Daughter's marriage-dowry	2.93	1.59	2.84
9. Maintenance mainly consumption expenditures	48.36	43.19	47.86
10. Medical treatment	5.06	5.05	5.06
11. Personal expenditures, fare during visits	65.27	72.91	66.01
12. Religious practices/charity	3.57	0.00	3.23
13. Purchase of land	11.67	3.18	10.85
14. Savings	0.00	1.71	0.16
15. Payment of loan	0.01	0.00	0.00

payment of dowry, demands more capital in the short run than yearly expenses in agriculture. Purchase of land also seem to be taking up less finance than construction and improvements of building though in terms of proportion of remitters they are similar.

The importance of consumption expenditure amongst the various uses of remittances has been revealed by all the other studies in Ludhiana, Delhi and Garhwal district. The major criticism of these studies is that the remittances have not been used for investment purposes. However use of remittances for consumption expenses can bring about an increase in demand for commodities, which in turn may give an impetus to increase in production. At the same time such an effect would depend upon the increase of prices for the commodities relative to the increase of income caused by remittances. Moreover, as pointed out in Chapter 2, the initial consumption pattern of the receiving households and areas will determine the sectoral benefit of the increase of demand.

On the other hand the use of the remittances in agriculture, construction and maintenance of residential buildings and investment in any form of self-employed activity can have an employment multiplier effect in the local economy, depending upon the level of mechanisation for these activities at the local level. The following sections will deal with these issues.

Table 5.11

Relative Importance of the Expected Use of Remittance in Terms of Proportion of Monetary Value of the Total Remittance

Use	*Percentage of total money channelled by:*		
	Male earning migrants	*Female earning migrants*	*Total earning migrants*
1. Agriculture	6.22	0.90	5.82
2. Education	7.37	9.04	7.50
3. Gift—festival, funeral	7.92	5.40	7.73
4. To finance self-employment	2.19	2.19	2.03
5. Construction/improvement of residential buildings	11.18	0.13	10.36
6. Salary to employees	0.13	0.00	0.12
7. Litigation	0.36	0.00	0.34
8. Daughter's marriage-dowry	16.47	3.22	15.48
9. Maintenance mainly consumption expenditures	29.95	37.45	30.51
10. Medical treatment	1.23	1.81	1.27
11. Personal expenditures, fare during visits	12.97	12.13	12.91
12. Religious practices/charity	1.48	0.00	1.37
13. Purchase of land	2.50	29.53	4.51
14. Savings	0.00	0.39	0.03
15. Payment of loan	0.03	0.00	0.03

Differences in the Use of Remittances in the Urban and Rural Areas

In terms of yearly remittance per earning migrant channelled to other urban centres, the highest amount is accounted for by the maintenance of relatives in the recipient areas (Rs. 402), followed by dowry (Rs. 284), personal consumption and fare during visits (Rs. 195), education (Rs. 170), gift (Rs. 108), construction and improvement of residential buildings (Rs. 88), finance for self-employed occupations (Rs. 67), medical treatment (Rs. 26) and purchase of land (Rs. 13).

The remittance received by rural areas (Table 5.12a) shows that the highest amount remitted per year per earning migrant is for the purpose of maintenance of relatives (Rs. 608) followed by construction and improvement of residential buildings (Rs. 255), personal fare and consumption expenditure (Rs. 232), dowry (Rs. 228), agriculture (Rs. 186), gift (Rs. 148), purchase of land (Rs. 136), education (Rs. 59), and salary to employees in property maintenance (Rs. 4). The proportion of remittance money used for various purposes in the urban and rural areas highlight the same trend in Table 5.12b. Table 5.12a further emphasises the differences in the propensity to transfer finance by an earning migrant

Table 5.12a

Differences in the Propensity to Remit for Different Purposes by the Earning Migrants

Use	*Money (Rs.) channelled per earning migrant to*		*Difference (Rural minus urban)*
	Urban areas	*Rural areas*	*(in Rs.)*
1. Agriculture	6.62	186.07	179.45
2. Education	170.14	59.27	−110.87
3. Gift—festival, funeral	107.78	147.98	40.20
4. To finance self-employment	67.11	0.00	−67.11
5. Construction/improvement of residential buildings	87.76	255.01	167.25
6. Salary to employees	0.0	4.11	4.11
7. Litigation	11.12	0.00	−11.12
8. Daughter's marriage-dowry	283.85	228.53	−55.32
9. Maintenance mainly consumption expenditures	401.58	608.21	206.63
10. Medical treatment	26.80	15.20	−11.60
11. Personal expenditures, fare during visits	195.27	232.06	36.79
12. Religious practices/charity	2.80	42.52	39.72
13. Purchase of land	13.26	136.11	122.85
14. Savings	0.96	0.00	−0.96
15. Payment of loan	0.00	0.93	0.93

for different uses between rural and urban areas. The important divergences are:

1. Yearly remittance per earning migrant to rural areas for maintenance of relatives exceeds that to the urban areas for the same purpose by Rs. 207 possibly because rural relatives may tend to remain more economically dependent on adult sons or male relatives.
2. Yearly remittance per earning migrant to rural areas for agriculture exceeds that to urban areas for the same purpose by Rs. 179 as agriculture is a non-urban occupation.
3. Yearly remittance per earning migrant to rural areas for construction and improvement of residential buildings exceeds that to the urban areas for the same purpose by Rs. 167. This may be due to the fact that rural areas tend to have a greater number of temporary structures which need frequent improvements. Moreover one of the respondents indicated that he had recently invested in the construction of a 'pucca' room so that his son would be more highly valued as a bridegroom, enabling him to demand higher dowry.
4. Yearly remittance per earning migrant to rural areas for purchase of land exceeds that to the urban areas for the same purpose by

Table 5.12b

Relative Importance of the Expected Use of Remittance in Urban and Rural Recipient Areas

Use	*Percentage of total money channelled to:*		*Difference (Rural minus urban)*
	Urban areas	*Rural areas*	
1. Agriculture	0.48	9.71	9.23
2. Education	12.37	3.09	−9.28
3. Gift—festival, funeral	7.84	7.72	−0.11
4. To finance self-employment	4.88	0.00	−4.88
5. Construction/improvement of residential buildings	6.38	13.31	6.93
6. Salary to employees	0.00	0.21	0.21
7. Litigation	0.81	0.00	−0.81
8. Daughter's marriage-dowry	20.64	11.93	−8.71
9. Maintenance mainly consumption expenditures	29.20	31.74	2.54
10. Medical treatment	1.95	0.79	−1.15
11. Personal expenditures, fare during visits	14.20	12.11	−2.89
12. Religious practices/charity	0.20	2.22	2.01
13. Purchase of land	0.96	7.10	6.14
14. Savings	0.07	0.00	−0.07
15. Payment of loan	0.00	0.05	0.05

Rs. 123. This may be due to three reasons: (*a*) value of land can be expected to be lower in the rural areas as compared to the urban areas, thus enabling more people to invest in purchase of land; (*b*) land as an asset may be more important in the perception of the rural people because of its agricultural value; (*c*) in the urban areas it may be more convenient to purchase a house or a flat and thereby avoid the hassles involved in first purchasing the land and then appointing builders and contractors to build the house; whereas in rural areas such accommodation may not be available.

5. Yearly remittance per earning migrant to rural areas for purposes of charity and religion exceeds its urban counterpart by Rs. 40.
6. Yearly remittance per earning migrant to rural areas for gift during festivals, funeral, marriage of relatives other than offsprings exceeds its urban counterpart by Rs. 40.
7. Yearly remittance per earning migrant to rural areas for personal expenses and fare during visits exceeds that to the urban areas for the same purpose by Rs. 37.
8. Yearly remittance per earning migrant to rural areas for payment of salary to employees supervising or maintaining property is Rs. 4, while no remittance for such purposes has been reported from the urban areas.

9. Yearly remittance per earning migrant to rural areas for the purpose of education is less than that to urban areas for the same purpose by Rs. 111. This may be because education is likely to be less expensive in the rural areas compared to the urban areas; siblings are likely to migrate to urban areas for higher education rather than rural areas; and education is likely to rank lower in the list of priorities in expenditures in the rural households compared to the urban ones.
10. Yearly remittance per earning migrant to rural areas for the purpose of financing self-employed occupation is less than that to urban areas for the same purpose by Rs. 67. About 5 per cent of the remittance to urban areas seems to be spent to finance self-employment termed as 'business' locally; all of them in the sample being investment in establishment of retail or wholesale occupations like electronic goods shop, clothing and dress material especially sari shop, stationery goods shop, door to door vending of garments and sari and supply of miscellaneous items to different shops etc. On the other hand no specific reference has been made about the use of remittance for such occupations in the rural areas possibly indicating that such occupations tend to have a greater viability in urban areas where consumer demand is more diverse and higher. Moreover in the rural areas the remittance may directly be used for other purposes, but may release money for small non-agricultural occupations which might not have been revealed in the survey.
11. Yearly remittance per earning migrant to rural areas for the purpose of medical treatment is less than that to urban areas by Rs. 12.
12. The urban areas receive about Rs. 11 per year per earning migrant for the purpose of litigation while the rural areas do not receive any money for that purpose.

From the above discussion it is apparent that, though consumption expenditure is likely to form the most important component of remittance use, it is likely to be more important in the rural than the urban areas. However some amount of money is being channelled to construction activity and a lesser amount to agriculture in the rural areas. The former is likely to create demand for construction labour and materials in the local economy, but does not constitute productive investment. The effect of remittance use in agriculture will however depend upon the inputs used in agriculture in the recipient areas and will be discussed later, but by any account ought to be productive.

Occupation of Earning Members of the Receiving Household

Definition and Categorisation of Occupations Represented in the Sample

Occupation defined as temporary or permanent employment which earns a remuneration in cash or kind has been divided into two broad categories with further subdivisions as given below:

Agricultural production employment: This broad category has been divided into the following sub-groups:

1. Owner of agricultural land which provides an income to the owner and the cultivation may be done by: (*a*) family labour; (*b*) agricultural wage labour; (*c*) a sharecropper.
2. Agricultural wage labour which in turn gets paid in cash or kind by the landholder-employer (the inputs are provided by the landholder).
3. Sharecropper who partly or wholly provides the inputs and the total product is shared by the sharecropper and the landholder, the ratio being determined by previous formal or informal negotiations based on the ratio of inputs provided by the two parties (the landholder provides land as the most important input).

Non-agricultural employment: This category includes production and distribution of non-agricultural commodities and various services and has been subdivided into the following subgroups:

1. Employees of specific employers especially formal organisations this group includes those employed by the owner of a business unit engaged in the production and distribution of secondary and tertiary commodities or distribution of primary products; the remuneration is in the form of monthly payment of wage.
2. Self-employed people who have no fixed and specific employer—this includes owner of a business unit engaged in production and distribution of secondary and tertiary goods and services and distribution of primary goods; the remuneration is not fixed and is in the form of piece rate. This group is further subdivided into the following sub-groups: (*a*) Shop-owner, wholesaler, hotel-owner; (*b*) Petty manufacturer—mason, blacksmith, painter, plumber, carpenter, sweet-maker, bandplayer, repairer, handicrafts manufacturer, spinning and weaving, tending to thread, reeling of yarn, *biri* making (major types provided by the responses); (*c*) Petty trader with no fixed outlet—seller,

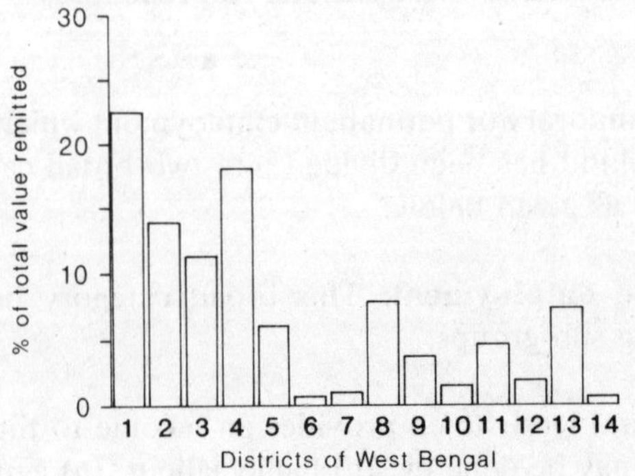

Percentage Distribution of Remittances
in the Districts of West Bengal
Fig. No. 5.04a

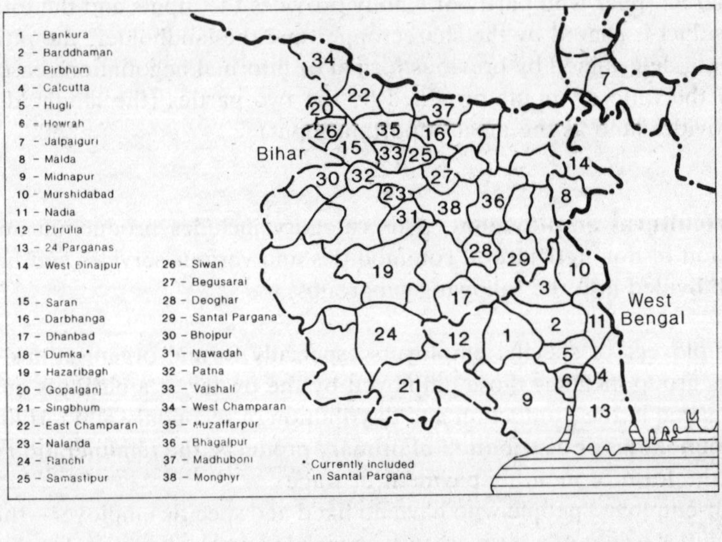

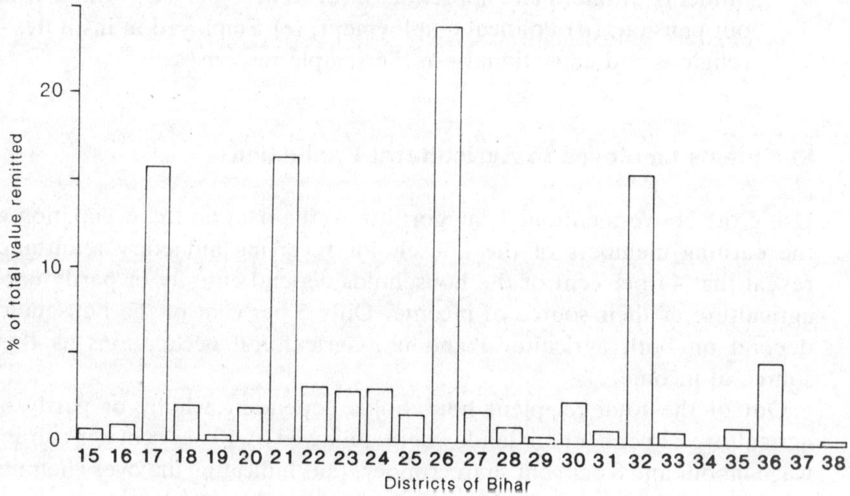

Percentage Distribution of Remittances in the Districts of Bihar

Fig. No. 5.04b

dealer, supply agent;[9] (*d*) Personal services—*dhobi* (person who runs informal laundry), tailor, porter, priest, *pir*, astrologer; (*e*) Rickshaw puller and van puller; (*f*) Taxi, *tempo*, auto-rickshaw, and lorry driver and someone engaged in transport business;[10] (*g*) Rentiers who earn an income by renting out accommodation; (*h*) Casual labour including construction labour with no benefits other than daily payments and in different types of jobs; (*i*) Contractor who is a middleman who takes large contracts from registered firms for supply of labour for particular jobs including construction jobs.

3. Contractor labour i.e., labour for different activities hired by contractors for a specified period of time or job receive benefits other than daily wages, for example, paid holidays, contributory provident fund, bonus etc. They are referred to as 'perennial contractor labour' and get employment either with the same contractor or same firm. Hence they enjoy a type of semi-guarantee of employment.

[9] Some respondents did not specify shop-ownership and have been included in this category.

[10] 'Rickshaw' puller, 'van' puller, driver of taxi, 'tempo' 'auto-rickshaw' and lorry as well as someone engaged in transport business include people who use own or hired vehicles; own vehicles may be hired out in transport business.

4. Others which includes: (*a*) Professionals like doctors, lawyers and advocates—doctors may be employed in hospitals as monthly wage receivers, but as they usually tend to have private practice as a professional, they have been included as a separate category. This category may be considered as highly technical self-employed; (*b*) Students, trainees and apprentices; (*c*) Retired persons with or without pension; (*d*) Political employment; (*e*) Employed in institutes—religious and educational—in the sample responses.

Recipients Employed in Agricultural Production

Using the above-mentioned categorisation, the data on the occupation of the earning members of the households receiving monetary remittance reveal that 44 per cent of the households depend entirely or partly upon agriculture as their source of income. Only 5 per cent of the households depend on both agricultural and non-agricultural occupations as their source of income.

Out of the total recipient households depending wholly or partly on agriculture 82 per cent are landowners, followed by 10 per cent agricultural wage labour and 8 per cent sharecropper, thus indicating the overwhelming dominance of landowners as recipients of monetary remittance compared to the two other groups (Table 5.13a). This suggests increased income for the landowners who can be expected to be economically better off than the two other groups. However it has been shown in Chapter 4 that a larger proportion of earning male migrants came from landholding households.

Table 5.13a

Control Over Land amongst Recipients Engaged in Agricultural Production Occupations

Occupational dependence of the recipient households	*% of total in agricultural production*	*% of total recipients*
Landowners	82.46	38.86
Agricultural labourers	9.84	–
Sharecroppers	7.69	–

Table 5.13b shows that 57 per cent of the landowners receiving monetary remittance are small farmers owning one to five acres of land. Another 26 per cent own less than one acre of land. Only 8.66 per cent of the recipient landowners have five to ten acres of land and 7.66 per cent own more than 10 acres of land. However this may reflect the size structure of landownership in the receiving areas, as the average size of landownership in West Bengal and Bihar is between one to five acres.

Table 5.13b

Size Structure of Landholdings of the Landowners Receiving Monetary Remittance

Size of land in acres	*% of total landowners who receive monetary remittance*
<1	26.47
1–5	57.41
5–10	8.66
10–15	4.40
15–20	2.55
>20	0.51
Total	**100.00**

Since majority of the recipients of monetary remittance have small landholdings as indicated above, there seems to be very little scope for mechanisation. 64 per cent of the landowning recipients seem to hire agricultural wage labour while only 26 per cent depend partly or wholly on family labour. 21 per cent depend only on family labour. 19 per cent have given some or all of their land to sharecroppers, whereas 16 per cent have all of their land cultivated by sharecroppers (Table 5.14). Hence a large proportion of investment in agriculture seem to be spent on wage payments to agricultural labourers which may imply demand for agricultural labourers and initiation of employment multiplier, though the rates seem to be quite low—Rs. 12–16 per day with food giving a monthly income of less than Rs. 500. Under the legislations on sharecropping in West Bengal the 'Barga' system may become increasingly important. The increase in the proportion of agricultural labourers around Durgapur in Barddhaman district as pointed out in Chapter 4 may reflect both supply and/or demand for agricultural labour.

Forty-six per cent of the cultivating households receiving monetary remittance do not invest money in the procurement of water as they depend upon rain, river or common facilities without having to pay anything. 14 per cent have their own ponds, canals, tubewells or pumps which might have required an initial or occasional investment for maintenance, but no running cost. On the other hand 42 per cent spend money either on purchase of pump water or payment of water tax for making use of government facility of tubewells or canals or hiring of pumps for short periods.[11] Thus approximately 40 per cent have a running cost for meeting the water requirement in agriculture (Table 5.15a).

[11] The percentage of cultivators receiving monetary remittances who have different facility of acquiring water with or without payment do not add up to 100 per cent because few of them purchase water or pay tax as well as hire pumps. Hence within 42.21 per cent the split of 4.55 per cent hiring pumps and 37.66 per cent paying tax and/or purchasing water are not mutually exclusive. Thus the total adds up to 102.6 per cent.

Table 5.14

Types of Labour Used by Cultivating Households Receiving Monetary Remittance

Type of labour used for cultivation	*% of total cultivators who receive monetary remittance*	*% of total cultivators who receive monetary remittance**
Agricultural wage labour	55.88	63.53
Sharecropper	15.88	18.82
Family labour	20.59	25.88
Wage labour/sharecropper	2.35	
Wage labour/family labour	4.71	
Wage labour/family labour/sharecropper	0.59	
Total	**100.00**	

* Percentage of total cultivating households using particular types of labour; as one cultivating household may use more than one type of labour the figures of each labour type is not mutually exclusive of each other.

Table 5.15a

Expenses Incurred for Procuring Water for Agriculture by the Cultivating Households Receiving Monetary Remittance

Expenses of procuring water for agriculture	*% of cultivating households receiving monetary remittance*
Yearly water tax, purchase of water at hourly or any other fixed rate	37.66
Payment of rent for hiring for short periods	4.55
Own means	14.29
No payment (rain, river or common facility)	46.10

Table 5.15b shows the relative proportions using water from different sources. Apart from the fundamental dependence on rain by 32 per cent and river by 5 per cent, pumps and tubewells seem to be most popular as 25 per cent use the former and 19 per cent use the latter. However 64 per cent of the pump users purchase water from pumps belonging to someone else at an hourly rate of Rs. 10–12; only 33 per cent have invested in the purchase of pump and are able to use their own pumps; while 18 per cent use hired pumps. Hence investment in pumps can subsequently become a source of increased income for those who can afford it. Similarly in the case of tubewells 66 per cent have to purchase water from others' tubewells or pay an annual tax to the government, while 21 per cent have their own tubewells and 14 per cent use common tubewells without having to pay (Table 5.15c).

Table 5.15b

Source of Water for Agriculture by the Cultivating Households Receiving Remittance

Source of water for agriculture	*% of cultivating households receiving monetary remittance*
Rain as only source	32.47
River	4.55
Pond	3.90
Well	1.95
Pond canal	14.93
River canal	5.84
Tubewell	18.83
Pump	25.32

Table 5.15c

Different Types of Access to Pumps and Tubewells by the Cultivating Households Receiving Monetary Remittance

Pump		*Tubewell*	
Method of procurement of water for agriculture	*% of total cultivating households using pumps*	*Method of procurement of water for agriculture*	*% of total cultivating households using tubewell*
Yearly tax, purchase at fixed rate	64.10	Yearly tax, purchase at fixed rate	65.52
Own	33.33	Own	20.69
Hired	17.95	Common (free)	13.79

Hence a large proportion of the remittance going to agriculture is likely to be used in the purchase of agricultural labour and water rather than mechanisation. Apart from labour and water, 42 per cent of the receiving households depending on agricultural landownership and sharecropping, seem to purchase seeds, 54 per cent purchase fertiliser and 49 per cent purchase pesticides. A very small proportion (1 per cent) seem to purchase or hire cows and ploughs.

Recipients Employed in Non-agricultural Occupations

Of the total households receiving monetary remittance 47 per cent depend partly or wholly on non-agricultural occupations including, trainee and apprentice. 24 per cent and 20 per cent of the receiving households depend partly or wholly on self-employment and employment under an employer in the non-agricultural occupations. Only 13 per cent of the receiving households have no source of income and consists of students (6 per cent), retired people with no pension (1 per cent) and households without an employed member (4 per cent).

Spatial Distribution of Monetary Remittance

State Level Receipts

Table 5.16 shows that only 2 per cent of the monetary remittance leaks out to countries outside India. 67 per cent of the remitters send money to areas within West Bengal, whereas 19 per cent send to areas in the neighbouring state of Bihar and 6 per cent send to the state of UP. These three states are the important contributors of labour force to Durgapur in the same sequence (as described in Chapter 4). In terms of value, 53 per cent of the remitted money goes to areas within West Bengal, while 30 per cent of the remitted

Table 5.16

Spatial Distribution of Remittances

States of India	*% of total no. of remitters remitting to areas within India*	*% of total value remitted to areas within India*	*Value remitted per remitter (in Rs.)*
Assam	0.17	0.00	100.00
Bihar	18.86	29.62	5592.07
Karnataka	0.50	1.04	7309.72
Delhi	0.45	0.12	946.22
Kerala	1.10	1.44	4628.14
Madhya Pradesh	0.32	0.06	500.00
Maharashtra	0.85	3.10	13024.62
Orissa	1.43	1.16	2898.90
Punjab	1.47	1.25	3047.70
Rajasthan	1.42	1.07	2675.07
Tamil Nadu	0.08	0.07	3250.00
Tripura	0.92	0.44	1700.00
Uttar Pradesh	5.63	7.15	4521.28
West Bengal	66.80	53.48	2849.77
Total	**100.00**	**100.00**	
Countries	*% of total no. of remitters*	*% of total value of remittance*	
Bangladesh	0.39	1.11	10123.96
Nepal	0.50	0.82	5897.22
India	99.11	98.07	–

money goes to Bihar, followed by 7 per cent to Uttar Pradesh. Hence these three states receive 90 per cent of the personal income transfer via remittance from Durgapur. However, the remitters to Bihar show a higher propensity to remit in terms of value as remittance per remitter amounts to Rs. 5592 compared to Rs. 4521 per remitter to Uttar Pradesh and Rs. 2850 per remitter to West Bengal.

Among these three states, the rural areas seem to get more monetary remittance than the urban areas, in absolute terms, in Bihar and Uttar Pradesh where the flow to the rural areas per earning migrant (in Durgapur), exceeds that to the urban areas by Rs. 281 per year and Rs. 189 per year respectively. On the other hand in West Bengal the urban areas seem to be getting more monetary remittance from Durgapur than the rural areas as shown in Table 5.17b, though the amount by which the flow to the urban areas exceeds that to the rural areas is relatively small, being only Rs. 44 per year per earning migrant in Durgapur. This rural bias in remittance link with Bihar and Uttar Pradesh can be expected because the labour force migration links have the same orientation as pointed out in Chapter 4.

The value remitted per remitter sending money to towns in Bihar is slightly higher than that to villages in that state as shown in Table 5.17a. A

Table 5.17a

Statewise Rural-Urban Distribution of Remittances from Durgapur within India

States	*Remittance to Urban Areas*			*Remittance to Rural Areas*		
	% of remitters who send money to urban areas	*% of total value sent to urban areas*	*Value per remitter to urban areas (in Rs.)*	*% of remitters who send money to rural areas*	*% of total value sent to rural areas*	*Value per remitter to rural areas (in Rs.)*
Assam	0.39	0.01	100	0.00	0.00	0
Bihar	15.12	24.84	5957	22.38	33.58	5405
Karnataka	0.00	0.00	0	0.90	1.84	7310
Delhi	1.08	0.28	946	0.00	0.00	0
Kerala	1.09	0.60	2000	1.15	2.09	6512
Madhya Pradesh	0.76	0.11	500	0.00	0.00	0
Maharashtra	1.89	5.75	11036	0.09	1.11	45000
Orissa	1.60	0.39	892	1.35	1.76	4711
Punjab	1.09	1.35	4500	1.80	1.19	2381
Rajasthan	1.92	0.61	1146	1.10	1.44	4688
Tamil Nadu	0.19	0.17	3250	0.00	0.00	0
Tripura	2.18	1.02	1700	0.00	0.00	0
Uttar Pradesh	3.48	1.85	1934	7.47	11.26	5433
West Bengal	69.20	63.01	3302	63.75	45.74	2585

Table 5.17b

Statewise Rural-Urban Difference in Value of Remittance Received from Durgapur

States	*Difference between remittance to rural areas and urban areas (in Rs.)*
Assam	−9.36
Bihar	16476.46
Karnataka	2067.61
Kerala	1831.86
Madhya Pradesh	−90.36
Maharashtra	−3688.86
Orissa	1643.33
Punjab	178.50
Rajasthan	1096.71
Tamil Nadu	−146.25
Tripura	−879.14
Uttar Pradesh	11095.56
West Bengal	−2640.61

similar trend is noted for remitters sending to areas within West Bengal, indicating that for these two states the earning migrants sending to other urban areas in the respective states, have a higher propensity to remit by value compared to those sending to rural areas in the respective states. On the other hand for Uttar Pradesh the remitters to rural areas in that state tend to send a higher amount of money than those sending to urban areas of that state.

However for both rural and urban areas remittance to towns/villages in Bihar per remitter is higher than corresponding figures of remittance per remitter to West Bengal (Table 5.17a). The amount going to urban areas per remitter to towns in Uttar Pradesh, is the lowest compared to that of Bihar and West Bengal, though the amount going to rural areas in Uttar Pradesh is the highest as shown in Table 5.17a. The above points indicate the following conclusions:

1. Remitters to Bihar have a propensity to remit a greater value compared to remitters to West Bengal to both rural and urban areas in the respective states.
2. The villages of Bihar and Uttar Pradesh are receiving more monetary remittance compared to the towns in these states; whereas the towns in West Bengal are receiving more monetary remittance compared to the rural sector in that state.

District Level Receipts

West Bengal: It is interesting to note that the district of Bankura, which has contributed labour force mainly from rural areas, receives the highest proportion of monetary remittances channelled from Durgapur (22 per cent) as shown in Figure 5.4a. This district ranks third (after Calcutta Metropolitan District and Barddhaman) in its contribution of the total labour force in Durgapur. The highly urbanised districts of Calcutta and Barddhaman (the latter being the district in which the town is located) account for another 18 per cent and 14 per cent of the remittances (Table 5.18a). Hence Bankura exemplifies a district where the impact of the remittances (if any) is likely to be felt in the rural areas. Since 44 per cent of the labour force from Barddhaman district has come from rural areas, remittances can be expected to affect both the rural and urban sectors of the district.

Table 5.18a

Distribution of Yearly Remittances from Durgapur to the Districts of West Bengal

Districts receiving remittances	*% of total value remitted*
Bankura	22.43
Barddhaman	13.95
Birbhum	11.35
Calcutta Metropolitan District	17.99
Hugli	5.96
Howrah	0.46
Jalpaiguri	0.89
Malda	7.76
Midnapur	3.62
Murshidabad	1.48
Nadia	4.50
Purulia	1.86
24 Parganas	7.26
West Dinajpur	0.52
Total	**100.00**

The two districts where the rural areas can be expected to receive large proportion of remittances from Durgapur viz. Bankura and Barddhaman are characterised by: (*a*) over 70 per cent of the agricultural labour force migrating from both the districts consists of owner cultivators as shown in Table 4.27. (*b*) While Bankura is characterised by a very high proportion of job-sought migrants, migrating labour force from Barddhaman consists of both job-sought and definite-job migrants.

Bihar: In contrast to West Bengal the highest proportion of the remittances flow into the district of Siwan (24 per cent), Singbhum (16 per cent), Dhanbad (16 per cent) and Patna (16 per cent) as shown in Table 5.18b and Figure 5.4b. Apart from Siwan (which had no representation in the labour force enumerated in the first phase survey), the three other districts have

Table 5.18b

Distribution of Yearly Remittances from Durgapur to the Districts of Uttar Pradesh

Districts receiving remittances	*% of total value remitted*
Saran	0.59
Darbhanga	0.91
Dhanbad	15.76
Santhal Pargana	2.18
Hazaribagh	0.27
Gopalganj	1.88
Singbhum	16.33
East Champaran	3.19
Nalanda	2.94
Ranchi	2.97
Samastipur	1.63
Siwan	23.79
Begusarai	1.79
Deoghar	0.90
Arrah	2.36
Nawadah	0.68
Patna	15.50
Vaishali	0.63
West Champaran	0.03
Muzaffarpur	0.84
Bhagalpur	4.63
Madhuboni	0.06
Monghyr	0.13
Total	**100.00**

contributed labour force mainly from urban areas in the respective districts (Table 4.32).

The most important district which has contributed the highest proportion of labour force from Bihar, as well as labour force from rural areas is Darbhanga (Table 4.32). It is interesting to note that this district receives only 0.91 per cent of all monetary remittances received by different districts of Bihar. It is characterised by: (*a*) out-migration of a higher proportion of agricultural labour compared to owner cultivators (Table 4.27), and (*b*) all out-migration to Durgapur as job-sought migrants.

Hence this district of Bihar (with rural out-migrants) presents a contrast to the rural district of Bankura in West Bengal in terms of receipt of remittances. If such a contrast exists at the aggregate level, when all remittances from all urban areas into the two districts are taken into consideration, it will be interesting to investigate their relative differences in economic development.

Table 5.18c

Distribution of Yearly Remittances from Durgapur to the Districts of Uttar Pradesh

Districts receiving remittances	*% of total value remitted*
Agra	13.08
Aligarh	0.14
Azamgarh	13.46
Ballia	5.83
Basti	1.42
Varanasi	1.52
Deonia	0.15
Etawah	30.82
Gazipur	12.75
Kanpur	4.72
Moradabad	14.00
Sitapur	1.68
Tehri Garhwal	0.42
Total	**100.00**

Implications of Money Transfer between Spatial Units

Changes in Purchasing Power

The most important implication of transfer and injection of money into the local economy of an area is the probable increase in the purchasing power of the recipients at the individual level and in the locality at the aggregate level (locality in geographical terms being defined in terms of settlement, district or state, at whichever level the data is available). However it must be pointed out and emphasised that changes in the purchasing power depends upon the relative rate of change of prices of commodities i.e., the rate of inflation and the wage rates or total income. Thus the following alternative conditions may result when money is remitted to an area which will also affect the demand for commodities and thereby affect the operation or non-operation of 'spread effect'.

1. If the increase in income caused by in-remittance is accompanied by a similar rate of increase in commodity prices, *ceteris paribus* there will be no increase in the purchasing power of the recipients in real terms, the demand for commodities will stagnate, the net effect being stagnant economic conditions.
2. If the increase in income caused by in-remittance is accompanied by a higher rate of increase in commodity prices, *ceteris paribus* the purchasing power in real terms will decline in spite of injection of monetary remittance.

3. If the increase in income caused by in-remittance is accompanied by no changes in commodity prices, only then will the in-remittance have a positive 'spread effect' in terms of increased purchasing power in monetary terms, increased demand for commodities, perhaps giving an impetus to increased production.

Though it is not possible in the present study to measure the rate of change of income due to in-remittance in the identified localities, for comparison with consumer price index, it is obvious that the absence of the existing remittance linkage would mean a lower level of purchasing power in all the alternative situations cited above. The effect would be conspicuously retrogressive in the first two alternative situations, with rising commodity prices as experienced in India. Moreover there may be regional variations in the rate of change of commodity prices as well as regional variations in the receipt of remittance which may affect the relative strength of 'spread effect' between localities. In order to have some understanding about the relative change in prices over time in the remittance receiving local economies, the consumer price index numbers for India have been used from 1970–71 to 1987–88. They have been calculated from consumption expenditure of three employment categories given below (by the Central Statistical Organisation and Labour Bureau, Government of India):

1. Calculated for agricultural labourers for different states of India, which is the only representative figure for rural areas;
2. Calculated for urban non-manual employees for selected urban centres in different states of India; and,
3. Calculated for urban industrial workers for selected urban centres in different states of India.

For this study the changes in prices in the states of Bihar and West Bengal have been focused upon, for consumption expenditure of agricultural labourers, representing rural India. For urban areas, the changes in Patna in Bihar have been compared with that of Calcutta in West Bengal as these were the two representatives of the respective states for the available values of consumer price index numbers for urban non-manual employees; the variation of consumer prices for industrial workers in Jamshedpur and Monghyr in Bihar have been compared with that of Calcutta and Asansol in West Bengal.

Figures 5.5a, 5.5b and 5.5c show the temporal variation in consumer price index calculated from consumption expenditure of three types of employment categories. The interesting point highlighted by the diagrams is that the increase in prices have been higher and more conspicuous in Bihar compared to West Bengal for agricultural labourers and urban non-manual employees. On the other hand, both the states seem to have almost

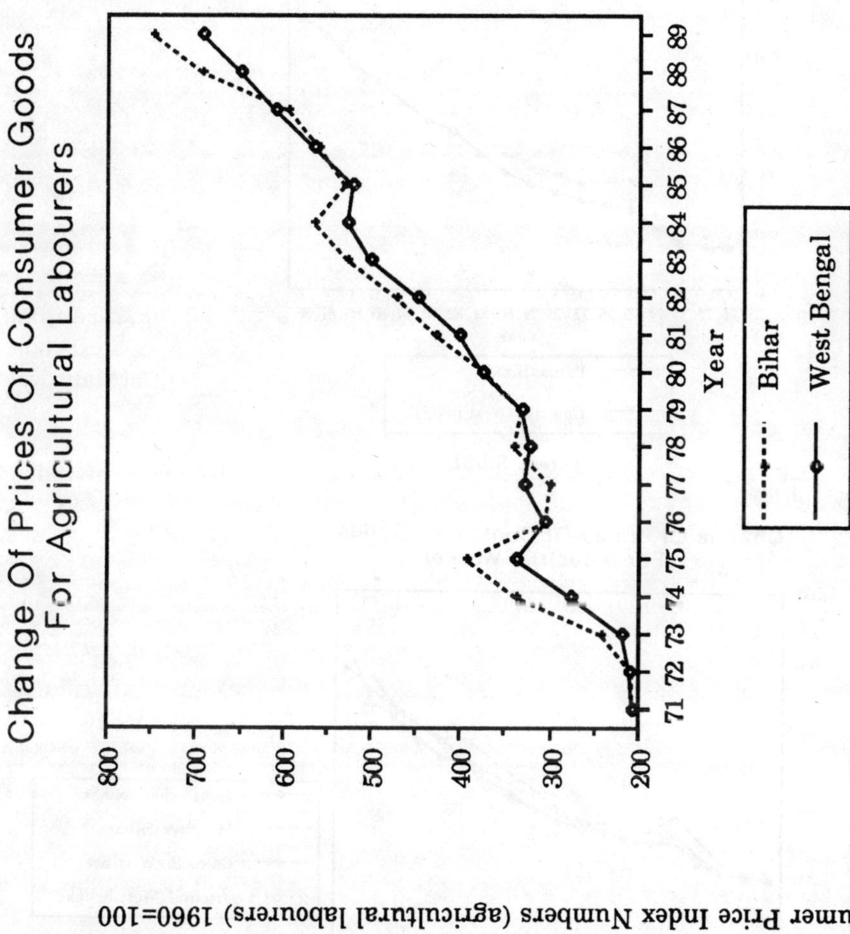
Change Of Prices Of Consumer Goods
For Agricultural Labourers
800
700
600
500
400
300
200
71 72 73 74 75 76 77 78 79 80 81 82 83 84 85 86 87 88 89
Year
Bihar
West Bengal
Consumer Price Index Numbers (agricultural labourers) 1960=100

Fig. No. 5.05a

Change Of Prices Of Consumer Goods
For Urban Non-Manual Employee

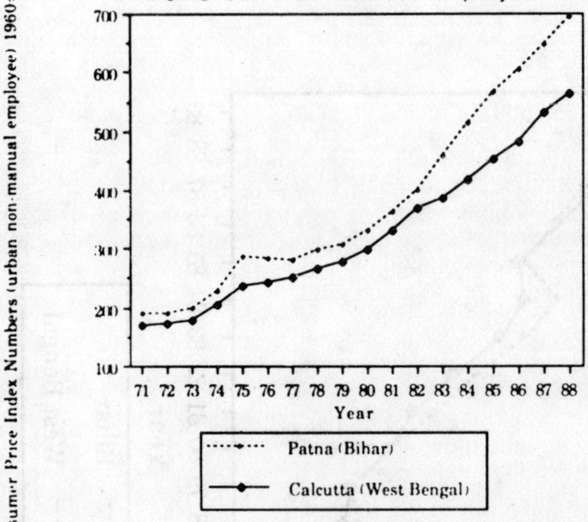

Fig. No. 5.05b

Change Of Prices Of Consumer Goods
For Industrial Worker

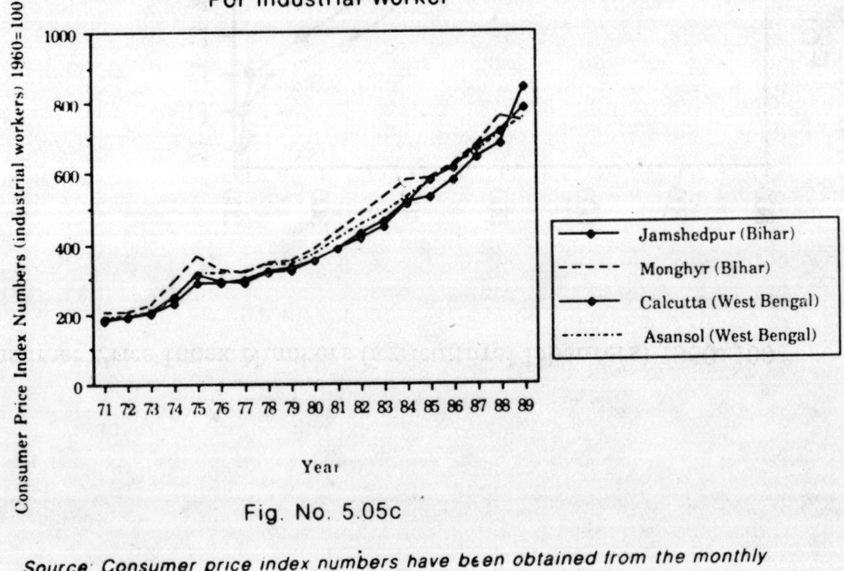

Fig. No. 5.05c

Source: Consumer price index numbers have been obtained from the monthly bulletins of Reserve Bank of India

identical trend for industrial workers. Hence for an equal rate of increase of income due to remittances flowing to agricultural labourers and urban non-manual employees of the two states, the impact on increase of purchasing power will be less discernible in Bihar compared to West Bengal. The survey in Durgapur has shown that the wage rate of agricultural labourers in remittance receiving areas in Bihar is similar or lower than that of West Bengal.

As pointed out earlier, though Darbhanga in the state of Bihar has experienced the maximum out-migration to Durgapur compared to the other districts, it receives very small proportion of remittance, whereas the districts of Singbhum, Patna and Dhanbad which can be expected to be more urbanised and economically developed receive the highest proportions of the remittances. That is the probable outcome of push migration from a place with high levels of poverty, when the primary gain of the area is in terms of consumption expenditure saved only.

Even in poverty-stricken rural areas, where increase in income may lead to increased demand for food items (as pointed out in Chapter 2), if local consumption increases then demand will have to be met in either of the following ways:

1. Increase in local production which will require increased investment. On the assumption that demand for agricultural products in the urban sector remains constant, the question that will be posed is what will be the source of investment?
2. If the local production fails to change, then release of surpluses to the urban and rural sector will be as follows: (*a*) If the rural area is well-connected to urban markets offering higher prices then the increased local demand will cause local price to rise provided the government does not interfere in the price mechanism. This will cause absolute poverty to persist in the rural area. In spite of in-remittance to the poorer section of the community the supply to the urban sector will not be reduced; (*b*) On the other hand if the rural sector is not well-connected with the high-priced urban markets the producers will be tempted to earn ready cash by selling more commodity to the local population while supply to the urban markets may fail to rise or even be reduced thus keeping the food prices high in that sector.

Hence in neither of the cases will remittance lead to an increase of demand for non-agricultural commodities. At the same time as production remains the same no additional employment can be generated in the retail or wholesale sector. This may partly account for the failure of remittances to spark off growth and thereby have little or no positive spread effect in the backward areas with high level of rural poverty like Bihar (Table 5.19).

On the other hand if the increase of income due to in-remittance takes

Table 5.19

Percentage of Population below Poverty Line (1983–84)

	Rural	*Urban*	*Combined*
West Bengal	43.8	26.5	39.2
Bihar	51.4	37.0	49.5
Uttar Pradesh	46.5	40.3	45.3

Poverty Line: Rs. 49.09 per capita per month at 1973–74 prices corresponding to daily calorie requirement of 2400 per person in rural areas and Rs. 56.64 per capita per month corresponding to the calorie requirement of 2100 in urban areas.
Source: Planning Commission of India.

place amongst people who are above the poverty line, especially landowners in the rural areas, it may trigger off very little impact on the demand and prices of agricultural commodities. On the other hand there will be greater scope for investment and employment multiplier to operate especially in the agricultural sector in rural West Bengal where the land sizes are too small for mechanisation. Both agricultural growth rate and rice yield are very high in the district of Barddhaman in West Bengal which is also a highly urbanised district. Though the level of urbanisation and agricultural growth rate are low in the district of Bankura in West Bengal, the yield of rice seems to be high (Dasgupta 1987a: 282). Perhaps in addition to all other physical factors, the level of in-remittance into the rural areas from the adjoining urban centres play a part in their development in terms of agricultural production.

Implications of Money Transfer in Terms of Consumption-Income Multiplier

The concept of investment multiplier, first introduced by Keynes in economics, implies that an increase in income may cause an increase in expenditure and that in turn, will cause a change in income which is greater than the initial change in expenditure. The multiplier is the ratio of the change in income to the change in expenditure that it brought about. This was derived at the national level and was applied to changes in national income. The ratio of change of consumption expenditure to the change in the income gives the marginal propensity to consume. It has been shown in Keynesian economics that: 'The value of the multiplier is the reciprocal of the marginal propensity to save or, what is the same thing, the reciprocal of unity minus the marginal propensity to consume' (Lipsey 1983: 536).

Hence an injection of additional income through in-remittance in a local economy would mean that a certain proportion of it will be spent on consumption expenditure, which will denote an income for an additional number of people who will, in turn, spend a certain proportion of it on consumption expenditure. On the assumption that all the rounds of consumption expenditure take place within the local economy which receives the remittances, an initial increase in money value of income will generate an additional amount of income which will gradually converge. Therefore, the multiplier becomes the sum of a convergent series (Lipsey 1983).

An attempt has been made to obtain an approximate idea of the gross impact of remittances in the generation of income in the local economy by using the following equation:

$$\sum_{j=1}^{n-1} M_{nj} = E^*\left(\sum_{j=1}^{n-1}\sum_{k=1}^{q} R_{njk}\right) = E^* \sum_{j=1}^{n-1} R_{nj}$$

where M_{nj} is the gross impact of monetary remittances flowing from town n to all other areas (rural and urban given by j = 1....n–1), E* is the consumption-income multiplier, R_{njk} is the money value of remittances from town n to all other areas (j = 1....n–1) for different uses (designated by k = 1....q). Though the multiplier effect of the injected money will vary according to the use to which it will be put, it is not an easy variable to measure especially with the difficulties of obtaining detailed micro-level data. Hence for practical calculation, the consumption-income multiplier has been used for multiplying with the total injected remittance to have a rough idea of a possible impact of the remittance injected in the local economy.

The definition of the term 'local economy', for calculating the multiplier, depends upon the level at which the data of per capita income and per capita consumption expenditure are available. In India the data of per capita consumption expenditure in rural and urban areas are available at the state level (estimated by the National Sample Survey Organisation, Government of India). On the other hand with respect to data on per capita income it has been pointed out:

> Income of the resident population of a state measures the totality of commodities and services produced during a given period of time within the geographical boundary of the state in monetary terms counted without duplication *plus* the net income received from other regions. Adjustment for net income from outside the state is almost impossible due to the open boundary of the states and the difficulty in collecting the relevant data regarding interstate transfer of goods and services and flow of funds. Thus estimates of income accruing to the normal residents of a state which incidentally provide a suitable measure of their welfare, are not possible to compile with the present availability of data. The state income estimates available are, therefore, the measures of income

originating within the boundaries of the state and are appropriately termed as net state domestic product at factor cost (Central Statistical Organisation, Government of India, October 1980: S–11).

Hence the per capita net state domestic product has been used as a substitute for per capita income in the selected states.

These two variables are required for calculating the marginal propensity to consume. On the basis of the data on per capita consumption expenditure, per capita net domestic product and population of the states under consideration a multiplier can be derived[12] which can then be multiplied with the estimated value of the remittances going to each state to give a rough idea about the amount of income generated in the different states via remittances from Durgapur. The underlying assumptions of this exercise are: (*a*) The consumption expenditure from all the rounds of income generated by the remittances received is confined within the state boundary; (*b*) The marginal propensity to consume is the same for both the initial income and remittance income for all the people receiving the remittance.

Table 5.20a shows that the marginal propensity to consume has decreased in all the three states viz. West Bengal, Bihar and Uttar Pradesh in a comparison of two values derived from (*a*) change in consumption expenditure and income between 1960–61 and 1970–71; (*b*) change in consumption expenditure and income between 1982–83[13] and 1986–87.

This has automatically resulted in a decrease in the value of the multiplier for all the three states and by 1982–83 the value of the multiplier in Bihar has reached that of West Bengal. This possibly reflects the production levels in the respective states. This is well-reflected in the case of Bihar because it seemed to be a state where the value of the total private consumption expenditure exceeded the value of the total net domestic product in 1960–61 and 1970–71 as shown in Table 5.20b. It emphasised the

[12] $\Delta C = Ct_1 - Ct_2$ where C is total private consumption expenditure per year and t_n is time (in terms of year), n = 1, 2;
$\Delta Y = Yt_1 - Yt_2$ where Y is income (given by total net domestic product per year) and t_n is time (in terms of year), n = 1, 2;
$MPC = \Delta C/\Delta Y$ where MPC is marginal propensity to consume;
$MPS = \Delta S/\Delta Y$ where MPS is marginal propensity to save and S is total private saving between two time periods;
Or $MPS = (\Delta Y - \Delta C)/\Delta Y = 1 - (\Delta C/\Delta Y) = 1 - MPC$;
$\text{Multiplier} = 1/(1 - MPC)$
Deflation by price index is not neessary as the same deflating value for consumption expenditure (numerator) and income (denominator) cancels each other. The results are at current prices.

[13] The per capita consumption figures of 1982–83 have been multiplied by the estimated population figure of 1982 and the per capita consumption figures of 1986–87 have been multiplied by the estimated population figures for 1986. Population estimates have been done on the assumption that the population growth rates between 1971–1981 remained the same for all the three states after 1981.

Table 5.20a

Probable Consumption-Income Multiplier Effect on Monetary Remittances Flowing from Durgapur

States	*Marginal propensity to consume*	*Marginal propensity to save*	*Multiplier*	*Estimated remittance per year (Rs.)*	*Total income generated (Rs.)*
	With 1960–61 and 1970–71 data				
West Bengal	0.55	0.45	2.22		
Bihar	0.74	0.26	3.77		
Uttar Pradesh	0.83	0.17	5.99		
	With 1982–83 and 1986–87 data			*1988–89*	
West Bengal*	0.48	0.52	1.94	133917573	259838630
Bihar	0.49	0.51	1.96	74182177	145167938
Uttar Pradesh	0.62	0.37	2.67	17904558	47862681

* Remittances flowing into areas outside Durgapur within the state of West Bengal.
Source: Based on data from National Sample Survey Organisation, Central Statistical Organisation, Govt. of India, *Sarvekshana* Vol. IX and XII Ministry of Planning, India.

Table 5.20b

Difference between Total Consumption Expenditure per Year and Net Domestic Product per Year of the States (in Rs. at Current Prices)

States	*1960–61*	*1970–71*	*1982–83*	*1986–87*
West Bengal	2710.41	11223.28	24205.31	60110.29
Bihar	−4328.11	−971.46	975.47	29939.99
Uttar Pradesh	183.64	4245.70	24404.71	59913.68

Note: Negative values indicate excess of consumption expenditure over state domestic product.
Source: Based on data from National Sample Survey Organisation and Central Statistical Organisation, Govt. of India, *Sarvekshana* Vol. IX and XII Ministry of Planning, India.

fact that until recently Bihar consumed more than it produced and the excess consumption could possibly have been financed by funds flowing in from outside the state, perhaps in the form of in-remittance from its labour force which has migrated to areas outside the state. However, the values for 1982–83 and 1986–87 highlight a more optimistic trend because Bihar's production seems to have exceeded its consumption (as understood from the available data).

Under the influence of the state level multiplier values given in Table

5.20a the monetary in-remittance from Durgapur is likely to generate a total income of over Rs. 260 million per year in the state of West Bengal outside Durgapur and this approximately amounts to 0.15 per cent of the net domestic product of West Bengal (after excluding the contribution of goods and services produced within Durgapur).[14] In Bihar it is likely to generate Rs. 145 million per year which roughly amounts to 0.10 per cent of the net domestic product of Bihar, while in Uttar Pradesh it generates about 0.03 per cent of the net domestic product of the state. Though these percentages seem to be quite low, it must be remembered that this income is generated only within a few districts of West Bengal, Bihar and Uttar Pradesh as shown in Tables 5.18a, 5.18b and 5.18c. Hence these proportions may be quite substantial at the district level and a single town such as Durgapur can hardly be expected to provide a substantially higher proportion.

However it must be remembered that this gives a very approximate idea of the effect of in-remittance into an area under a number of assumptions as stated earlier. Moreover the multiplier may vary from area to area at a smaller and local level than the state. Under the data limitations, (which is a natural phenomenon in a very large country like India), attempt has been made in this study to use the available data in the best possible way.

Concluding Remarks

This chapter has shown that there is a substantial development of remittance linkage from this new town via the migrants especially the male migrants. Though the female earning migrants have comparable propensity to remit, the low participation of females in the labour force limits their role in the transfer of money as remittance. Therefore both the studies in Ludhiana and Durgapur seem to indicate that towns having a higher proportion of female migrants can be expected to have a lower potential to develop remittance linkages. The villages receiving low or negative remittances in the 1950s and 1960s in Rajasthan and Tamil Nadu, highlighted by Lipton, seem to be located in parts of India, characterised by the development of Low Migration Towns mostly dominated by female migrants as shown in Chapter 3.

Contrary to Lipton's view only 4 per cent of the migrants in Durgapur seem to be receiving remittances from rural areas. The net remittance from

[14] Durgapur's goods and services have been estimated by (*a*) weighting the per capita net domestic product by the ratio of per capita urban consumption expenditure to the average per capita consumption expenditure, since the per capita consumption expenditure in urban areas can be expected to be more than the average; (*b*) then multiplying the weighted per capita consumption expenditure figure with the per capita net state domestic product and the total population of Durgapur. However it must be noted that the assumption is that the savings rate in all urban areas within the state is the same.

Durgapur to rural areas is high and positive as indicated both by money order record as well as the sample data. The net inflow into a particular rural area will however depend upon its linkages with other urban settlements which is beyond the scope of the present study.

Hence it seems that a linkage is developing, without perhaps having a discernible spread effect of growth of purchasing power and production in all the receiving areas. That however may be due to inflation which can prevent the growth of purchasing power in real terms. Such inflation may result from bottlenecks in other types of linkages highlighted by Rothermund (1980) and discussed in the next chapter. Hence more attention should be given to the price mechanism (which in turn is related to international terms of trade, money supply, mismatch between demand and supply of commodities, factor costs etc.). It is likely that there are variations in the degree of spread effect via remittances in different regions of India, closely connected to variations in the rates of price increase or inflation in the different regions.

In spite of the fact that in Durgapur at present the majority of the labour force has in-migrated from urban areas, the town seems to have developed a stronger link in monetary terms with the rural areas compared to the urban areas as 86 per cent of the total remittance (in terms of monetary value at current prices) is channelled to rural areas. However, compared to other towns which have a higher proportion of rural migrants as shown in Chapter 3, the relative strength of its link with the rural sector may be weak.

Amongst the various uses of the remittances, consumption expenditure, construction activity and agricultural production seem to be important. Consumption expenditure accounts for only 44 per cent of the remittances that flow into the rural areas from the town, unlike Lipton's evidence that it accounted for 90 per cent and data from Ludhiana, where it seems to account for 85 per cent. On the other hand investment in agriculture and construction which represents productive investment accounts for 23 per cent of the remittances flowing into rural areas from Durgapur, compared to 3 per cent recorded in Ludhiana. The definitional differences of 'remittances' in the different studies pointed out in this chapter makes direct comparison of figures unreliable. Moreover, as pointed out by Lipton (1980) there is not much systematic evidence on the use of marginal income derived from remittances which is a very difficult topic to study.

It seems that the districts contributing a higher proportion of owner-cultivators than landless agricultural labourers seem to receive the bulk of the remittances along with the districts which have higher levels of urbanisation. It is possible that this has an effect on the relative development of the districts. Though this partly supports Lipton's point that remittances tend to benefit the better-off, the majority of the remittance-receiving landowners seem to be small farmers with less than five acres of land.

However empirical data from one town will not be able to show the aggregate trend in the rural areas as they are likely to receive remittances from other rural and urban areas. Moreover at the aggregate country level, since the proportion of urban population in India is only 26 per cent, the aggregate figure for urban to rural remittance cannot be very high.

This study of remittance linkage from Durgapur only highlights the potential of an industrial town to develop remittance linkages with other rural and urban areas. When planning other similar towns this potential can be envisaged from the beginning and an attempt can be made to monitor the migration and remittance hinterland. This may enable the development of other supporting linkages to meet the increased demand for commodities which the remittance linkage can be expected to initiate. From the remittance hinterland identified for Durgapur it is evident that increases of demand are likely to take place mostly in the districts of Barddhaman, Bankura and Calcutta area in West Bengal. In Bihar, remittances from Durgapur are likely to trigger off demand mainly in the urbanised districts of Dhanbad, Singbhum and Patna. However Darbhanga in Bihar which has mainly contributed landless labourers receives little or no remittances from Durgapur. Perhaps this district represents an area where the remittance linkage at the aggregate level for the district is also poor and if so the policies undertaken for that area are bound to be different from those to be undertaken in the remittance-receiving areas. In planning, priority should be given to districts like Darbhanga which happen to contribute labour force, but do not receive any monetary inflow.

Lipton's arguments have been put forward from an aggregate and rural perspective and hence the local and urban perspective of this study is unable to either prove or contradict the theory about the impact of remittances at that level. As pointed out in Chapter 1 investment in rural areas in non-primary occupations (depending upon the potential of the particular area) is likely to create new urban areas which are likely to, not only absorb the local labour, but may also attract labour from other areas, given the size of India, degree of regional inequality existing in the country and employment characteristics of the urban areas being created. Even if Lipton's points about the negative aspects of migration holds good, such a process is inevitable in the real world and a knowledge of the migration and remittance potential of different types of urban units characterised by different types of employment opportunities is essential for planning purposes.

Lipton's argument about the low rates of migration to urban areas as exemplified by Calcutta (Lipton 1980) does not show the average trend because towns cannot be expected to absorb migrants indefinitely nor is it desirable that they should do so, as it would result in rising cost of civic amenities and congestion. In the Calcutta area concerted effort has been made to divert migration away to other urban centres like Durgapur and hence it is not surprising that the in-migration rate to that metropolis has fallen. That does not mean that investment in non-primary occupations in rural or urban areas will not trigger off migration with the consequent development of a remittance linkage.

6

Conclusion

The focus of this research has been to examine the potential of urban units to absorb migrants and to throw new light in doing so, on the models and theories of migration and new understanding on spread effects, particularly through remittances. Specifically it has highlighted the potential of an industrial new town to absorb different types of migrants in different phases of town growth. The Harris–Todaro model in economics emphasises the in-migration of the labour force, with the expectation of finding a job, and their contribution to the growth of squatter colonies at a theoretical level, and takes into consideration only economic variables while neglecting the effect of temporal variation within a defined space. In this study an attempt has been made to project values of the proportion of this type of migration in different phases of town growth in a post-Independence steel town, Durgapur, in West Bengal in eastern India. Usually this component of migration is not taken into account during the physical planning of a town and therefore this research emphasises the need to allocate space and government funds from the beginning of the development of a town in order to control the unplanned growth of squatters.

Second, all the new post-Independence towns in India have been criticised for failing to achieve the desired 'spread effect' of development in their hinterland due to the failure of the growth of the desired linkages. Contrary to Lipton's assertions, this study shows that there is a substantial development of remittance linkage from this new town especially to rural areas via the migrants as 86 per cent of the remittances flow into rural areas. Like Delhi, a very small proportion (approximately 4 per cent) of the migrants in Durgapur seem to receive monetary remittance. It seems that a linkage is developing, without perhaps having a discernible spread effect of growth of purchasing power and production in all the receiving areas. That, however, may be the result of inflation which may prevent the growth of purchasing power in real terms when incomes or wage rates fail to rise at the same rate. Hence more attention should be given to the price mechanism (which in turn is related to international terms of trade, money supply, mismatch between demand and supply of commodities, factor costs etc.). Moreover 23 per cent of the remittances to rural areas is being spent in productive activities like agriculture and construction which is higher than the figure for remittances from Ludhiana where only 3 per cent goes to productive investments. Only 44 per cent of the remittances from Durgapur is being spent on consumption expenditure, contrary to Lipton's figure of 90 per cent and Ludhiana's figure of 85 per cent. First, it must be remembered that Lipton's figure is at an aggregate rural level and, therefore, is different from the proportional use of remittances flowing from Ludhiana and Durgapur. Second, in the earlier chapters it has been pointed out that there are definitional differences in the empirical studies which makes direct comparison of figures unreliable.

It is likely that there are variations in the degree of spread effect via remittances in different regions of India, closely connected to variations in the rates of price and wage increase in the different regions. While the survey in Durgapur shows that the agricultural labourers of Bihar receive similar or slightly lower wages compared to those of West Bengal, the rise in consumer goods prices is higher in Bihar compared to West Bengal. Therefore, the rise in purchasing power due to inflow of the same amount of remittances to the respective states is likely to be lower in Bihar than West Bengal. Moreover certain areas like Darbhanga district of Bihar may be contributing migrant labour force from agricultural labourers, but may be receiving little or no remittances compared to other areas like Barddhaman and Bankura district of West Bengal which contributes labour force from owner cultivators and receive higher amount of remittances. It must be noted that Barddhaman is agriculturally the most developed district, which has undergone a 'green revolution' in agriculture between 1972–73 and 1985–86 (Bhattacharya, Chattopadhyay and Rudra 1987) and both Barddhaman and Bankura have high yield rates for rice. Perhaps this development can be partly attributed to the development of a strong remittance linkage of these areas compared to other districts of West Bengal. Barddhaman is a highly urbanised district and like Durgapur, the migration and remittance linkages of other urban centres of the district may be confined to the districts immediately surrounding the urban centres, thereby partly accounting for the development of the district. This is in accordance with Ravenstein's laws of migration according to which migration is inversely proportional to distance and it has been pointed out by Harriss that villages in close proximity to towns are more developed: 'those villages which have made most striking recent agricultural progress and are not "stagnant" are generally in areas traditionally progressive, and well endowed both with natural resources and with towns' (J.C. Harriss 1976, cited in Harriss 1976: 65). However to prove this point further research is required regarding the relative development of two or more districts on the one hand and the migration and remittance characteristics of the urban centres in the vicinity.

Remittance link development is likely to be lower in the hinterlands of towns which are characterised by higher levels of female in-migration and those which have been categorised as Low Migration Towns in Chapter 3, especially in areas characterised by low levels of urban/rural population potentials (indicating the absence of smaller towns). It is important to give priority to these areas for planning purposes and enquire into the alternative methods of increasing the purchasing power of the population. The rural-urban terms of trade in such areas should be taken up for investigation. It has been shown in Chapter 3 that the villages with low and negative net remittances cited by Lipton (in the Rajasthan–Gujarat area) are located in areas with a regional concentration of Low Migration Towns, most of them dominated by female migrants. A very different conclusion might emerge if villages are taken up for study in the regional enclaves of High Migration Towns in Maharashtra or south-eastern Bihar or Punjab–Haryana area. However as Figure 3.1a shows, towns categorised as Low Migration Towns, Older Migrant Centres and Stagnant Recipients of Migration seem to dominate the structure of the urban system of large towns in India. This perhaps limits the growth of migration and remittance linkages at the national level. It is a pity that data on smaller sized towns are not available to reveal their regional variation.

However Lipton writes: 'My partial evaluation certainly cannot justify anti-migratory policies. Yet it does suggest strongly that past and present policies are producing frustrated migrants, unintended damage, and few prospects that migration will often benefit the places of origin' (Lipton 1980: 16).

He however acknowledges (Lipton 1980) that migration is chiefly in response to deep-seated inequalities and rigidities in the communities of origin. Rural emigration is a response to decades of public policy biased, in both investment allocation and price manipulation, against agriculture. Such inequalities and policies, however, may vary from region to region within a country with a federal government structure. A theory at the aggregate level will be unable to solve the problems of empirical realities at the local or the regional level. Harriss has pointed out that in Tamil Nadu the terms of trade have shifted in favour of agriculture (Harriss, 1984), where till 1971 large High Migration Towns have not developed, though the high urban/rural population potentials indicated the existence of larger number of smaller sized towns.

In order to control the growth of population in large sized towns planning policies have highlighted the necessity to reduce in-migration to these towns. That can be effected either by increasing employment in the rural hinterland or by injecting employment-creating investment in smaller and new urban centres. It must be noted that injection of investment in rural areas for the promotion of non-primary activities, (which may be necessary, depending upon the local conditions of agriculture and commodity demand) may gradually cause it to become an urban unit. It has been shown that within the High Migration Towns those with higher proportion of rural migrants are associated with higher levels of rural poverty. In areas which are also characterised by high levels of urban/rural population potentials, a rural-oriented policy will be more effective in reducing migration. However such a policy will not be effective in the hinterland of towns receiving more urban migrants. In such areas alternative urban centres are required and this group constitutes most of the High Migration Towns identified in Chapter 3.

At the same time planning policies should give priority to the regional enclaves characterised by the development of Low Migration Towns. Especially when combined with lower levels of urban/rural population potentials, these areas identify regions where towns are not playing a significant role in the labour transfer mechanism. Increase of employment opportunities in the large Low Migration Towns may help to reduce unemployment amongst the indigenous population of the towns, but will fail to absorb migrants and will have little impact on the hinterlands.

In such areas attention should be given to the growth of small sized production-oriented towns rather than market-oriented towns only. Perhaps emphasis should be laid on low priced consumer commodities which will be readily consumed by final demand from the local population. It has already been shown that Bihar's aggregate private consumption expenditure exceeded the net domestic products in 1960–61 and 1970–71. Perhaps this deficit was financed partly by remittances flowing into the state from the migrants. The investment and linkage development have possibly improved in that state to catch up with the increased demand initiated by remittances, as the trend has reversed since 1982–83.

While assessing and commenting on the role of a settlement through the development of 'linkages', it is essential to question and define the term 'linkage' in specific terms and to distinguish between the actual linkage and its expected or realised effects at both the ends of the linkage in consideration. In this study, linkages have been defined in terms of 'migration' and 'remittances', which identify two types of hinterland viz., migration and remittance hinterlands. The expected economic effect on such a hinterland can be measured in terms of increase in purchasing power. There may be various types of linkages with different effects and the physical manifestations of the effects may be linked together to present the overall regional problem of 'backwardness'. However, in my opinion, solution of such a huge problem demands an understanding of each of the components of the 'problem', the linkages in-between the components in terms of socio-economic variables, space and time.

Rothermund (1980), while explaining rural stagnation in relation to rapid urban growth around the coalfields in Dhanbad has highlighted that bottle-necks and weaknesses in the interconnections between the linkages also affect the smooth functioning of the system. He has emphasised the absence of physical linkage and factors like caste, religious affiliation, marketing charges, ordinary and additional charges like bribes which affect the commodity linkage resulting in local differences in prices of consumer goods and isolation of small markets which affects the farmers. The lowest prices seem to have been recorded in the urban area of Jharia coalfield as the wholesalers could benefit from increased sale and then transport the surplus to distant markets because they had better means of transport. The high price differences confirm split market of which the produce-sellers and vegetable farmers are the main victims. The absence of an integrated market limits the market of vegetable farmers and their surplus products considerably. Price arrangements are thus primarily made when purchasing farm products and such arrangements are not made while selling the products, so that the individual wholesaler is free with the price policy.

He points out that the people of the rural hinterland are absent amongst the entrepreneurs in the coalfield, implying the lack of development of a commuter linkage, but a stronger link with distant areas indicating the development of a migration linkage. There seems to be a commuter linkage of industrial workers, but their investment in agriculture has played a marginal role. However this book shows that Dhanbad contributes migrants to Durgapur from urban areas and receives 16 per cent (highest proportion) of the remittances flowing into Bihar from Durgapur, though at the state level rural areas receive a higher proportion of the remittances.

Dienemann's study (1980) of mining and industrial workers in Dhanbad district in 1970 has shown that more than 77 per cent of the mine workers and 52 per cent of the industrial workers were transferring cash to rural areas. However only 7 per cent of the cash was transferred to rural areas within the district. Moreover more than 80 per cent of the remitted money was used for consumption expenditure. Therefore, at the aggregate level, the remittance linkage of the rural areas in Dhanbad district may be weaker than that of Barddhaman district and the investment in agriculture is also likely to be lower than that in Barddhaman district. Such low outflow of remittances into Dhanbad from the mining and industrial workers in the district exists in spite of the fact that the district accounts for two-thirds of the employees. The study also shows that the pay-scales of employees from Dhanbad district in the industrial sector are conspicuously below average (possibly due to qualificational differences) and compared to the migrants from Uttar Pradesh a smaller number of migrants are single-member households.

All these studies highlight the necessity to study migration and remittance linkages in detail and correlate their effect on consumer goods' prices at the local level.

Lipton suggests the following three ways to correct inequities in the field of migration: (*a*) rural labour exchanges and loans to permit the acquisition of simple skills usable elsewhere, (*b*) transport to, and temporary homes in remote rural areas with different seasonal labour peaks, and (*c*) redistribution of control over rural land and capital, which would reduce both migration and the maldistribution of such rural benefits as it may bring. Rural labour exchanges suggest identification of priority areas, what type of labour and what type of 'skills usable elsewhere'. The second point about 'transport to' also has a spatial dimension as policies will have to determine 'from where' and 'to where'.

Perhaps the migration and remittance linkages of Durgapur suggest a need for a deeper enquiry into the problems and potentials of Darbhanga district in Bihar. On the other hand, investigation should be carried on about the wage rates, labour demand and labour supply in the agricultural and non-agricultural areas of the districts which receive higher amounts of remittances via the landholders, for example, Barddhaman and Bankura. It has been pointed out that the incidence of agricultural labour has increased in the Barddhaman district, but this may not represent an excess of labour supply. Such an increase may have resulted from an increase in demand for labour due to remittances being used to hire labour, especially in small holdings where mechanisation is not feasible. It has been shown in Chapter 5 that the bulk of the landholders receiving monetary remittance are small farmers having less than five acres of land.

On the basis of the findings of the enquiries regarding labour supply, wage rates, demand for commodities, exchange of rural labour may be arranged, perhaps with Darbhanga. Though investment is required in agriculture and rural-based industries, at the same time it must be remembered that some of the commodities produced in the heavy investment urban sector are required by all countries for various reasons, for example, defence needs. The critical problem is to strike a balance between rural and urban development, the choice of importing or producing both producer and consumer goods within the country; emphasis to be given to the different types of commodities needed by the country in general and individual local consumers in particular.

This study of migration and remittance linkages from Duragapur only highlights the potential of an industrial town to develop migration and remittance linkages with other rural and urban areas so that when planning other similar towns this potential can be envisaged from the beginning and an attempt can be made to monitor the migration and remittance hinterland so that the other supporting linkages can be developed to meet the increased demand for commodities which the remittance linkage can be expected to initiate. India has different types of towns which can be expected to have different types of migration and remittance linkages. Compared to Durgapur, the other steel towns of eastern and central India viz., Jamshedpur, Bokaro, Rourkela and Bhilai seemed to have a higher proportion of rural migrants (according to 1971 data) and consequently they can be expected to have a stronger linkage with the rural areas than does Durgapur. It is necessary to understand which type of town has what type of remittance linkage so that it will be possible to estimate the demand which such a linkage can generate after the inception of the urban units.

As pointed out in Chapter 2 if the linkage is with people below the poverty line, the demand for food is likely to increase, while if it is mainly with people above the poverty line and landholders, the consumer demand will have a different structure. While the migration linkage of Durgapur with Darbhanga has possibly failed to initiate demand for commodities, especially non-food items, there is a possibility that it has partly contributed to an increase in demand for consumer goods in Barddhaman district. Though micro-level village studies have been made on changes in consumption expenditure in Barddhaman, Birbhum and Purulia, they have mainly monitored changes between 1972–73 and 1985–86. In order to understand the impact of remittances on initiation of demand for commodities, comparison should be made with consumption expenditures that prevailed in the 1950s (prior to the development of Durgapur and associated growth of urban employment and remittance linkages in the district). It might be possible to train and transfer labour to different productive sectors and spatial units depending upon the trend of local demand for commodities.

This study emphasises the role that remittances can play in initiating demand for commodities which in ideal conditions should lead to increase in production and other types of linkages, which in turn should increase employment, purchasing power and demand until the income elasticity of demand for different types of commodity decline. However if there is a bottle-neck in the other types of physical, commodity and service linkages due to various factors, which may prevent the increase of production and availability of the desired commodity, inflation will result and the spread effect will not materialise. The inflationary forces unleashed in Kerala has been partly attributed to the increased demand for commodities brought about by the inflow of remittances from Gulf countries (Rigg 1990; Amjad 1989).

Harriss (1984) in her study on commodity linkages of Arni in south India has estimated that about Rs. 50 million was paid to rural dwellers as wages by business units in Arni (thus implying transfer of capital via commuters) and only 20 per cent of the businessmen of Arni, owning agricultural land, have invested in agriculture (the average size of landholding being 7.5 acres). On the basis of this she has remarked that the 'town does have generative functions in relation to its hinterland—*pace* Mellor's proposition—these have not developed primarily as a result of the expansion of agricultural production in the region' (Harriss 1984: 99).

Mellor's argument was as follows. Increased agricultural production, based on cost decreasing technology can make net additions to national income. This income will accrue to large cultivators, who tend to spend a large percentage of it on non-agricultural commodities. The consumer goods industries stimulated by rising rural incomes are likely to be relatively labour intensive compared to the capital intensive producer goods industries (Mellor 1976). Thus increased agricultural production by the wealthier landowning classes generates demand for more non-agricultural production and so brings about increased employment. The expanded employment of the lower income labouring classes, who spend the bulk of their increased incomes on food, provides the demand for further increases in food production. The strategy calls for an industrial policy which conserves capital which is made available for agricultural investment and taps new sources of savings. It would facilitate expansion of consumer goods production and encourage decentralised small-scale industry.

Harriss (1984) emphasised in her empirical study of Arni that the initial increase in demand was not the result of expansion of agricultural production as envisaged by Mellor, but the result of flow of capital via the urban wage-earners residing in the rural areas. However she did not estimate the possible transfer of finance as remittances sent by migrants. Perhaps this small town in Tamil Nadu did not have a high proportion of migrant labour force like Durgapur. In towns like Durgapur with high labour absorption capacity, remittances might play a greater part in initiating an increase in demand in the rural hinterland. Contrary to Mellor's proposition the remittance linkage from Durgapur seem to be channelling finance to small farmers whose scope for investment in agriculture is limited to purchase of water, seeds, fertiliser and hire of labour. If the consequent agricultural production does not produce a marketable surplus to generate profit for re-investment, then the agricultural production will be sustained only in the short run when the remittance linkage exists. Moreover the small land-holders may not belong to an income level where the income elasticity of demand for non-agricultural commodities is high. Hence the demand for commodities may not register drastic changes as envisaged by Mellor. The hired labour may however create demand for food. Therefore attention has to be given to innovation of new agricultural technology or double-cropping which are likely to create agricultural surplus for marketing.

It has been shown that in spite of the green revolution in agriculture in Barddhaman district between 1972–73 and 1975–76 the per capita consumption of cereals stagnated and was roughly equal to the districts of Purulia and Birbhum (Bhattacharya, Chattopadhyay, Rudra 1987). The other food items show a similar trend of stagnation in all the studied districts. In consumption of non-food items Barddhaman ranks first followed by Birbhum and Purulia and there has been an increase over time in all the districts. Increase has mainly been noted in clothing and footwear in all the districts and medicine has increased in Barddhaman. Amongst consumer durables considerable increase has taken place in the consumption of non-traditional items like radio, torch, wrist-watch, bicycle, stainless steel dining plates though district-wise break-ups are not given. The white-collar class has largely responded to incorporate the non-traditional items in their consumption patterns. Acquisition of these items increases as land possessed by households increases, except for torch lights which are in demand amongst all types of people. The overall per capita consumption seems to be low for all items and according to the authors the picture seems to be dismal.

However as pointed out earlier such stagnation may not be attributable to the lack of operation of spread effect via remittances as the observed consumption levels in Barddhaman may be higher than the level prevalent prior to the development of remittance linkage, which cannot be investigated with the available data. Moreover income level is not the only determinant of consumption which may also depend upon availability of commodities at low prices as well as the value system in the society which may affect the pattern of desired demand. Harriss writes:

> in those areas where irrespective of social inequalities, there are significant rural-urban differences in average effective demand, it has been found that towns to a large extent serve and are served by other towns and to a small extent serve and are served by those elements in the rural 'hinterlands' who can afford to avail themselves of urban facilities (Harriss 1975, cited in Harriss 1976).

In Arni Harriss (1984) has pointed out a similar increase in the consumption of non-traditional commodities like cold drinks, poultry eggs, cosmetics, ready-made goods and steel furniture. Unlike rural Bengal there has been an increase in the consumption of a wide range of consumer plastics which may reflect the local taste and their value system. These products are mainly procured from the big cities and therefore Mellor's concept of decentralised production has not materialised. Rothermund's study in Dhanbad has also shown that the trade of food items is handled by large wholesalers who have links with distant markets and supply areas, which therefore limits the market for local products. However Harriss thinks that in an open market economy: 'our study clearly supports the view that the urban centre of Arni is "parasitic" rather than "generative" . . . there must be no illusions about the practical and political difficulties involved in implementing a policy of small scale industrialisation for the production mainly of consumer goods' (Harriss 1984: 100).

In Durgapur the 'parasitic' role may be partly offset by the flow of remittances by both migrants and commuters, though the net effect of all types of flow is yet to be studied. In West Bengal an attempt has been made to introduce spinning and weaving of cotton saris, garments etc., in the rural areas, though detailed study of such projects do not exist. Lipton's argument that remittances are used to finance education which leads to out-migration of bright, young people from villages (Lipton 1977, 1980), cannot be substantiated with data from an urban area study. However such migration can partly be offset by changing the structure of education so as to include subjects like agriculture, veterinary and pisci-culture from the primary level. Harriss has pointed out while criticising the 'growth centre' concept in India:

> If employment generation is regarded as politically expedient and morally good we face the problems that growth centres, to judge from the services to be provided (Pilot Research Project on Growth Centres 1973), will cater for the educated unemployed from existing towns, while the rural unskilled will only find temporary labour in construction (Harriss 1976: 265).

On the other hand if the rural unemployed are trained in the above-mentioned skills, they may become permanently employed in the agro-service centres which may be promoted in the new growth centres (rural and urban). This can diversify the employment structure and prevent them from vying for general urban education which only tends to create a glut for white collar low paid jobs as pointed out by Lipton (1968, 1980). All these multi-faceted issues are likely to affect the relative strength of the different types of linkages, thereby having both a short and longer term impact on the levels of economic development at the micro-level.

The discussion of remittance linkage shows that the impact of remittance linkage is likely to depend upon:

1. Strength of the linkage;
2. Its capacity to generate demand for different types of commodities which will depend upon: (*a*) income level and initial consumption of the recipient family, (*b*) knowledge of the range of commodities available, (*c*) availability of the commodity at the local level at attainable prices, (*d*) local constraints on the use of certain commodities due to historical, social and environmental factors together with the value system of the receiving household.

Increase of consumption expenditure due to inflow of remittances as exemplified by most of the studies is likely to increase the demand for consumer goods, which even if imported from urban areas is likely to give rise to trading activities thus implying the operation of an employment multiplier. However if remittances or the increased demand arising from it fails to increase production and income, then the positive impact is likely to be a short run one as the demand will fall once the remittance linkage declines. In agriculture, if the investment of remittances does not result in the production of a marketable surplus, the profit from which can be re-invested, then again the impact of remittances is likely to be a short run one. Remittance in order to have a longer term effect must be matched by increase of production which will lead to more production independent of the remittance linkage. Similarly increase of construction activity is likely to increase demand for construction workers and construction materials.

Do generalised comments (as given below) or quoted earlier in the previous chapters really pinpoint the structure of the 'problem' and the linkages of its components? 'In India the development of major resource industries, while contributing effectively to the government's import substitution policy, appears to have had little effect in slowing migration to large cities or inducing spread effects to the hinterlands of the new industrial towns' (Taylor and Williams 1982: 328).

This quotation has been taken from the conclusion of a book with an article 'Durgapur: Case Study of an Indian New Town' which focuses primarily on the physical planning of Durgapur and has no definition or investigation of linkages which can be expected to develop from a new town and their possible spread effect. Nor does that study investigate the declining population growth rate of Calcutta. There are no proofs that Durgapur which was conceived to function as a 'counter-magnet' to Calcutta in terms of absorption of migrants has, in reality, failed to do so. The fact remains that Durgapur has provided employment to a large number of migrants and Calcutta's population growth rate has declined to 4 per cent between 1971 and 1981. The authors can hardly predict that in the absence of Durgapur the migrants would not have flocked to any other large city in search of employment. Moreover this study shows that a large proportion of migrants in Durgapur have come from Calcutta. Such out-migration must have decreased the population growth rate in the metropolis of Calcutta.

The problem that arises is the same as that of any other newly growing town; it cannot be expected to function as a counter-magnet indefinitely nor is it desirable that it should, since it will then replicate all the problems which the planners try to escape in a large city and in an urban system characterised by increasing primacy. Therefore, after a specified period of time, since the inception of an urban centre, it is necessary to divert migration away from it.

Amitabh Kundu (1986) has shown concern about the decreasing mobility of both rural and urban population. He writes:

> The decreasing mobility of both the rural as well as urban population poses the major challenge for the development strategy being followed in India and the development perspective for the twenty-first century. The policy of unbalanced development if maintained despite this ominous trend, now distinctly visible can be extremely dangerous (Kundu 1986: 2008).

Though the proportion of male migrants from rural to urban areas to the total migrants have not declined between 1961 and 1981 at intra-district, inter-district and interstate-levels, the faster growth of intra-state rural to urban migrants compared to the interstate component suggests that the urban centres are drawing larger proportions of the migrants from within the states. He has pointed out that since a large part of the state has received a small share of the total investments and labour productivity in agriculture has stagnated or gone down, except in a few selected pockets, the intra-state inequality has sharpened and encouraged migration of people from rural to urban areas within the state. At the same time the interstate inequality in various socio-economic dimensions of development are noted to be on the rise. So he concludes: 'A slowing down of the interstate mobility specially for the male population on the face of rising disparity in terms of per capita income and labour productivity is indeed very alarming' (Kundu 1986: 2008).

Hence rural labour mobility is expected to respond to two levels of inequality: (*a*) intra-state; and, (*b*) interstate. The relative significance of these two levels of inequalities are likely to be dependent on: (*a*) the actual difference in the amount of inequality between the two levels, and (*b*) perception of that inequality by the migrant which will affect the expected rural-urban differences in earnings at the two levels.

First, if the inter-district difference is higher than the interstate one, then step migration is more likely to be confined within the state. Second, as pointed out by the author, the state level development activities may create new intra-state destinations for the migrants and deter them from migrating to other states with different cultures and languages. Third, within the already developed states if investment takes place in towns with large indigenous unemployed labour supply or in towns which have already received labour force migrating from within the same state, then the probability of finding a job on the part of a job-sought migrant is likely to decline. It has been shown in the case of Durgapur that 75 per cent of the migrating labour force from rural areas consist of job-sought migrants. Fourth, with increasing communication in physical terms, the migrating labour force may be more aware of: (*a*) the difficulties of finding a job and (*b*) perhaps a smaller difference in incomes in real terms as the expenses in the towns are likely to be higher and the rise of prices in all the states may reduce the relative advantage of a particular state in the perception of a migrant.

Hence the policy of unbalanced development, if carried out, has to be examined and implemented at both the levels. However, unbalanced development in terms of injecting growth in the advanced areas may be effective only up to a certain point, after which attention has to be given to the policies of development of backward areas. At the initial stages accentuation of unbalanced development may help to improve productivity and growth at sectoral and national levels, whereas with the passage of time emphasis should perhaps shift towards investment and development of backward areas with a close examination of their potentials and alternative possibilities. Moreover the pricing policies at different levels for different commodities have to be given serious consideration.

The statement of Taylor and Williams quoted earlier seems to be sceptical about the Indian policy of 'import substitution'. This is of course a large field of controversy, which does nevertheless have a bearing on migration, since the type of industrialisation affects the growth rate and labour market characteristics of towns and thereby migration itself.

As pointed out in Chapter 4, indicators like lack of electricity or assured water supply, lack of educational facilities beyond primary level, lack of irrigation and incidence of agricultural labourers (in the face of declining proportion of workforce in primary activity), persistence of subsistence agriculture in an area with poor soil conditions (as mentioned by Jagannathan 1987) do not indicate the characteristics of the linkages or their strength. Use of such facilities by the inhabitants of an area demands two requirements: (*a*) their provision by the different authorities including the administrative unit in charge of the particular spatial unit; and, (*b*) their use by the inhabitants which might require purchasing power of various types.

The lack of provision can hardly be attributed to lack of linkage of the area with the nearest urban centre. The effect of linkage directly comes into operation with regard to the second point. Hence while assessing the development of an area these two components have to be taken into consideration separately. However, it must be noted that economics operate within the context of space, time, societal norms and value system of the people and the above-mentioned indicators have to be judged with reference to the specific context, for example, in a sparsely populated rural area people may not be aware of the necessity of formal sanitation facilities and it may not present an acute problem of hygiene as a similar situation would in a densely populated urban area.

Thus this study emphasises the need for micro-level studies for local planning within the context of a broad theoretical understanding. It must be remembered that macro level theorisation, though necessary up to a point, will not be able to solve local level problems in a vast and diverse country like India. Practical policy implications need scientific collection of local information and formulation of local level policies suitable to deal with the local constraints.

Research is a frustrating exercise as it always tends to begin and end with unanswered questions! This study represents a very small part of a fascinating area of research and enormous scope remains for developing a model. As hypothesised in the first chapter different towns may develop different types of remittance linkages both in strength and characteristics which may be a factor behind regional development. It remains for future research to establish the hypothesis by testing it in different types of towns in different regions. However it must be remembered that the building of a model requires comparable data-sets collected with identical definitions, which in reality becomes difficult for individual and independent researchers.

Appendices

Appendix 1: Changes in Census Definitions

It is important to note that the definition of 'worker' in the census data has undergone a change between 1971 and 1981. According to the 1971 Census definition:

> A worker is a person whose main activity is participation in any economically productive work by his physical or mental activity. Work involves not only actual work but effective supervision and direction of work. The reference period is one week prior to the date of enumeration in the case of regular work in trade, profession, service or business. If a person had any such regular work on any one of the days during this reference period and this has been returned as his main activity the person will be categorised accordingly . . . . There are certain types of work which are not carried on throughout the year . . . . A person's main activity should be ascertained with reference to such work, in last one year even if he was not economically active in the week prior to enumeration (Census of India, 1971, Series 23, Part XIII-B, p. 4).

In the 1981 Census workers have been divided into (*a*) main workers (*b*) marginal workers. The town level analysis in Chapter 3 uses nine categories of main workers. Main workers have been defined as: '. . . somebody who has done economically productive work for at least 183 days during the year preceding enumeration' (Census of India, 1981, Series 23, Part XIII-B, p. 4).

Hence the data on occupation proportions for 1971 are not exactly comparable with the data for 1981. However under the constraints of non-availability of analogous data, it has been assumed that the occupation proportions for main workers and marginal workers are not likely to be very different. The percentage figures can then be expected to give a rough idea about the type of changes that are taking place in the urban system. Amongst the nine occupation categories, three of them viz., (*a*) cultivators, (*b*) agricultural labourers and (*c*) livestock, forestry, fishing, hunting, plantations, orchards and allied activities, have been added to give the figures for primary activity.

Appendix 2: Questionnaire of First Phase Sample Survey

FIRST PHASE OF QUESTIONNAIRE SURVEY
(Question sheet to be attached with the answer sheets)

Location: Town—Durgapur State—West Bengal Country—India

Purpose: Identification and selection of migrants for the second phase of questionnaire survey.

Person to be Interviewed: Any Adult member of the household

Definition of household: Persons (relatives, servants etc.) who usually sleep under the same roof and take main meals from a common kitchen and persons who sleep in one place and take meals at another, should be considered a normal member of the household where they sleep. A lodger who occupies a separate room in the dwelling, caters for himself and pays rent should not be considered as a member of the household.

Answers are to be filled in the answer sheets attached herewith

Q1. Please give the names of all persons who usually live in this house (including servants, friends, relatives. Please mention Mr./Miss/Mrs.).

Q2. Was each member born in Durgapur?
If the answer is No (N) ask Q3.
If the answer is Yes (Y) ask Q4.

Q3. Did he/she come to stay in Durgapur before he/she was 9 years old?
If answer is No (N) ask Q5.
If answer is Yes (Y) do not ask any more questions.

Q4. Was he/she brought up in Durgapur until the age of 9 years?
If the answer is No (N) ask Q5.
If the answer is Yes (Y) do not ask any more questions.

Q5. In which year did he or she come to Durgapur?

Q6. Please can you give the place of last residence of the members who have answered Q5? (Write the names of the vill./town, district, state, country, its administrative status when you moved away to Durgapur if possible).

Q7. Please give the date of birth or age of each person.

Q8. What was the purpose of his/her coming to stay in Durgapur?
*W/J/E/D/O/T/R/M/A/Other (specify)

Q9. What does he/she do now or wants to do?
*W/J/E/D/O/T/R/M/A/Other (specify)

Q10. Does he/she receive any of his/her earning from employment centres located in Durgapur?

Q11. Please give the name of the concern in which he/she works. If no fixed place please specify the reason or exact job.

Q12. Please give the address of his/her place of work. If there is no fixed place, specify.

Q13. Give the designation of his/her job (for example, general manager, assistant clerk, cobbler, domestic cook, etc.) in order to help contacting in the place of employment.

Q14. Please give the name of the department in which he/she works in order to help contacting.

Q15. Please give your residence phone number.

Q16. Please give the office phone number of the household members wherever applicable (to help contacting them in the office).

Q17. If he/she is to be contacted in the office, is it necessary to have an appointment?

Q18. What are the office hours of each member (wherever applicable)?

Q19. Name the holidays in a week of each member please.

Q20. Which caste (for example, brahmin, scheduled caste etc.) does he/she belong to?

Q21. What was his/her educational qualification when he came to Durgapur?

Q22. What was his/her occupation in the place of last residence (for example, general manager, assistant clerk, landless labourer, tenant cultivator, owner cultivator of three acres/ten acres, cobbler, shopowner etc.).

* *Meaning of Letters*

W - hoping to find a job
J - employment
E - education
D - dependent
O - Office tour
T - tourist
R - refugee
M - marriage
A - age

Questionnaire 1

QUESTIONNAIRE SURVEY 1

Answer Sheets

Interviewer's name: ______________________________

Household No.: . ... Date: .... Month: .... Year: ....

Address: ....

....

Member No.: ...... Q1. Name: Miss/Mr./Mrs. (delete and use block letters please)

....

Q2. Birth Place: Durgapur? Y/N — Q3. Came before 9 years? N/Y

:

Q4. Lived till 9: Durgapur? N/Y :

Q5. Year of arrival (exact year or how many years back) ....

Q6. Last residence: Vill./Town............... District ....

State .... Proximity to ....

(imp. road/dam/barrage/lake/nearest town).

Q7. Date of birth or age: ....

Q8. Purpose: W/J/E/D/O/T/R/M/A/Other ....

Q9. Present occupation: W/J/E/D/O/T/R/M/A/Other ....

Q10. Place of earning: Durgapur? Y/N

:

Q11. Name of concern of employment: ....

Q12. Address of place of work: ....

....

Q13. Office Designation ....

(for example, general manager, assistant clerk, cobbler, servant etc.)

Q14. Department: ....

Q15. Res. Phone No.: .... Q16. Office Phone No.: ....

Q17. Office appointment necessary? Y/N

Q18. Office Hours: ....

Q19. Weekly holidays: ....

Q20. Caste: ....

Q21. Educational qualification (at arrival in Durgapur): ....

....

Q22. Past occupation: ....

Appendix 3: Questionnaire of Second Phase Sample Survey

SECOND PHASE OF QUESTIONNAIRE SURVEY
(Schedule A)

Location: Town—Durgapur State—West Bengal
Country—India

Person to be Interviewed: Selected migrant worker employed in Durgapur if concentrating only on the outflow data. It may be preferable to question only male members, but it depends on the proportions of respondents in different groups identified by the first phase of survey.

Purpose: Determine gross remittances flowing out of the urban centre and to determine the employment, income and family status of the recipients.

PLEASE NOTE THAT YOUR NAME AND ADDRESS ARE NOT REQUIRED. YOUR IDENTITY CAN REMAIN A SECRET. ANSWERS GIVEN WILL GIVE STATISTICAL INFORMATION FOR RESEARCH. THERE IS NO POSSIBILITY OF IDENTIFYING THE RESPONDENT LATER ON AS THE NAMES AND ADDRESSES ARE NOT BEING NOTED.

Answers to be filled in the answer sheets attached

Q1. Did you send any money/goods to places outside Durgapur in the last 1 year? Please fill in the tables attached herewith indicating the details of any transfer of money or goods. Monthly details are required starting from the current month in which the interview is taking place. The months go back to January 1988 (if the survey starts in January 1989). If your answer to this question is *yes* for any of the months answer the next questions please (all to be filled in the tables). If you have taken money/goods yourself please answer the section marked B in this question sheet of schedule A.

Q2. To whom did you send the money/goods? Please give the names and mention Miss/Mrs./Mr.

Q3. Where did you send them? Please give the address if possible.

Q4. Please give the age of the person to whom you send the remittance?

Q5. What is your relationship with the person to whom you send the remittances (for example, father, mother, friend etc.).

Q6. (*a*) What type of remittance did you send good/money?
(*b*) How frequently do you send back goods or money (weekly, monthly, quarterly)?

Q7. Please give the details of the goods/money sent i.e., the exact items, their value, intended/actual use (for example, buying food, clothes, i.e., consumption items, for farming, purchase of land there or elsewhere, land improvement, marriage, purchasing house, paying for house maintenance, paying for dwelling, pay off debt of others, pay off own debt, pay off his or her schooling etc.) and method of sending (by money order through post office/with friends or relatives/by cheque through bank).

Q8. Please give the occupation of the person.

Q9. Please give his place of work.

Q10. If work is agriculture indicate how many acres/hectares he cultivates in the table.

Q11. Is his/her work permanent?

Q12. Please indicate his or her income status.

Q13. Please indicate his/her family status i.e. the nonearning members who are supported by him/her

Q14. Please give me the names or relations who live in his/her place of residence.

SECOND PHASE OF QUESTIONNAIRE SURVEY
(Schedule B)

Purpose: Determine the family status of the migrant/migrant worker

Q1. Can you please give the following information about your family? Please fill in the table below.

	Age Yrs.	*Occupation*	*Earns an income/pension*	*Please give the names of their current places of normal residence*		
				Vill/Town	*District*	*State*
Father						
Mother						
Sisters						
1						
2						
3						
4						
5						
Brothers						
1						
2						
3						
4						
5						
Sons						
1						
2						
3						
4						
5						

Daughters

1 ____________________

2 ____________________

3 ____________________

4 ____________________

5 ____________________

Other relations dependent on you:

Other relatives living with you:

Answer Sheets of Schedule A of Second Phase of Questionnaire Survey

---

Interviewer's name: .... Household No. ....
Date of interview: .... Year of migration ....

Q1. Y/N

:

:

Person No. .... to whom the remittance is sent (write the name below):

Q2. Miss/Mrs./Mr. ....

Q3. Address (if possible) ....

or ....

Vill/Town .... Dist ....

State .... Country ....

Proximity to (imp. dam, barrage, river, nearest metalled road, lake etc.)

....

Q4. Age of the person .... Q5. Relation to you ....

Q6a. Type - goods/money (please tick). Q6b. Frequency ....

Schedule A

Q7. Please fill in the table below:

Month and year of sending	*Goods/money (exact items)*	*Value in Rs.*	*Intended/actual use*	*Method of sending*

Q8. Occupation of the person (give designation; if occupation is agriculture mention if he is landholder—employer/landholder own account/day, casual wage labour/long term wage labour/unpaid family worker/unpaid non-family worker/labour service tenant/cash paying tenant/other tenant/sharecropper part of family workforce/sharecropper, other type/other specify).

....

Q9. Place of work: ....

Q10. If work is agriculture please fill in the table below with how many acres of land does he/she own/cultivate.

Acres/hectares of land

Landholder—employer	Landholder	Tenant	Sharecropper (not family)

Q11. His job is permanent/temporary/mention for how long he has been employed.

....

....

Q12. What would you consider his/her income status relative to other members of the village/town of residence? Please tick below.

Very rich / Rich / Upper middle / Lower middle / Poor / Very poor

Q13. Can you indicate his family status i.e. how many nonearning members he has to support for their living? (for example, father, mother, unmarried sister, brother, son, daughter, servants etc.)

....

....

Q14. Who lives with him in his place of residence (including the number of servants). If you are a seasonal migrant mention who lives in the place where you go every year.

....

....

....

Schedule A

Answer this section B of this page if you took the goods/money yourself

A. Do you go back to your hometown or to visit any relative or friend or to any place you own a property every year? Y/N

B. When did you last go? .... (give month and year).

C. Where did you go? Please give the address if possible in Q3 of the general answer sheets attached herewith.

D. Could you please indicate the purpose of your going (harvesting, holiday)? ....

E. Did you take any goods/money the last time you went for use in the place you visit every year? Y/N

F. Could you please give the details of the items (goods/money) you took for gift/investment/spending in the place where you went? Please fill it in table of Q7 in the general answer sheets attached herewith.

G. Could you please give the value of the goods/money you took back and used there and indicate their use in the Q7 of the answer sheets.

SECOND PHASE OF QUESTIONNAIRE SURVEY
(Schedule A2)

Q1. Do you receive any money or goods from outside Durgapur?

Y/N

:

:

Q2. Please tell me how much money/goods you receive per year (please try to mention the value of the goods received).

....

....

....

....

....

Q3. From which town/village (please tick) do you receive them? Please give the names of the town/village, district and state.

Town/Village .... District ....

State ....

SECOND PHASE OF QUESTIONNAIRE SURVEY
(Schedule C)

Purpose: Determine the employment status of the migrant/migrant worker

---

Answers to be filled in Table No. 1

Q1. What is your present occupation, when did you join it and where have you been working for the last year/month/week/day (delete please)? Fill in the table below. Specify all types of income earning occupations that you are involved in.

Q2. Who owns the concern(s) where you work? What is your office designation and nature of work? If you are employed in agriculture mention if you are landholder-employer/landholder, own account/day, casual wage labour/long term wage labour, unpaid family worker/unpaid non-family worker/labour service tenant/cash paying tenant/other tenant/sharecropper, part of family workforce/sharecropper, other type/other (specify) in the column given for designation. Specify the types of crops grown in the column given for nature of work. In other types of occupation mention your official designation or occupation (for example, general manager, assistant clerk, cobbler, shop-keeper, salesman etc.).

Q3. How many employees worked in the place where you worked last year/last month/last week/day/other (specify) ....

Answers to be filled in Table No. 2

Q4. How long have you been engaged for? Please tick as appropriate.

Q5. Could you please give details about the contract of your employment? (for example, no contract/verbal/written/witnessed/drawn by a lawyer/other (specify) for column 2; and dismissal arbitrary/with prior notice/cannot dismiss/none to dismiss/other (specify) for column 3; and suspend arbitrarily/with notice/cannot suspend/other specify for column 4.

Q6. How often do you go to work? (every day/alternate days/once a week/other (specify), if the number of days of work/week is indefinite tell me how many days did you go to work/week in the last two weeks.

Answers to be filled in Table No. 3

Q7. Does your concern have a registration or license (col. 1), does your concern require any registration or license (col. 2), do your occupation have any registration or license (col. 3), does your occupation require any registration or license (col. 4)? Answer Yes/No/Do not know in the table below.

Q8. Does your unit of occupation has any of the following accounting system? Answer Yes/No/Do not know.

Q9. What is the function(s) of your concern (e.g. manufacturing , selling smaller agents i.e. wholsaling, retailing to individual consumers, teaching, etc.). What are the final products or services manufactured or sold (for example, steel sheets, coke tar, old clothes, new clothes, new furniture etc., graduates, engineers etc.).

Table No. 1 [Schedule C]

Occupation	*Year of joining*	*Name of concern(s)*	*Not fixed (give reasons e.g. casual labour or vendor etc.)*	*Owner of your concern (govt./private/self/ famiy partnership etc.)*
1.				
2.				
3.				
4.				
5.				

Designation/occupation	*Remarks regarding nature of your work if any*	*No. of employees*
1.		
2.		
3.		
4.		
5.		

Table No. 2 [Schedule C]

Job No.	*1 day*	*1 week*	*3 months*	*6 months*	*Till retiring*	*Other specify*	*Contract*	*Dismissal*	*Suspend*
1.									
2.									
3.									
4.									
5.									

	Regular/irregular	*Days/week*
1.		
2.		
3.		
4.		
5.		

Table No. 3 [Schedule C]

Job	*Concern has*	*Concern requires*	*Occupation has*	*Occupation requires*	*Audit*	*Bookkeeping*	*Other (specify)*
1							
2							
3							
4							
5							

	Functions	*Final Products*
1		
2		
3		
4		
5		

Answers to be filled in this sheet

Q10. Do you work fixed hours? (tick) Y/N
Q11. How many hours do you work per day? ....
Q12. Would you like to work for longer hours per day? Y/N/do not know.
Q13. Please give reasons for wanting to work for more hours (e.g. require more money/bored/pleasure/other (specify).
....
Q14. Would you like to work for more days per week? Y/N/do not know
Q15. Please give reasons for wanting to work for more days (e.g. require more money/bored/pleasure/other (specify).
....
Q16. Can you take the protection of the following laws? Please tick the applicable law.
Industrial Disputes Act ....
Factory Act ....
Minimum Wages Act ....
Provident Fund Act ....
Any other law to protect the terms of your employment (specify) ....
....

SECOND PHASE OF QUESTIONNAIRE SURVEY
(Schedule C continued)

Q17. Do you have any tools or equipment that you use currently in the work you do? Name them.
....
....
....
....

Q18. If answer to Q17 is 'yes' then answer this question.
(*a*) Do you own them yourself? ....
(*b*) Do you hire them from your employer or supplier of goods? ....
....
(*c*) Do you hire them from some other source e.g. a bank? ....
....

Q19. Do you have any working capital currently for the conduct of your business (e.g. cash, raw materials)?
If so, (*a*) How much is your own? ....
(*b*) How much is on loan or credit? ....
(*c*) Who gave the loan or credit? (Employer/supplier of goods/ bank/ friends/relatives) ....
....

Q20. If self-employed, do you have to pay for your place of work (i.e. rent for plot, bribe for pavement squat, tax etc.)? How much?
....

Q21. To whom do you sell your product or service?
(*a*) to the general public ....
(*b*) to one single buyer—and if so to whom (e.g. to your supplier of goods)? ...
....
....

Q22. What type of contract do you have for supplying your products?
(*a*) verbal (*b*) written (*c*) nil (*d*) any other ....
(*e*) Time period for supplying your products according to the contract ....
....
(*f*) What happens after that (renew the contract, look for new customers)? ...
....

SECOND PHASE OF QUESTIONNAIRE SURVEY
(Schedule D)

Purpose: Determine the income status of the migrant/migrant worker

---

Q1. Could you please indicate the type of earning you have and how frequently you receive your earning?

Job	Profit/Wage/ Commission/Piece rate/ Other (specify)	Daily/weekly/monthly/ other (specify)
1.		
2.		
3.		
4.		
5.		

Q2. What other facilities do you receive from your work? Please tick.

Dearness allowance .... Children's education facilities...............
House allowance .... Pension after retirement ....
Car .... Entitled to gratuity ....
Medical facilities .... Entitled to provident fund ....
Other (specify) ....

Has your company given you a bonus in the last 12 months? Y/N
Do you expect to get a bonus in the next 12 months? Y/N

Q3. Do you sleep at night at your place of employment? Y/N
Q4. Is the accommodation (sleeping facility) free of cost? Y/N
Q5. Do you eat at your place of employment? N/Y
Q6. Is it free? Y/N
Q7. Does your earning vary daily/weekly/monthly/yearly? ....
Q8. Could you please give your monthly income? Rs. ....
(if you do not wish to say the exact amount could you please indicate any of the range given below? Please tick)

Less than Rs. 75 .... Rs. 1001–2000 ....
Rs. 100 – 500 .... Rs. 2001–3000 ....
Rs. 501 – 1000 .... Rs. 3001–4000 ....
More than Rs. 4000 ....

Q9. What type of accommodation do you have? Please tick below.

Owner of pucca house .... Rented house (pucca/kancha) ....
Owner of kancha house .... Rented flat (pucca/kancha) ....
Owner of a flat .... Rented room (pucca/kancha) ....
Owner of a room (pucca/kancha) ....
Grade of company accommodation (if applicable) ....
Meaning or ordering of grading ....
....

Q10. Do you or your landlord pay tax for your landholding? Y/N/Do not know
Q11. What is the roof made of (from observation)?
Thatch/tin/tile/concrete/other (specify) ....

Q12. What are the walls made of?
Brick/plastered brick/tin/mud/straw/other (specify) ....

Q13. Is the house or accommodation owned one storeyed/two storeyed/three storeyed/other (specify)? ....

Q14. Do you have servants or cook or gardener etc.? Please specify and mention if he/she is permanent (i.e. sleeps at night and eats in the house) or temporary (i.e. who does daily work but do not eat or sleep in the house). Please give the total number of each type.
....
....
....

Q15. Do you have cars (if yes mention how many)? ....
Q16. Do you have bicycles (if yes mention how many)? ....
Q17. Do you have any other vehicles rented/owned (specify)? ....
....

Q18. Do you have the following items in the house? (Please specify how many).
TV ....
record player ....
cassette player ....
radio ....
transistor ....

Q19. What do you use to cook? Please tick.
coal fire/gas fire/electric heater/oil stove/wood/dung/other (specify)
....

Q20. Do you have electricity in all rooms? Y/N specify ....
Q21. Do you have fans in all rooms except kitchen and bathrooms?
(Y/N specify) ....
Q22. What type of toilet do you have? (flushable new type/flushable old type/non-flushable/no sanitary facility)
....

Q23. Does your house have corporation water supply to taps? Y/N/specify
....

Appendix 4: Occupation Types Identified in the Sample Surveys

Code	*Occupations*
1	Personal services—maidservant, servant, helper, cook, animal-keeper, gardener, Dhobi, tailor, porter
2	Petty manufacturer—mason, blacksmith, painter, plumber, carpenter, sweetmaker, bandplayer, weaving, spinning, tending to thread
3	Beggar
4	Casual labour, contractor labour, construction labour
5	Seller, dealer, agent with no fixed outlet of sale
6	Shop-owner, hotel-owner
7	Rickshawpuller, vanpuller, coachman
8	Driver, conductor
9	Owner cultivator
10	Agricultural labourer
11	Professionals—doctor, lawyer, advocate
12	Clerk, Head assistant, accountant, cashier
13	Chargeman, chargehand, foreman
14	Chemist, physicist, pharmacist, scientist, statistician
15	Engineer, assistant engineer, process controller, metallurgist
16	Administrative—Vice chairman, director, executive, manager, superintendent, administrator, officer, controller
17	Inspector, sub-inspector, verificator, estimator, surveyor, timekeeper, storekeeper, storeman, supervisor, salesman, station master, shift-in-charge, camp-in-charge
18	Personal assistant, confidential assistant, stenotypist, telephone assistant, teleprinter
19	Attendant, lab. assist., lab. attendant, peon, sweeper, messenger, unskilled shop assistant, canteen boy, conditioning assist., counter assistant, petrol pump filler, porter, cycle repair shop worker
20	Guard, checking vehicles, constable, police, security guard, officer, navy, fire rescue, defence
21	Contractor
22	Draftsman, designer, programmer
23	Mechanic, fireman, driller, pump operator, melter, fitter, electrician, furnaceman, technician, wireman, keyman, machinist, rigger, meter reader, technical, moulder, optical, plumber, plater, printer, yard master, master, welder, roadfitter, crane operator, asst. op. technician, washer, turner, setter, oilman, crane driver
24	Midwife, nurse
25	Teacher
26	Trainee, apprentice
28	Priest/pir, astrologer
29	Landlord
30	Student
31	Sharecropper
32	Subeditor, vaccinator
90	Income earner, but exact occupation unknown
91	Nil
92	Unemployed and searching for employment

Appendix 4 (Continued)

Note: Codes 12–23 include employment for the payment of wage on a monthly basis in specific employment units. Some of the occupation names are terms used in specific industries especially in the categories 13, 16, 17, 22 and 23. Casual and contractor labourers coded as 4 are usually paid on a daily basis.

This is a very rough categorisation to understand absorption of migrant labour force in different occupations as represented by the first phase sample survey. Further details regarding employment conditions were collected during the second phase survey, though they have not been analysed in this book.

Appendix 5: Major Manufacturing Firms in Durgapur

Abbreviation	Manufacturer
DSP	Durgapur Steel Plant
ASP	Alloy Steel Plant
MAMC	Mining and Allied Machinery Corporation
DPL	Durgapur Projects Limited
DVC	Damodar Valley Corporation
ABL	ACC-Babcock Limited
DCL	Durgapur Chemicals Limited
FCI	Fertiliser Corporation of India
PCBL	Phillips Carbon Black Limited

Appendix 6: List of Programs Used for Computing

1. Fortran programs of Q-analysis by Prof. G.P. Chapman.
2. Fortran programs written by me.
3. Statistical and graphics packages.
   (*i*) Minitab on mainframe.
   (*ii*) Excel (version 2.2) on Apple Macintosh.
   (*iii*) Statview (version 1.1) on Apple Macintosh.
   (*iv*) Cricket Graph (version 1.3) on Apple Macintosh.
   (*v*) Mac Draw II on Apple Macintosh.
4. Word processing package - Microsoft Word (version 4.0) on Apple Macintosh.

Bibliography

Amjad, Rashid (ed.). (1989). *To the Gulf and Back*. International Labour Organisation. Asian Employment Programme (ARTEP): New Delhi.

Asansol–Durgapur Development Authority. (October 1983). *Zonal Development Plan for Benachity and Bhiringi Area*, pp. 3–16. Durgapur.

Asia 1990 Yearbook, p. 6. 'Far Eastern Economic Review', Hong Kong.

Baker, Randall and **Barbara Harriss.** (March 1980). '*Urban Bias in Developing Countries: Two Views*'. Development Studies Discussion Paper No. 67. University of East Anglia: UK.

Banerjee, Biswajit. (1981). 'Rural-Urban Migration and Family Ties: An Analysis of Family Considerations in Migration Behaviour in India', pp. 321–55. *Oxford Bulletin of Economics and Statistics*, Vol. 43.

Barro, J. Robert. (1984). *Macroeconomics*, pp. 151–97. John Wiley & Sons: New York.

Berry, B.J.L. (1964). 'Cities as Systems within Systems of Cities', pp. 147–61, *Papers of Regional Science Association* Vol. 13, University of Illinois.

Berry, B.J.L., E.C. Conkling and **M.D. Ray**. (1976). *The Geography of Economic Systems*, pp. 477–84. Prentice Hall: New Jersey.

Bhattacharya, Nikhilesh, Manabendu Chattopadhyay and **Ashok Rudra**. (11 July 1987). 'Changes in Level of Living in Rural West Bengal, Private Consumption', pp. 1149–50. *Economic and Political Weekly*, Vol. XXII, No. 28.

————. (15 August 1987). 'Changes in Level of Living in Rural West Bengal, Social Consumption', pp. 1410–11. *Economic and Political Weekly*, Vol. XXII, No. 33.

————. (5–12 September 1987). 'Changes in Level of Living in Rural West Bengal, Housing Conditions', pp. 1559–60. *Economic and Political Weekly*, Vol. XXII, Nos. 36 and 37.

————. (31 October 1987). 'Changes in Level of Living in Rural West Bengal, Consumer Durables, Clothing and Footwear', pp. 1871–73. *Economic and Political Weekly*, Vol. XXII, No. 44.

Bilsborrow, R.E., A.S. Oberai and **G. Standing.** (1984). *Migration Surveys in Low Income Countries*, pp. 14–534. Croom Helm: London & Sydney.

Bourne, L.S. and **J.W. Simmon** (eds.). (1978). *Systems of Cities: Readings on Structure, Growth and Policy*, pp. 18–52. Oxford University Press: New York.

Buch, M.N. and **P. Pathak.** (1985). 'The role of the informal sector in the development of small and intermediate cities of India'. A Summary paper presented at The Round Table Conference on the Informal Sector in the Economy of small cities. 17–27 February.

Byres, T.J. (1979). Review Article of Neo-Populist Pipe-Dreams: Daedalus in the Third World and the Myth of Urban Bias, pp. 210–44. *The Journal of Peasant Studies*. Vol. 6, No. 2. Frank Cass & Co. Ltd.: London.

Census of India. (1971). *Migration Tables*, Series 1, Part II D (i). Government of India.

————. *General Economic Tables*, pp. 131–46, 487–521. Series 1, Part II B (i). Government of India.

Census of India. (1971). *General Population Tables*, pp. 237–79. Series 1, Part II A (i). Government of India.

———. (1981). *Bihar, General Population Tables*, p. 78. Series 4, Part II A. Government of India.

———. *General Economic Tables*. Series 2–22, Part III A & B. Table B3. Government of India.

———. *Uttar Pradesh, General Population*, p. 11. Series 22, Part II A. Tables. Government of India.

———. *West Bengal, District Census Handbook, Barddhaman District, Village & Townwise Primary Census Abstract*, p. 10. Series 23, Part XIII-B. Government of India.

———. *West Bengal, General Population Tables*, p. 79. Series 23, Part II A. Government of India.

Central Statistical Organisation. (October 1980). Monthly Abstract of Statistics, pp. S11–S19. Ministry of Planning, Government of India.

Chand, M. and **V.K. Puri.** (1983). *Regional Planning in India*. Allied Publishers Pvt. Ltd.: New Delhi.

Chapman, G.P. (1983). 'The Growth of Large Cities in India 1961–71,' *Geoforum*. Vol. 14, No. 2, pp. 149–59, Pergamon Press Ltd.: Oxford.

———. (1986). 'A Modern Theory of Classification: and The Question, Who is a Migrant?' A paper prepared for the workshop on Urbanisation and Migration, Office of the Registrar General of India, New Delhi.

Chapman, Graham and **Sudhir Wanmali.** (1981). 'Urban-Rural Relationships in India: A Macro-Scale Approach Using Population Potentials', pp. 19–43: *Geoforum*. Vol. 12, No. 1. Pergamon Press Ltd.: Oxford.

Chatterji, Ruchira. (1989). *The Behaviour of Industrial Prices in India*. Oxford University Press: Delhi.

Chaudhuri, B.K. (1988). *Administrative Report*. Durgapur Notified Area Authority. Durgapur.

Connell, J., B. Dasgupta, Roy Laishley and **M. Lipton**. (1976). *Migration from Rural Areas: The Evidence from Village Studies*, pp. 2–220. Oxford University Press: New Delhi.

Dasgupta, Biplab. (14 February 1987a). 'Urbanisation and Rural Change in West Bengal', pp. 276–87. *Economic and Political Weekly*, Vol. XXII, No. 7.

———. (21 February 1987b). 'Urbanisation and Rural Change in West Bengal', pp. 337–44. *Economic and Political Weekly*, Vol. XXII, No. 8.

De Grazia, R. (1984). *Clandestine Employment*. International Labour Office: Geneva.

Dienemann, G. (1980). 'Labour Force and Wage Policy: An Analysis of their Structural Characteristics and Patterns of Development', pp. 271–345: D. Rothermund, E. Kropp, G. Dienemann (eds.) *Urban Growth and Rural Stagnation*. Manohar Publications: New Delhi.

Dobhal, G.L. (December 1981). 'Money-order Remittances and Outmigration—A Case Study of Pauri Garhwal District', pp. 76–97: *Annals of National Association Geographers of India*, Vol. I, No. 2.

Durgapur Notified Area Authority. (1984). *Revised Budget (1982–83) and Budget Estimate (1983–84)*.

Elkan, W. (1967). 'Circular Migration and the Growth of Towns in East Africa', pp. 581–89. *International Labour Review*, December, Vol. 96, No. 6. International Labour Organisation: Geneva.

Gaude, J. and **P. Peek**. (1976). 'The Economic Effects of Rural-Urban Migration', pp. 329–38. *International Labour Review*, Vol. 114, No. 3. International Labour Organisation: Geneva.

Gershuny, J.I. (1978). *The Self Service Economy*, Frances Printer: London.

Gershuny, J.I. and **R.E. Pahl.** (1979). 'Work Outside Employment: Some Preliminary Speculations', pp. 120–35. *New Universities Quarterly*. Vol. 34, No. 1.

Glasson, John. (1978). *An Introduction to Regional Planning*, pp. 63–121, 171–94. Hutchinson: London.

Goon, A.M., M.K. Gupta and **B. Dasgupta.** (1983). *Fundamental of Statistics*. Vol. 1. The World Press Private Ltd.: Calcutta.

Gould, P.R., J.H. Johnson and **G.P. Chapman.** (1984). *The Structure of Television*. Pion Ltd.: London.

Government of India (April 1986 and April–June 1989). *Sarvekshana*, Vol. IX and Vol. XII. Department of Statistics, Ministry of Planning.

Government of India (June 1988). *Estimates of State Domestic Product (1970–71 to 1986–87)*, pp. 3–5. Central Statistical Organisation, Department of Statistics.

Hansen, Niles M. (ed.). (1972). *Growth Centres in Regional Economic Development*. The Free Press: New York.

Harriss, J.R. and **M.P. Todaro.** (1970). 'Migration, Unemployment and Development: A Two Sector Analysis'. *American Economic Review*, Vol. 60, No. 1, pp. 126–42.

Harriss, B. (1976). 'The Indian Ideology of Growth Centres', pp. 263–69; *Area*. Vol. 8, No. 2. Institute of British Geographers: Dorchester.

——— (1984). *State and Market*, pp. 37–68. Concept Publishing Company: New Delhi.

Harriss, B. and **J. Harriss.** (April 1984). '"Generative" or "Parasitic" Urbanism? Some Observations from the Recent History of a South India Market Town'. *The Journal of Development Studies*, pp. 82–101. Vol. 20, No. 3. Frank Cass & Co. Ltd.: London.

Harriss, J. (1982). 'Studies of Small Scale Enterprise and Urban Labour in South India', *Development Studies Occasional Paper*, No. 19, pp. 1–78. University of Norwich.

Hermansen, Tormod. (1972). 'Development of Poles and Development Centres in National and Regional Development', in Antoni Kuklinski, *Growth Poles and Growth Centres in Regional Planning*, pp. 1–68. Mouton & Co.: Paris.

Hirschman, A.O. (1958). *The Strategy of Economic Development*. Yale University Press: New Haven.

Hugo, C.J. (1978). *Population Mobility in West Java*, p. 274. Godjah Mada University: Yogyakarta.

Jagannathan, Vijay N. (28 March 1987). 'Planning in New Cities, The Durgapur Experience', pp. 553–58. *Economic and Political Weekly*, Vol XXII, No. 13.

Johnson, G.E. and **W.E. Whitelaw.** (April 1974). 'Urban-Rural Income Transfers in Kenya: An Estimated Remittances Function' in Bert F. Hoselitz (ed.), *Economic Development & Cultural Change*, Vol. 22, No. 3, pp. 473–79. The University of Chicago Press: Chicago.

Joshi, H. and **V. Joshi.** (1976). *Surplus Labour and the City: A Study of Bombay*, pp. 1–182. Oxford University Press: New Delhi.

Kuklinski, Antoni. (1972). *Growth Poles and Growth Centres in Regional Planning*. Mouton & Co.: Paris.

Kuklinski, A. and **R. Petrella.** (eds.). (1972). *Growth Poles and Regional Policies*. Mouton: The Hague.

Kundu, Amitabh. (15 November 1986). 'Migration, Urbanisation and Inter-regional Inequality, The Emerging Socio-Political Challenge', pp. 2005–8. *Economic and Political Weekly*. Vol. XXI, No. 46.

Lipsey, Richard G. (1983). *An Introduction to Positive Economics*, pp. 534–36. Weidenfeld and Nicholson: London.

Lipton, Michael. (1968). 'Strategy for Agriculture: Urban Bias and Rural Planning', in Paul Streeten and Michael Lipton (eds.). *The Crisis of Indian Planning*, pp. 83–147. Oxford University Press: London.

———. (1977). *Why Poor People Stay Poor*, Temple Smith: London.

———. (1980). 'Migration from Rural Areas of Poor Countries: The Impact on Rural Productivity and Income Distribution', *World Development*, Vol. 8, pp. 1–24. Pergamon Press Ltd.: Great Britain.

Lozano, B. (1983). 'Informal Sector Workers: Walking Out the Systems Front Door', *Journal of Urban and Regional Research*. Vol. 7, No. 4, pp. 449–70. Edward Arnold: UK.

Mellor, John W. (1976). *The New Economics of Growth, A Strategy for India and the Developing World*. Cornell University Press: New York.

Mingione, E. (1983). 'Informalisation, restructuring and survival strategies of the working class', *Journal of Urban and Regional Research*. Vol. 7, No. 3, pp. 311–39. Edward Arnold: UK.

Misra, R.P. (1972). 'Growth Poles and Growth Centres in the Context of India's Urban and Regional Development Problems', in Antoni Kuklinski, *Growth Poles and Growth Centres in Regional Planning*, pp. 141–68. Mouton & Co.: Paris.

Moseley, Malcolm J. (1974). *Growth Centres in Spatial Planning*. Pergamon Press: Oxford.

Myrdal, Gunnar. (1957). *Economic Theory and Under-Developed Regions*, pp. 3–38. Gerald Duckworth & Co. Ltd.: London.

Norcliffe, G.B. (1982). *Inferential Statistics for Geographers*. Hutchinson, London.

Oberai, A.S. and **E. Bilsborrow.** (1984). 'Theoretical Perspectives on Migration', in R.E. Bilsborrow, A.S. Oberai, G. Standing, *Migration Surveys in Low Income Countries*, pp. 14–30. Croom Helm: London.

Oberai, A.S. and **M.H.K. Singh.** (1980). 'Migration, Remittances and Rural Development; Findings of a Case Study in the Indian Punjab', *International Labour Review*. Vol. 119, No. 2. March–April, pp. 229–41. International Labour Organisation: Geneva.

———. (1981). 'Urban Inmigration and Remittances; A Case Study of Ludhiana in Indian Punjab', *World Employment Programme Research*; Working Paper No. 97, pp. 1–32, International Labour Organisation: Geneva.

Oberai, A.S. and **H.K.M. Singh.** (1983). *Causes and Consequences of Internal Migration*, Oxford University Press, Delhi.

Odimuku, C.L. and **J.B. Ridell**. (1979). 'Remittances in Southeastern Nigeria'. *Area*. Vol. 11, No. 1, pp. 58–62. Institute of British Geographers: Dorchester.

Pahl, R.E. (1980). 'Employment, Work and Domestic Division of Labour', *Journal of Urban and Regional Research*, Vol. 4, No. 1, pp. 1–19. Edward Arnold: U.K.

Peek, Peter and **Guy Standing**. (1979). 'Rural-Urban Migration and Government Policies in Low Income Countries', *International Labour Review*. Vol. 118, No. 6, pp. 747–59. International Labour Organisation: Geneva.

Perroux, F. (1964). *La notion de la pôle de croissance, l'économie de xxème siècle*. Second edition, Paris.

Perspective Planning Division, Planning Commission, Government of India (June 1986), *A Technical Note on the Seventh Plan of India (1985–90)*, pp. 10–16, and annexures for percentage of people below the poverty line for 1972–73, 1977–78 and 1983–84 (Provisional), pp. 1–33. United Nation's Centre for Regional Development, Nagoya, Japan.

Prabhu, P.N. (1956). 'A Study of the Social Effects of Urbanisation'; in UNESCO, *The Social Implications of Industrialisation and Urbanisation*. Oxford Printing Works: Calcutta.

Rempel, Henry and **Richard A. Lobdell**. (April 1978). 'The Role of Urban-to-Rural Remittances in Rural Development', *Journal of Development Studies*. Vol. 14, No. 3, pp. 324–41. Frank Cass & Co. Ltd.: London.

Reserve Bank of India Bulletins (1972–1989), Reserve Bank of India, Bombay (India).

Rigg, Jonathan. (1990). 'Perspectives on Migrant Labouring and the Village Economy in Developing Countries', *Progress in Human Geography*, pp. 66–82. Edward Arnold: UK.

Rossi, Peter H., James D. Wright and **Andy B. Anderson.** (eds.). (1983). *Handbook of Survey Research*, Academic Press Inc.: San Diego.

Rothermund, D. (1980). 'Epilogue: Urban Growth and Rural Stagnation', pp. 453–63; in D. Rothermund, E. Kropp, G. Dienemann (eds.), *Urban Growth and Rural Stagnation*. Manohar Publications, New Delhi.

Rothermund Dietmar, E. Kropp, and **G. Dienemann**. (eds.). (1980). *Urban Growth and Rural Stagnation*. Manohar Publications, New Delhi.

Roy, B.K. (Direction) (1979). *Geographic Distribution of Internal Migration in India*, Census of India.

Roy, B.K. (Editing & Direction) (1989). *Geographic Distribution of Internal Migration in India 1971–81*, Census of India.

Ryan, B.F., B.L. Joiner and **T.A. Ryan** Jr., (1976). *Minitab*. PWS Publishers: Boston.

Sanghvi, P. (1969). *Surplus Manpower in Agriculture and Economic Development*, pp. 1–171. Asia Publishing House: Bombay.

Sethuraman, S.V. (1976). 'The Urban Informal Sector: Concept, Measurement and Policy'. *International Labour Review*. Vol. 114, No. 1. International Labour Organisation: Geneva.

Shaw, R.P. (1980). 'Bending the Urban Flow: A Construction Migration Strategy', *International Labour Review*. Vol. 119, No. 4. International Labour Organisation: Geneva.

Shepperdson, Mike. (1979). 'Urban Bias and Rural Poverty', Occasional Paper No. 8, Centre for Development Studies, University College of Swansea: U.K.

Sivaramakrishnan, K.C. (1976–77). *New Towns in India, A Report on a Study of Selected New Towns in Eastern Region*. Indian Institute of Management: Calcutta.

Sivaramakrishnan, K.C. (1982). 'Durgapur: Case Study of an Indian New Town', John L. Taylor and David G. Williams (eds.). *Urban Planning Practice in Developing Countries*, pp. 145–59. Pergamon Press: Oxford.

Standing, Guy. (1984). 'Income Transfers and Remittances', in R.E. Bilsborrow, A.S. Oberai, G. Standing, *Migration Surveys in Low Income Countries*, pp. 264–316. Croom Helm: London.

Steel, W.F. and **Y. Takagi**. (1976). *The Intermediate Sector, Unemployment and the Employment-Output Conflict*. Vanderbilt University: Nashville, Tenn.

Taylor, John L. and **David G. Williams**. (ed.). (1982). *Urban Planning Practice in Developing Countries*. pp. 3–44, 145–58, 321–49. Pergamon Press: Oxford.

The National Sample Survey Organisation, 16th Round (1960–61), No. 101, *Tables with Notes on Consumer Expenditure (Preliminary)*, pp. 1–5, 26, 48–50, 68–69, 90–93.

The National Sample Survey Organisation, 28th Round (1973–74) No. 240, *Tables on Consumer Expenditure*, pp. 1–3, 22, 34, 35, 86, 99, 100.

The National Sample Survey Organisation, 38th Round (1982–83) and 42nd Round (1986–87), *Tables on Consumer Expenditure*.

Thirlwall, A.P. (1978). *Growth and Development*, The Macmillan Press Ltd.: London.

Thomas, J.J. (1983). *An Introduction to Statistical Analysis for Economists*. Weidenfeld and Nicholson: London.

Todaro, P.M. (1976). 'Rural-Urban Migration, Unemployment and Job Probabilities: Recent Theoretical and Empirical Research', in A.J. Coale (ed.). *Economic Factors in Population Growth*, pp. 367–93. Macmillan: London.

————. (1980). *Internal Migration in Developing Countries*, pp. 1–90. International Labour Office: Geneva.

United Nations Organisation (May 1990), *Monthly Bulletin of Statistics*, p. 3, Vol. XLIV, No. 5.

Wanmali, Sudhir. (February 1983). *Service Provision and Rural Development in India: A Study of Miryalguda Taluka*. Research Report 37. International Food Policy Research Institute.

Webcon. (1981). *A 10 Year Perspective Plan for Industrial Development of Durgapur*, Vol. I (for Asansol-Durgapur Development Authority, Durgapur).

Whittaker, William. (1984). 'Migration and Agrarian Change in Garhwal District, Uttar Pradesh', T. Bayliss Smith and Sudhir Wanmali (eds.), *Understanding Green Revolutions*, pp. 109–35. Cambridge University Press: Cambridge.

